WORDS MADE FLESH

OTHER BOOKS BY DAVID JAUSS

FICTION

Glossolalia: New & Selected Stories
Nice People: New & Selected Stories II
Black Maps
Crimes of Passion

POETRY

You Are Not Here
Improvising Rivers

NONFICTION

*Alone With All That Could Happen: On Writing Fiction
(Revised & Expanded Edition)*

ANTHOLOGIES

*Words Overflown by Stars: Creative Writing Instruction
and Insight from the Vermont College of Fine Arts
MFA Program*

*Strong Measures: Contemporary American Poetry
in Traditional Form*

The Best of Crazyhorse: *30 Years of Poetry and Fiction*

WORDS MADE FLESH

THE CRAFT OF FICTION

DAVID JAUSS

Press 53
Winston-Salem

Press 53, LLC
PO Box 30314
Winston-Salem, NC 27130

First Edition

Copyright © 2024 by David Jauss

All rights reserved, including the right of reproduction in whole or in part in any form except in the case of brief quotations embodied in critical articles or reviews. For permission, contact publisher at editor@press53.com or at the address above.

Cover image, "Sonoran Desert at Sunset, 35,000 Feet,"
Copyright © 2018 by Catherine Helland Watson,
used by permission of the artist.

Cover design by Kevin Morgan Watson and Claire V. Foxx

Library of Congress Control Number
2024941479

ISBN 978-1-950413-85-0

For my students, who taught me how to teach

Acknowledgments

I am grateful to the editors of the following journals, in which earlier versions of these essays first appeared:

Grist: A Journal of the Literary Arts
 "The Flowers of Afterthought: Premises and Strategies for Revision"

Short Fiction in Theory & Practice
 "'What We See With': Redefining Plot"

The Writer's Chronicle
 "Homo Fictus vs. Homo Sapiens"
 "Who's Afraid of the Big Bad Abstraction?: Conveying Emotion in Fiction"
 "The Art of Description"
 "Returning Characters to Life: What Chekhov Teaches Us About Endings"

I am also grateful for the support and encouragement of my students and colleagues at Vermont College of Fine Arts, where early drafts of these essays were delivered as lectures. I owe special debts of gratitude to my teachers, Frederick Busch, Philip Dacey, Stephen Dunn, George P. Elliott, Delbert Wylder, and Edith Wylder, all of whom contributed to my understanding of the craft of fiction, and to my life, in ways above and beyond the call of duty and, even, friendship. Finally, I am thankful beyond measure to my wife, Judy, for more than five decades of love and support.

Contents

Preface	xiii
Homo Fictus vs. Homo Sapiens	1
Who's Afraid of the Big Bad Abstraction?: Conveying Emotion in Fiction	27
The Art of Description	53
"What We See With": Redefining Plot	79
Returning Characters to Life: What Chekhov Teaches Us about Endings	127
The Flowers of Afterthought: Premises and Strategies for Revision	153
Notes and Works Cited	181
Author Biography	213

Fiction is so very much an incarnational art.

—Flannery O'Connor

Preface

The premise behind this book is the same as that behind my previous collection of essays on the craft of fiction, *Alone with All That Could Happen: On Writing Fiction (Revised & Expanded Edition)*: in order to improve our fiction, we need first to recognize and understand the vast panorama of techniques and strategies available to us. Unfortunately, many creative writing textbooks and essay collections take a prescriptive rather than a descriptive approach to matters of craft and thus restrict our sense of what's possible in fiction. In the six essays in this book, I have tried to expand our understanding of the craft of fiction by describing what writers have actually done rather than by prescribing what they should do. As a result, the essays take issue with some of the reigning dogmas of the day, as expressed both in standard creative writing guides and in the practice of many contemporary fiction writers.

In "Homo Fictus vs. Homo Sapiens," I challenge the oft-repeated advice that writers need to know "everything" about our characters' inner and outer lives, from their deepest thoughts to their preferred brand of underwear. I argue that this advice leads us to create characters whose inner lives lack the complexity and mystery of real people and whose outer lives are so dense with naturalistic detail that we lose sight of the characters' essence. I call the attitude behind this advice "Positive Capability," in contrast to Keats's "Negative Capability," which he defines as the all-important ability of "being in uncertainties, mysteries, doubts, without any irritable reaching after fact and reason." I also dispute conventional claims about the "roundness" and "reality" of fictional characters and the notion of a fixed, singular desire as the sole motivation for a character's behavior.

In "Who's Afraid of the Big Bad Abstraction?: Conveying Emotion in Fiction," I question the ubiquitous admonition to "go in fear of abstractions," as Ezra Pound advised, and the likewise ubiquitous commandment to avoid what John Ruskin dubbed "the pathetic fallacy." The essay defines and provides examples of a wide range of strategies—abstract, concrete, and figurative—for conveying emotion and examines their pros and cons.

In "The Art of Description," I go beyond the commonplace observation that literary description is "painting in words" to draw parallels between five specific movements in visual art—realism, impressionism, expressionism, post-impressionism, and cubism—and their equivalents in fiction, thereby defining and illustrating five different approaches we can take to write effective description.

In "'What We See With': Redefining Plot," I discuss the limitations of the standard monolithic definition of a plot and its focus on causality, character change, and what Jane Alison calls "masculo-sexual structure," then I provide definitions, examples, and analyses of seven alternative non-causal forms of plot that have been employed by masterly fiction writers throughout literary history and that can enrich our own fiction.

In "Returning Characters to Life: What Chekhov Teaches Us About Endings," I critique the narrow definition of closure that underlies the vast majority of endings in contemporary fiction and analyze twelve alternative strategies for endings that Chekhov invented and that we can consider using in our own stories and novels.

And, finally, in "The Flowers of Afterthought: Premises and Strategies for Revision," I point out that what many writers consider revision is actually little more than editing (and usually premature editing) and I present a comprehensive survey of ten premises and fourteen specific strategies that will help us revise our work effectively.

There is another premise behind this book besides the one I've described above, and it is a premise Jean Rhys beautifully expressed in her *Paris Review* interview. "Listen to me," she said. "All of writing is a huge lake. There are great rivers that feed the lake, like Tolstoy and Dostoyevsky. And there are mere trickles, like Jean Rhys. All that matters is feeding the lake. I don't matter. The lake matters. You must keep feeding the lake." I second Rhys's injunction that we feed the lake of literature, though not her overly modest opinion of her own contribution to it. If her extraordinary fiction added only a mere trickle to the lake of literature, few of us can claim to have added more than a single molecule of water. I have done my best to feed the lake through my fiction, but I have also tried to feed it through my nearly five decades of teaching. I hope the information and advice in this book will help you feed the lake.

Homo Fictus vs. Homo Sapiens

1. Hamlet's Brain

If you've been wondering why Hamlet is so darn indecisive, you can stop wondering now. The eminent scientist Jacob Bronowski has given us the answer. It turns out that Hamlet's fatal indecision isn't due to moral scruples, madness, an unresolved Oedipus complex, or any of the myriad explanations that literary scholars have inflicted on us over the centuries; rather, it's the result of his brain's underdeveloped frontal lobes. According to Bronowski, it takes our frontal lobes, which control long-term decision-making, twenty-plus years to develop fully, and because Hamlet is still a teenager, his frontal lobes haven't developed enough to allow him to make the decision to avenge his father's murder. "It is pointless of the Ghost to keep on nudging him and saying 'Revenge, Revenge,'" he says. "The fact is that Hamlet as a youth is simply not mature. Intellectually or emotionally . . . he is simply not ready for an act of that magnitude in boyhood."

Since the play makes it clear that Hamlet is in fact thirty years old, Bronowski is wrong to consider him a teenager—either that or he's the second-oldest teenager in the history of the world, after Dick Clark. (Act V, scene 1 reveals that the sexton has been a "grave-maker" for thirty years, ever since "that very day that young Hamlet was born," and that Yorick, upon whose back the young Hamlet rode, has been dead for "three and twenty years."[1]) But more importantly, Bronowski is wrong to think that Hamlet's frontal lobes are underdeveloped; after all, Hamlet doesn't *have* frontal lobes, or any other biological organs for that matter, since he is composed entirely of words—and none of those words is *frontal* or *lobes*. Some Shakespearean scholars may have had insufficiently developed frontal lobes, but I can guarantee that the character himself does not.

Bronowski's explanation of Hamlet's behavior illustrates a common mistake we encounter in talk about fictional characters—the tendency to treat Homo sapiens and Homo fictus not as "allied species," as E.M. Forster calls them, but as a single species. This tendency is so prevalent that authors of books and essays on fiction writing typically feel the need to point out, sometimes at considerable length, that fictional characters aren't real. Forster devotes an entire chapter of *Aspects of the Novel*—twenty-one pages—to proving this seemingly common-sense fact, and William H. Gass spends much of his seminal essay "The Concept of Character in Fiction" making the same point. Even John Gardner, who famously disagreed with virtually everything Gass ever said, agrees that nothing sensible can be said about characterization until we make "the crucial observation . . . that, except as creatures of the imagination, characters in fiction do not exist."

This point may seem obvious to most of us, but many general readers, students, literary scholars, and even writers themselves have been known to talk about characters as if they have a life outside of fiction, speculating about their childhoods, their futures, and what they would do in such and such a situation. And W.J. Harvey, the author of the influential study *Character and the Novel*, has even said flat-out that "we may legitimately talk of the reality of fictional characters." Homo sapiens and Homo fictus certainly bear a family resemblance—they're like fraternal twins born to different parents—but for all their similarities, they are two very different species.

That readers confuse the real and the fictive is inevitable, perhaps, given the fact that we, as writers, do everything within our powers to make our characters seem real, but we need to make sure that we don't make this mistake ourselves. If we want to create successful characters, we need to understand the differences between the two species. As Richard Cohen points out, since "characters are made of language rather than protoplasm," they rarely, if ever, need to eat, drink, or go to the bathroom, and they "have a much higher pain threshold than physical human beings"—so high, in fact, it's virtually "nonexistent." Furthermore, he adds, they have "a lower threshold of psychic pain than real people": "Any flesh-bound character who felt as much emotion as a fictional character would probably not have much time to get any work done." But, of course, fictional characters don't need to worry about getting any work done since they rarely have jobs, and even if they do, "Ninety percent of fiction takes place in the off-hours." To Cohen's list of differences, we could add the fact that characters tend to be active whereas most people are passive, they seek out conflict whereas people generally do their best to avoid it, they watch a lot less TV, and they tend to have more unusual names: life gives us a lot more Tom Joneses than fiction, and fewer Huckleberry Finns and Humbert Humberts.

But there are two other differences between Homo fictus and Homo sapiens that are far more important, and they are the differences we most need to keep in mind when we create our characters. First, unlike real people, fictional characters often have inner lives we can witness. And second, compared to actual human beings, fictional people are, as Gass has said, "mostly empty canvas"—we know relatively little about their physical appearance, their behavior and relationships, their past histories, and so forth. Homo fictus, then, consists in large part of the *presence* of something that *can't* be observed in real people—the inner life—and the relative *absence* of things that *can* be observed—the outer life. Paradoxically, the characters who feel most "real" to us are those who differ from real people in these two very important ways—provided we don't take these differences too far. If we presume to know absolutely everything about our characters' inner lives, including every motive for their behavior, or make them entirely empty canvases, their realism diminishes significantly.

All of the differences between the two species result in one overall difference that we need first to acknowledge and then to fight against: compared to real people, literary characters are almost ludicrously simple, barely two-dimensional—far more flat than round. It may be that, as the old joke has it, deep down we're all shallow, but even the shallowest human being is infinitely more complex than any fictional character. As the novelist Rabih Alameddine has said, "Everybody believes that a good fictional character is three-dimensional and rounded. If that's true, then a real person is one hundred dimensional. We're all a lot more complex than we let the world see, and we're all a lot more complex than even we know." In his book *Incognito: The Secret Lives of the Brain*, neuroscientist David Eagleman supports Alameddine's claim that we're more complex than we know. He says the human brain is like a representative democracy with a "multiple-party system" and its many selves comprise a "team of rivals" who compete over how best to proceed in any given instance—and they compete under the radar of the conscious mind, as if they're on a "black ops mission." As Eagleman points out, "consciousness is the smallest player in the operations of the brain," so small that he compares it to a "stowaway on a transatlantic steamship, taking credit for the journey without acknowledging the massive engineering" below decks that actually keeps the ship running.

Whereas human beings are more complex than we can begin to suspect, fictional characters are far simpler than we often acknowledge. As James Wood notes, "Even the characters we think of as 'solidly realized' in the conventional realist sense are less solid the longer we look at them." They're so unsolid, in fact, that Wood questions the value of distinguishing between round and flat characters. "I would be quite happy," he says, "to abolish the very idea of 'roundness' in characterization, because it tyrannizes us—readers, novelists, critics—with an impossible ideal. 'Roundness' is impossible in fiction, because fictional characters, while very alive in their way, are not the same as real people."

I agree. It's time for us to get real about the reality of characters. We need to recognize that when we talk about characters who "come to life," we are, quite frankly, talking nonsense. But we shouldn't abandon the "impossible ideal," however tyrannical it is. Even though Homo fictus and Homo sapiens are two different species, I believe we should do our best to make our characters as realistic as possible—except, of course, when we're writing satire or farce or some other literary genre that requires unrealistic characters.

There's nothing unusual about this belief; virtually everyone shares it. Unfortunately, conventional wisdom about characterization only makes the impossible ideal more impossible to achieve. As I see it, much of the advice we encounter in creative writing textbooks and MFA workshops is counterproductive because it encourages us to make our characters drastically different from real people when they should be relatively similar and drastically similar when they should be relatively different. The conventional advice is to know *everything* about our characters' inner and outer lives. This advice leads us to create characters whose inner lives lack the complexity and mystery of real people and whose outer lives are, like real people's, so dense with naturalistic detail that we lose sight of the characters' essence.

2. A Visible Secret Life

No one would argue that we need to know everything about actual human beings before they seem real to us. After all, we know far from everything about our parents, significant others, children, and closest friends—not to mention ourselves—yet we are quite convinced of the reality of all of the above. It seems odd, then, that authors of fiction writing guides regularly assert that characters don't become "real" until we know everything there is to know about them. Forster is one of the principal proponents of this notion. Despite all of his talk about characters not being real, he asserts that "a character . . . is real . . . when the novelist knows everything about it." This kind of total knowledge is possible, he says, because of "the fundamental difference between people in daily life and people in books": the fact that people in books belong "to a world where the secret life is visible." "In daily life," he says,

> we never understand each other, neither complete clairvoyance nor complete confessional exists. We know each other approximately, by external signs, and these serve well enough as a basis for society and even for intimacy. But people in a novel can be understood *completely* by the reader, if the novelist wishes; their inner as well as their outer life can be exposed. And this is why they often seem more definite than characters in history, or even our own friends; we have been told all about them that can be

told; even if they are imperfect or unreal *they do not contain any secrets*, whereas our friends do and must, mutual secrecy being one of the conditions of life upon this globe. (emphases mine)

To an extent, of course, what Forster says is very true. By exploiting this major difference between fictional characters and real people, we can indeed create the impression of a similarity between them. The fact that omniscience, an inherently unrealistic technique, is capable of creating the illusion of reality is a paradox that all writers—and readers—have experienced. As Andre Dubus has said,

> I have never known anyone as deeply as I know a character who comes to me through the work of writing a story, because I have never been able to feel absolutely what another human being is feeling. The perception of a character in a story written with compassion is, for both the reader and the writer, a perception closer to divine than human.

But what neither Dubus nor Forster acknowledges is that the closer the perception comes to the divine, the *less* realistic the character becomes. There is a point where the presentation of a character's inner life can stop creating the impression of reality and begin having the reverse effect, and that point is reached when we presume to understand a character with godlike completeness. Forster is wrong, I believe, to suggest that a character we know completely seems more real than a character we know only partially. In my opinion, a character who does not "contain any secrets" lacks the mystery that most characterizes our fellow human beings and is therefore just too far removed from reality to seem real.

Robert Boswell argues this point very persuasively in his brilliant essay "The Half-Known World." The goal of the fiction writer, he argues, should be "the creation of a half-known world," not a fully known one. "To accomplish this," he says, "the writer must suggest a dimension to the fictional reality that escapes comprehension. The writer wishes to make his characters and their world known to the reader, and he simultaneously wishes to make them resonate with the unknown" because, unlike the real world, "A fully known world is devoid of mystery." If we know too much about our characters, then, they will be too simple to seem real. "Here's another definition of stereotype," Boswell says: "any character that is fully known."

Forster, of course, saw it exactly the other way around: a fully known character was a round character to him. You may agree, but for my money, Boswell's got it right: knowing everything about your characters can only exaggerate the difference between them and real people. Even though Forster starts out by affirming a valuable difference between Homo fictus and Homo sapiens—the role a visible secret life can play in creating the impression of reality—he exaggerates that difference to the point that he winds up arguing that we should make the two species differ in a way they shouldn't.

3. Mostly Empty Canvas

While applying the principle of "knowing everything" to our characters' inner lives leads us to make characters different from real people when they should be similar, applying this principle to our characters' outer lives leads us to make them similar to real people when they should be different. As Gass has pointed out, successful literary characters differ from real people most conspicuously by the fact that so much of their outer lives is absent. "Characters in fiction are mostly empty canvas," he says. "I have known many who have passed through their stories without noses, or heads to hold them." Their personal histories, too, are mostly empty canvas. The fact that our knowledge of fictional characters is far less than complete does not weaken characterization; rather, it strengthens it. Indeed, I believe the relative emptiness of the fictional canvas is one of fiction's main glories, not to mention one of its principal advantages over film and drama and—dare I say it?—reality. By giving us only those details that matter, we can see the *essence* of a character more accurately than we can see any human being. As Georgia O'Keeffe said, "Nothing is less real than realism. Details are confusing. It is only by selection, by elimination, by emphasis that we get the real meaning of things."

The kind of description that film and drama of necessity

show—and the kind of description that we find in far too many short stories and novels—actually *conceals* character more than reveals it. In those forms, the canvas is so full we see not only the significant details, but also many insignificant ones that distract us from the essential nature of the character. To illustrate this point, just imagine two very different actors—John Wayne, say, and Johnny Depp—playing the same role; even though they'd say the same words, perform the same actions, and wear the same clothes, I guarantee we'd have very different responses to the character, all of which would distract us from the character's essence. Film, drama, and life give us a superfluity of accidental characteristics, in short, but fiction gives us only the essential ones—or at least that should be its goal. One of the most important ways successful fictional characters differ from real people, then, is that their essences are manifest.

As we all know, of course, readers often respond to the relative emptiness of the fictional canvas by "filling in the blanks" with their own descriptions and backstory. I had a student once who confessed that she always pictured the main male character of a story as Brad Pitt and the main female character as Jennifer Aniston. I wasn't able to persuade her to stop—though I suspect that she, like Mr. Pitt, later replaced Aniston with Angelina Jolie. (And who knows who's taking Ms. Jolie's place in her head now?) Gass warns us against this kind of misreading, saying that "it's important to . . . resist any inclination we may have to elaborate" the author's depiction of the character because such elaboration "destroy[s] the work as certainly as 'touching up' and 'painting over'" destroy a painting.

Unfortunately, readers aren't the only ones who are guilty of the literary equivalent of painting a mustache on the *Mona Lisa*. Many writers do likewise, defacing their own canvases with inconsequential details. This is especially true of the so-called maximalists, who have responded to the austerity of minimalism with what I consider misguided prodigality. In the work of David Foster Wallace and William T. Vollmann, for example, characters frequently disappear under the mountain of information we're given about them. The maximalists are not entirely to blame, however; after all, they, like the rest of us, have been repeatedly told that the accumulation of details and information is essential to creating lifelike characters.

Let's look at this advice and its implications. And let's start with the book that has justly been the most popular, respected, and influential fiction writing textbook for the past forty-plus years: Janet Burroway's *Writing Fiction*. I admire this book—as I admire Burroway, and all the writers with whom I'm about to quarrel—but it contains some advice that I consider antithetical to the creation of truly realistic characters. In it, she tells us to

> know everything about your character whether you use it or not. Before you put a character in a story, know how well that character sleeps. Know what the character eats for lunch and how much it matters, what he buys and how the bills get paid, how she spends what we call working hours. Know how your character would prefer to spend evenings and weekends and why such plans get thwarted. Know what memories the character has of pets and parents, cities, snow, or school. . . . When you know these things, you will have taken a step past invention toward the moment of imagination in which you become your character, live in his or her skin, and produce an action that, for the reader, rings universally true.

And when you know these things, you will also have created a very full canvas, not a mostly empty one. Burroway seems to want that canvas to be as full as possible, at least in the initial stage of characterization; she even goes so far as to suggest that we imitate actors schooled in the Stanislavski Method and compose biographies of our characters. John Dufresne, who also believes "You can never know too much about your characters," likewise recommends the Stanislavski Method, devoting an entire chapter to its use in his book *The Lie That Tells a Truth*.

Burroway and Dufresne are far from being the only writers to recommend that we fill the entire canvas when we create our characters, of course. You can find similar advice in virtually every creative writing guide ever written, many of which offer sample questions we should ask ourselves about our characters in order to create them.[2] And if those sample questions aren't enough for you, there's an entire book—Eric and Ann Maisel's

What Would Your Character Do?—that consists of (as its subtitle says) *Personality Quizzes for Analyzing Your Characters*. This book contains more than 230 pages of questions that'll help you nail the lid on the coffin of your character's personality.

Some writers swear by this pack-rat approach to characterization. T Cooper, for example, reports that he created the characters in his novels by writing their names at the top of a page and then just

> vomit[ing] out all the details about them I could possibly conjure. Down to the kind of soft cotton boxers they wore in high school . . . How they talk, what they look like, what music they like, sports they're good at, secrets they have, food allergies, how they'll die, what their relationship with their mother was like, and so on.

He did this, he explains, because "it's important to know all of these details about . . . characters before putting them in motion in the narrative."

Note that Cooper, like Burroway, not only says that we should know everything about our characters but that we should do so *before* we put them in a story. If you ask me, this is putting the proverbial cart before the horse, requiring us to invent a character before we invent the circumstances and events that create him or her. I believe, with Boswell, that making "a list of traits that define a character . . . in advance of real narrative exploration tends to cut a character off at the knees." Just as Ezra Pound advised that poets should "think with the poem," so fiction writers should think with the story. Tobias Wolff is one writer who clearly thinks with the story, creating his characters as he writes rather than plugging in information from some predetermined list of traits. "Characters generally rise up out of the work of the writing," he says. "As I write, the character begins to coalesce and take on particularity. . . . I've even changed the gender of my characters halfway through a story." I believe that this kind of dramatic redefinition of a character is possible only when we think with the story, not with the list. Thinking with the list closes the imagination down; thinking with the story opens it up.

Since the effect of following Burroway and Cooper's advice

is to create a character who exists before the first word of the story is even written, it strikes me as an attempt to duplicate the situation we're in if we base a character on a real person. It's no surprise, then, that Robin Hemley, the author of *Turning Life into Fiction*, supports this approach to characterization. Like Burroway, he says that we should know everything about our characters—and he seems to mean that as literally as she does. He says,

> You should be able to answer any question, no matter how seemingly insignificant, about your character. If asked, 'What do the curtains in Shorty's bedroom look like?' you should be able to answer, 'There aren't any curtains in his bedroom,' or whatever you think best fits his character.

Kim Edwards likewise argues that we should know everything about our characters, including what they would do in any given situation, even one unrelated to the story. "Even if this character doesn't cause a car accident or lose a parent or leave a spouse," she says, "the author must have a clear sense of what he or she would do in such situations—and readers must, as well." I don't know about you, but unless I had actually done these things, I wouldn't know what I would do, much less what anyone else would do in these situations. I'd have to live through those events before I'd know the answer, and if I were imagining those things happening to a character, I'd have to live through those scenes by writing them before I'd have even an inkling of an answer. The implication that we can know anything, much less *everything*, about a character without writing is utterly alien to me. And the idea that we need such total knowledge at *any* point in the writing process strikes me as preposterous. In short, the creation of lists of factoids about our characters seems like busy work to me, work that can do nothing but distract us from the task of creating the essence of a character.

To their credit, all of the writers I've just quarreled with are well aware of the danger of the clutter they urge us to create. Even as they tell us to "know everything" about our characters, they warn us that the vast majority of this knowledge will be unnecessary. Hemley, for example, stresses the need to select from the "flood of details" the ones that are, or can become, significant. Any detail that isn't truly significant, he notes, "becomes a red herring, a false clue, a detail that serves no purpose other than the author's whim." His advice, like everyone else's, is to use only those details that matter. But if our goal is to convey the essence of a character, why first imagine everything that's inessential? If you ask me, creating an encyclopedia of facts about our characters is like preparing to paint a bedroom by painting the rest of the house.

Also, the more inessential details we invent, the more we're likely to use. If we make the mistake of thinking that characters should be as fully known as real people, we'll almost inevitably include a great deal of inessential information about them—full-scale head-to-toe descriptions, résumé-like backstory, all the trivial events of their lives, every stray thought that wafted through their heads on a midsummer day, etc. I can't think of anything more detrimental to the creation of successful characters than the mere accumulation of information. As Boswell has said, accumulated details don't bring characters to life, they "flatten" them "with their weight." They do so, as Flannery O'Connor argues in "The Nature and Aim of Fiction," because such details are naturalistic, and naturalism and realism work at cross purposes. "In a strictly naturalistic work," she says, "the detail is there because it is natural to life, not because it is natural to the work. In a work of art we can be extremely literal, without being in the least naturalistic. Art is selective, and its truthfulness is the truthfulness of the essential . . ." And it is the essence of the character that we want to convey, after all.

How, you may be wondering, do I account for the fact—and it is most definitely a fact—that Forster, Burroway, Dufresne, Cooper, Hemley, Edwards and many other writers who tout the "know everything" approach to characterization have created so many characters whose essence is *not* obscured by the presence of a plethora of inessential information? I confess I have a sneaking suspicion that they don't always, or maybe even ever, follow their own advice, but if they do, they clearly have an extraordinary gift for determining which of the "flood of details" should be cut and which kept. This is not, I can attest, a gift that very many of the students I've taught over the past five decades have (and it's definitely not a gift I have, either). The "know everything" approach may work for those writers who have the willingness to cut most of what they've invented, and the wisdom to know just what to cut, but I don't believe it works for most writers. In my opinion, Forster and Company succeed at creating excellent characters not *because* of their know-everything approach but *in spite of it*, and they do so because they know, instinctively if not consciously, that the fact that actual people are mostly full canvases doesn't mean that our characters should be too. They know that the relative absence of our characters' outer lives is one of the essential differences between Homo fictus and Homo sapiens, a difference we should exploit, not destroy. For if we don't exploit it, selectivity and "the truthfulness of the essential" will suffer, and we will be in danger of proving that Voltaire was right when he said, "The secret of being a bore is to tell everything."

4. Likely Glove Locations vs. All that David Copperfield Kind of Crap

If compiling a list of traits and attributes isn't the way to create a character, what is? A more effective way, I'd argue, is to let the imagination supply the details as the needs of the story arise— and during the actual composition of the story, not in advance. As Gass points out, the imagination is driven by concepts, and it naturally ignores details unrelated to those concepts. (These concepts need not be conscious; indeed, characters arise largely from unconscious concepts.) To illustrate his point, Gass describes the process by which he tries to remember where he left his gloves. "I ransack a room in my mind until I find them," he says. "But the room I ransack is abstract—a simple schema. I leave out the drapes and the carpet, and I think of the room as a set of likely glove locations." Similarly, when we create characters, our concepts about them lead us to create the details that most convey their essence. It is precisely because the imagination works in this way that the best characters are "mostly empty canvas."

Take Holden Caulfield, for example. Holden is, like Gass's "likely glove locations," a relatively simple schema: he consists of a handful of physical details, a couple of days of conversations and interactions with fewer than a dozen characters, and snippets of memories of three or four past events (principally, the death of his brother Allie). As *The Catcher in the Rye*'s famous first sentence makes clear, Salinger is not interested in giving us the kind of detailed, expansive information conventional advice calls for, information he dismisses as "all that David Copperfield kind of crap." Rather, he wants to give us only the information that conveys the essence of his character. For simplicity's sake, I'll focus here on Salinger's physical description of Holden; suffice it to say that he is just as sparing with the other modes of characterization (i.e., thought, dialogue, and action) as he is with this one.

In the course of the novel, Salinger gives us only seven descriptive details about Holden, and all serve to reveal the essence of his character. Here are the details:

1. He has a deep voice;
2. he's unusually tall for a sixteen-year-old;
3. he's had "millions of gray hairs" on one side of his head since he was a kid;
4. he wears a crew cut even though it's out of date and girls encourage him to grow his hair longer;
5. he wears a red hunting hat backwards;
6. he has a sore on the inside of his lip; and
7. he's unable to make a fist with his right hand because he broke it while knocking out all the windows in his family's garage after his brother died.

The first three details—his deep voice, atypical height, and gray hair—underline the fact that in some ways he's prematurely old (and perhaps, as the gray hairs may suggest, precociously wise). The crew cut indicates that he's hesitant about change and reluctant to leave his childhood. The hunting hat reveals that he refuses to follow the crowd (no one else wears hunting hats on the streets of New York City in 1950), and the fact that he wears it backwards tells us that he's the opposite of a hunter, a protector (he worries about what happens to the ducks in Central Park in winter and fantasizes about standing in a field of rye on "the edge of some crazy cliff" and catching children before they fall off). The sore on the inside of his lip, which makes him worry he has cancer, serves to reveal his fear of dying like his brother. And his damaged hand illustrates the fact that his anger at the world and its phoniness and sorrows hurts only himself (he is, after all, narrating the novel from a sanatorium, where he's recuperating from a breakdown).

Salinger's description of Holden works because the details convey the essence of his character, not just "paint a picture." It's possible, of course, that Salinger created Holden in the roundabout way Burroway and others recommend, but I suspect it's far more likely he simply used his imagination in the way Gass describes. If he hadn't, I believe, the novel would be littered with far more details about Holden's appearance—and far more incidents, relationships, and backstory as well. In short, we would have found out where Holden was born and what his lousy childhood was like and how his parents were occupied and all before they had him, and all the rest of "that David Copperfield kind of crap."

5. The Fourth Dimension

While conventional wisdom tells us we should know everything about our character, there's one thing in particular we're told we absolutely must know: our character's motivation. In virtually every creative writing guide, workshop, and author interview, motivation is discussed as if it were the be-all and end-all of characterization. Without motivation, we're told, the character simply can't be plausible and the story is doomed to fail. As Rick DeMarinis has testified, "If *motive* is missing, your character can go through all sorts of delightful or hair-raising adventures and it won't add up to a hill of beans." But if motivation is present—and not only present but clearly defined—well, that's when a character becomes "real." Or so says John Emmons, who claims "Characters come alive... when their motivation is apparent to readers," and Dufresne, who claims characters can be "convincing" only when readers "know why they do what they do." Adam Sexton goes so far as to say that motivation is "The fourth dimension of characterization" and without it a character cannot truly "come to life."

The advice-givers are not only certain that understanding motivation is essential, they're also certain what it is: desire. Every discussion of character I've encountered equates motivation and desire. Tom Bailey, for example, quotes Aristotle, who said "man is his desire," then says, "This desire, the need that makes him or her, can be termed the character's motivation."

Burroway is also a representative voice on this subject. She says "the importance of desire in creating character can scarcely be overstated," for understanding a character's desire is "the first principle to grasp in the creation of character." Robert Olen Butler agrees, though he finds the word *desire* too sedate for his taste: he prefers *yearning*. For him, understanding a character's yearning is so essential that he says, "Until a character with yearning has emerged from your unconscious, I don't encourage you to write at all." Without a clearly defined desire to motivate a character's behavior, he suggests, we might as well not bother visiting our writing desk, for motivation is not only the key to character, it's the key to plot. Plot, he says, echoing virtually everybody from Aristotle on down, consists of "the attempt to fulfill the yearning and the world's attempt to thwart that." Butler has certainly defined one very valid kind of plot (and written numerous excellent stories and novels that employ that plot), but it's far from being the only kind of plot, or even, in my judgment, the best kind of plot. I tend to prefer plots in which the conflict is internal rather than external. I find *Hamlet* far more compelling and complex than *Romeo and Juliet*, for example, precisely because Hamlet's desires are in conflict more with themselves than with the world.

And Butler, like the others who tout the desire-based view of character and plot, seems to think of desire as something singular and fixed. Burroway certainly does. Everything that occurs in a story should be "in the service of a fixed desire," she says. Brandi Reissenweber likewise calls for "one driving desire" and says "the storyline will grow organically" from this desire. And Julia Fierro argues that the protagonist's desire should not only be singular and fixed but *unique*: it should be "Not what *all people* want, but what *that character*, and absolutely no other, wants," for "It is the uniqueness of the character's desire . . . that will make both you and the reader confident that the character is a genuine person."

Let me get this straight: even though human beings are composed—or so both experience and neuroscience tell me—of numerous conflicting and ever-changing desires, a character should have just one fixed desire, and it has to be a desire that no other character in literature or human being in history has ever had?

This sounds like a formula for creating an utterly implausible character, not a realistic one. Making a character's desire singular, fixed, and unique is exactly the sort of simplification that reduces the character's realism. I don't believe that human beings have fixed, unitary, unique selves, and hence I also don't believe they have fixed, unitary, unique desires. In my opinion, it would be more accurate to say that characters are motivated by multiple, shifting, and conflicting desires, most of which they share with the majority of their fellow humans, but even that definition of motivation strikes me as inexact and incomplete.

In any case, while desire certainly has a longstanding and legitimate role in motivating characters throughout literary history, there are other motives, and therefore other plots, available to writers. If we think of character and plot solely in terms of desire, especially a fixed desire, we significantly limit both of these essential elements of fiction.

I see at least six serious problems involved in the assumption that desire is, or should be, the sole motivation in fiction.

First, equating desire and motivation ignores the question of what motivated the desire. Why is one character afflicted with a certain desire and another one not? Why does Ahab want to wreak vengeance on Moby-Dick for taking his leg while Captain Boomer, who lost an arm to the same whale, doesn't?

Second, many characters' desires change in the course of the story (so much for the notion of a fixed desire) and that change is either motivated by something other than the initial desire or not clearly motivated at all. In Joyce Carol Oates's "Where Are You Going, Where Have You Been?," for example, the desire that drives Connie at the beginning of the story—her self-absorbed desire to escape her family's influence and control—turns, at the end, into a self-less desire to save the lives of her family, including her mother, whom she had earlier wished was dead. And while Connie's change is motivated in part by her confrontation with Arnold Friend, her love for her family and her capacity for self-sacrifice, which have apparently been submerged parts of her character all along, are not—and they, more than anything Arnold Friend says, are what motivate her behavior at the story's end.

While Connie has at least some motivation for her change in desire, characters in other stories sometimes change their desires without any motivation whatsoever. In Chekhov's "The

Lady with the Dog," for example, Gurov's rakish desire for a brief affair with Anna turns into a loving desire to spend his life with her, and Chekhov doesn't pretend to show or even tell us what motivates his change of feeling; he merely asserts that it happens. And since Gurov wants to remain his rakish self, his change occurs in direct opposition to his desire: he changes *in spite of* his desire, not *because* of it. What motivates his new desire is never specified or even hinted at. He falls in love with Anna, sure—but why? We can invent our own explanations for his change of heart, of course, but if we do, we're no longer reading Chekhov's story, we're writing our own.

Third, some stories begin with a character motivated by desire but end with him or her motivated by something else. Take O'Connor's "A Good Man Is Hard to Find," for example. For most of the story, the grandmother's behavior is clearly motivated by two straightforward desires: first, the desire to go where she wants to go for a vacation rather than where the rest of the family wants to go, and second, the desire to avoid being murdered by the Misfit. But neither desire motivates her behavior in the story's climactic moment. Indeed, we could even say that what motivates her behavior there is the abrupt *disappearance* of desire, for it's only when she's free of the petty desires that have driven her throughout the story that she's open to what O'Connor calls "the action of grace" and therefore is able to recognize her "kinship" to the Misfit and achieve a kind of salvation. (At least that's O'Connor's explanation of her story's climactic moment in her essay "A Reasonable Use of the Unreasonable.") At the climax of "A Good Man Is Hard to Find," any equation between desire and motivation simply vanishes. The same thing happens at the climax of Raymond Carver's "Cathedral." There, the narrator's desire that he not have to deal with his wife's blind friend vanishes and he achieves a sort of communion with him, a communion that he hadn't desired any more than the grandmother desired her feeling of "kinship" with the Misfit. And if the most crucial moment of a story isn't motivated by desire, why should we privilege desire as the be-all and end-all of motivation?

Fourth, some characters never discover what, exactly, they desire; the desire that motivates them, then, is the Chinese box-like desire to know what they desire. That's a plausible desire, of course, but I don't think it's what Aristotle had in mind when he said "man is his desire" or what Burroway and Butler have in mind when they say desire is what determines a story's plot. Kafka's "A Hunger Artist" is an example of this kind of story. At its end, the Hunger Artist reveals what has motivated his fasting. In part, he confesses, it's the desire for his audience's admiration—he says, "I always wanted you to admire my fasting"—but he acknowledges a much deeper motive: he never found the food he desired. If he had found it, he says, "I should have made no fuss and stuffed myself like you or anyone else." When the story ends, then, he's no closer to knowing just what he desires than at any other point. His desire remains undefined, elusive, his motivation a mystery to him as well as to us.

Fifth, while a character may have a clearly defined desire, the author may be far more interested in a desire he or she *lacks*. The prostitute protagonist of Chekhov's "A Gentleman Friend," for example, wants nothing more than some fancy clothes so she can ply her trade at a swanky nightclub called the Renaissance, but as the name of the nightclub ironically suggests, what Chekhov—and, therefore, the reader—desires is that she be "reborn" and change her life. What is a happy story from her perspective—she ultimately gets the clothes she wants—is a sad story from Chekhov's perspective, for she fails to replace her trivial, materialistic desire with a meaningful, spiritual one. The surface plot of the story, then, deals with the presence of one desire while what we can call the "shadow plot" cast by the surface plot deals with an absent one. And it is the absent desire that truly matters.

Finally, in some stories, desire does not drive either the character or the plot. What desire motivates Nick Adams in Hemingway's "Indian Camp" or "In Another Country"? Or Anders in Tobias Wolff's "Bullet in the Brain"? Or Fuckhead in Denis Johnson's "Car Crash While Hitchhiking"? The list could go on, but you get the point: some stories are about things that happen to characters, or things they witness, not events their desires initiate. This seems an obvious thing to say, but judging from my survey of creative writing guides, no one seems to be saying it.

In my opinion, the best creative writing advice is not prescriptive but descriptive; it lets us know what writers have done, and therefore what we might do, rather than make claims about what we should or should not do. The prescriptions we find in creative writing guides are often belied by the actual practice of fiction writers, and it is their practice that I suggest we attend to. If we do, we'll see that, while many stories—the majority, no doubt—are indeed driven by a character's desire, and end with her achieving that desire, or failing to achieve that desire, or merely discovering what she has been desiring all along, other stories—including some of the best ever written—follow very different plot patterns and employ very different motivations.

6. Half-Known Characters

Despite the evidence that desire and motivation aren't inherently synonymous, writers and teachers seem content to assert that a character's desire motivates all of his behavior, not just some of it. But however we define motivation, do we really need a complete understanding of our characters' motivations? I would say no. In fact, I'd say it's actually a good thing if we *don't* understand, at least not fully, our characters' motives. The best characters, in my opinion, are those whose motivation is, as Boswell would say, half-known. A fully known motivation would inevitably limit the realism of the character and, therefore, the story. In real life, we may *pretend* to know someone's motive—this pretense is most apparent in gossip and courts of law—but who is really all that certain about anyone's motives, even our own? As Aimee Bender says, "We've been trained to believe that psychology is cause and effect, but, actually, our motivations are complicated and messy, and how our actions tie into our motivation isn't always clear." We've been taught a plot is causal—i.e., it traces the cause-and-effect relationship of its events—and that motivation is the through-line that ties the events together. But if cause and effect aren't this overt in life, should fiction suggest that they are?

The desire-based theory of character implies characters actually *do* know what they desire, that their motivation *is* clear, and that each effect has a definable, understandable cause. Interestingly, the most intriguing characters in literature are those whose deepest motivations are impossible to parse. Witness Hamlet. We're still arguing about his motivation. And Hamlet himself—perhaps because of growing pains in those pesky frontal lobes—doesn't understand why he delays avenging his father's murder. He asks himself during one of his soliloquies,

> ... Now, whether it be
> Bestial oblivion, or some craven scruple
> Of thinking too precisely on th' event—
> A thought which, quartered, hath but one part wisdom
> And ever three parts coward—I do not know
> Why yet I live to say 'This thing's to do,'
> Sith I have cause, and will, and strength, and means,
> To do't.

Various critics have glommed on to one or another of the motives he lists, but it's clear that none of them is the "answer." All we know for sure is that Hamlet's desire to kill the king must be matched by an equally strong desire not to kill him, for there is no compelling external reason for his delay. But what, exactly, prevents him from following his "will" to kill Claudius? And why does his father's charge that he kill his uncle lead him to consider killing *himself*? According to conventional advice about characterization, we should be able to answer these questions—and every other question the play raises about Hamlet—because we should know everything about our characters. But if we could answer these questions, Hamlet would be a fully known character, not a half-known one, and a fully known character is, paradoxically, not fully human, for human beings are too complex and opaque to be completely understood.

In his book *Will in the World: How Shakespeare Became Shakespeare*, Stephen Greenblatt argues that the absence of a clear motive for Hamlet's delay is intentional—and an important artistic discovery. He points out that the source material for *Hamlet*—and for Shakespeare's subsequent tragedies—contains clearly defined motives for the characters' behavior, motives that provide "a familiar, comforting rationale that seems to make it all make sense." But Shakespeare not only refused to include these motives, he refused to replace them with other, similarly explanatory ones. In writing *Hamlet*, Greenblatt says,

> Shakespeare found that he could immeasurably deepen the effect of his plays, that he could provoke in the audience and in himself a

peculiarly passionate intensity of response, if he took out a key explanatory element, thereby occluding the rationale, motivation, or ethical principle that accounted for the action that was to unfold. The principle was not the making of a riddle to be solved, but the creation of a strategic opacity.

This "strategic opacity," created by the "excision of motive," is what makes Hamlet a half-known character. By making something that's too often transparent in literature—the character's motivation—opaque and unknowable, as it often, maybe even always, is in real people, Shakespeare created the first truly realistic character in literature. As K.L. Cook has said,

> Throughout the play, [Hamlet] seems both brilliant and foolish, spiritual and crude, melancholy and manic, empathetic and callous, indecisive to the point of paralysis at one point and then suicidally impulsive at others. There is a mysterious contradiction at the center of his character that is both consistent and unfathomable.

I suspect that even those who claim we need to know our characters' motives inside and out find Hamlet a compelling and believable character precisely because they *don't* fully understand his motivation. Methinks, in short, they doth protest too much.

T.S. Eliot may be an exception. Shakespeare's "strategic opacity" seems to have irritated him as much as it impresses Greenblatt. In his essay "Hamlet and His Problems," he says that "So far from being Shakespeare's masterpiece, the play is most certainly an artistic failure" because Shakespeare did not "impose" a motive on his principal character. He argues that "the delay in revenge is unexplained on grounds of necessity or expediency" and hence he compares the play unfavorably to Thomas Kyd's earlier play *Hamlet*, in which Hamlet's motive was revenge, pure and simple, and the delay in achieving it was caused merely "by the difficulty of assassinating a monarch surrounded by guards." Clearly, Eliot wanted the play to follow the same internal-desire-vs.-external-obstacles dynamic that

Butler and others recommend, but why he, or anyone, would favor such a reductive and simplistic motive and plot over the mystery and complexity of Shakespeare's play is beyond me.

As I see it, Hamlet is a more powerful character, and his play all the more a masterpiece, for the very reason that we can't find a one-to-one—or even a two- or three- or four-to-one—correspondence between his motives and his behavior. And I'm far from alone in holding this view. As Charles Baxter notes, "Gertrude Stein shrewdly remarks that the reason people still talk about *Hamlet* has to do, not with what people understand about it, but with what they continue, down through the years, not to understand." As Boswell might say, what makes Hamlet such a great character is that he is half-known—he is composed of both what we understand about him and what we don't—and what we don't understand is what makes him so fascinating. And not just him. As Rust Hills has said, "With some exceptions, all the intriguing characters in literature have very unclear motivation."

Our uncertainty about Hamlet's motivation is what makes him resonate with something akin to the complexity of real people. Certainty about motives, on the other hand, leads to a reductive sense of who your character is. To equate a character with a single desire—or even a couple of conflicting desires—tends to simplify the character, make him flatter than he needs to be. As Bender says, explaining behavior in this way not only "reduces fiction and . . . the human mind. It also demeans the character." If, as Forster says, the "test of a round character is whether it is capable of surprising in a convincing way," how could any character defined by a single fixed desire pass that test? Wouldn't such a character, by definition, be incapable of surprising us? If you ask me, the only characters who are truly capable of surprising us in a convincing way, the way people in real life are capable of surprising us, are those whose motivations remain at least partly mysterious. Tim O'Brien agrees. Convincing characters are achieved, he says,

> not through a "pinning down" process but rather through a process that opens up and releases mysteries of the human spirit. The object is not to "solve" a character—to expose some hidden secret—but instead to deepen and enlarge the riddle itself. Too often, I believe, characteriza-

tion fails precisely because it attempts to characterize. It narrows; it pins down; it explicates; it solves. . . . This sort of characterization has the effect of diminishing the very mystery that makes us care so passionately about other human beings.

As I hope I've shown, knowing everything about our characters, especially their motivations, makes them differ from real people in a way that prevents them from being truly realistic. When it comes to fiction writing, the old cliché about a little knowledge being a dangerous thing is false. What's most dangerous in fiction is having too much knowledge. It's dangerous because it leads us to include information that distracts the reader, and us, from the essence of the character and because it leads us to think we understand more than we actually do, or can, about our characters and their motivations. Quite literally, creative writing guides are trying to make us know-it-alls, at least when it comes to characterization. I hope we'll resist that temptation.

7. A Great Step Forward

It's been more than four hundred years since Shakespeare discovered the principle of strategic opacity, but still the vast majority of people who comment on characterization have failed to recognize the value of that principle. However, writers—consciously or not—have learned from Shakespeare's example and created characters who are "half-known worlds" unto themselves. This has never been truer than it is now. Even DeMarinis, who is a strong proponent of desire-based characterization and plot, admits that many characters in contemporary fiction lack a clearly defined desire that motivates their behavior. Indeed, he says that much of contemporary fiction is about "[a] character who wants something he or she can't define." Darren Townsend, the protagonist of Benjamin Percy's "Meltdown," is a good example of this kind of character. As Percy says, "Darren occasionally gets the feeling—this dread surging through him—that he is never going to find what he wants, even though he doesn't know exactly what he wants." DeMarinis notes that characters who don't know what they want "populate the work of Alice Munro and Joyce Carol Oates and countless others," including Flannery O'Connor, Raymond Carver, and Tobias Wolff. He says, "Sherwood Anderson might well be the godfather of this kind of story," but I'd give that title to Chekhov, whose stories frequently comment on the inscrutability of human motivation. In "The Darling," for example, the otherwise omniscient narrator reports that Olenka, the title character, loves the son of a former lover so much that she "would give her whole life" for him, then he asks himself, and us, "Why?" His answer is that there is no answer: "Who knows why?" Chekhov's stories often end with the main character unable to understand what motivated his or her actions. See, for example, the conclusion of his woefully underread masterpiece "Terror," in which the protagonist exclaims, "Why have I done this? . . . Why has it turned out like this and not differently?" These are the questions that resonate throughout Chekhov's fiction, and to his everlasting credit, he refuses to pretend he knows how to answer them.

Like Shakespeare, Chekhov had the quality Keats called Negative Capability, the ability to remain "in uncertainties, mysteries, doubts, without any irritable reaching after fact and reason." Whether they realize it or not, the proponents of knowing everything about our characters, from their motivations to their favorite brand of underwear, are proponents of irritably reaching after fact and reason. In their advice, if not (thank goodness) in their own fiction, they champion what could be called *Positive* Capability, the ability to know everything, without any irritable reaching after uncertainties, doubts, and mysteries. Ironically, the proponents of knowing everything claim to be proponents of Negative Capability; they quote Keats's comment regularly and always approvingly. Some things are *both/and*s, not *either/or*s, but this one's an *either/or*: either a writer's greatness stems from acknowledging uncertainty, mystery, and doubt or it stems from knowing and understanding everything. The two attitudes toward reality, and human beings, are mutually exclusive. If you ask me, Negative Capability is the key to creating truly round, realistic characters, whereas Positive Capability can lead only to the creation of characters of varying degrees of flatness. I like George Saunders's definition of a successful character: the "sum total of moments we can't explain."

Chekhov most certainly did not believe he, or anyone else, could know everything about his characters or parse their motivations. In a letter, he wrote,

> It is time for writers to admit that nothing in this world makes sense. Only fools and charlatans think they know and understand everything. The stupider they are, the wider they conceive their horizons to be. And if an artist decides to declare that he understands nothing of what he sees—this in itself constitutes a considerable clarity in the realm of thought, and a great step forward.

This is a step that now, more than a century after his death, we have just barely begun to take. It is high time more of us took it.

Who's Afraid of the
Big Bad Abstraction?:
Conveying Emotion in Fiction

1. Be Afraid. Be Very Afraid

Most creative writing instruction is inevitably negative—it's a lot easier to tell apprentice writers what they should avoid doing than what they should do—but few aspects of craft are taught more negatively than the all-important subject of conveying emotion. The most influential and oft-repeated advice on this subject is, no doubt, Ezra Pound's imperial imperative "Go in fear of abstractions." The fact that he phrased this advice as a commandment, echoing the exhortations of Biblical prophets (and their contemporary cousins, TV evangelists) to "Go in fear of the Lord," might explain why so many writers have taken his advice as holy writ. Leaving aside the fact that his admonition to avoid abstractions is itself abstract, it is nonetheless largely sound advice. But the argument he uses to support his advice reveals the danger of taking it as an unbreakable commandment. "Don't use such an expression as 'dim lands *of peace*,'" he says. "It . . . mixes an abstraction with the concrete. It comes from the writer's not realizing that the natural object is always the *adequate* symbol." Oh, really? If the writer just wrote "dim lands," the reader would automatically think of *peace*? Maybe Pound would, but I wouldn't. All I'd think of is, well, *dim lands*.

Pound's advice has been repeated as gospel by many writers and teachers, but no one has seconded it with as much fervor as

Robert Olen Butler. If Pound sounds like a televangelist, Butler sounds like a pope. Speaking *ex cathedra*, Butler doesn't suggest that good abstractions might go to heaven, the unbaptized ones to limbo, and all the rest to purgatory or fiery hell; no, they're all damned, and right from the get-go. (For a pope, Butler is quite the Calvinist.) "Absolutely never name an emotion," he says in *From Where We Dream*; "never start explaining or analyzing or interpreting an emotion."

In short, be afraid. Be very, very afraid.

Me, I get nervous when I hear the word *never*. And when someone tells me never to do something, I'm liable to want to do it even more. Furthermore, an excellent case can be made for the judicious use of abstractions; in fact, Stephen Dunn has already made that case very persuasively in his essay "Some Reflections on the Abstract and the Wise." But even though I think Butler seriously overstates his case, I'm ultimately more a disciple of his than a reprobate. There are, after all, extremely good reasons to be afraid of abstractions—at least afraid enough to respect them and handle them with care. As Butler stresses, "*emotions reside in the senses.*" Without some appeal to the senses, then, it is very difficult, if not downright impossible, for us to make our readers experience our characters' emotions. Virtually all authors of craft books—including, of course, Butler—have made this point and rightly advised writers to convey their characters' emotions via the senses. Relatively few have provided positive, successful examples of sensory expression of emotion, however, and none, to my knowledge, has defined the various modes of conveying emotion available to writers and extrapolated principles for their use, as I hope to do in this essay.

The primary ways writers can convey emotion through the senses are body language and metaphor, each of which can convey emotion either by itself or in combination with the other. And, as I hope to show, both body language and metaphor can also be combined with abstractions, for although Pound inveighs against mixing the abstract and the concrete, that is in fact often an effective way to convey emotion—and so, in some cases, is mixing the abstract with the abstract.

But even though I believe abstractions can be used effectively in certain circumstances, I think it's important to acknowledge the value of Pound and Butler's negative advice. More often than not, abstractions *do* undermine rather than aid our attempts to convey what our characters are feeling. So before I discuss the positive modes of conveying emotion, I will look first at some of the reasons we should have a healthy fear of abstractions.

2. The Misuse of Abstractions

Sensory Bypasses

All too often, we use an abstraction as a sort of shortcut to conveying emotion. Instead of creating on the page the physical sensation of fear, for example, we simply say "fear." But a shortcut for the writer is a longcut for the reader. When we bypass the senses and go directly to an abstraction, we are asking the reader to do the hard work of imagining the physical sensations of the emotion for us, and readers aren't any less susceptible to laziness than we are, so more often than not the reader doesn't take the longcut: she just skips the trip entirely. Either that or she gets lost. (Or my analogy does . . .)

Let me illustrate this problem with three examples of such shortcuts, all taken (with permission) from stories by my undergraduate students:

> Jason was delighted.
> Trisha's anxiety rose.
> There was anger in Evan's voice.

Do you feel Jason's delight, Trisha's anxiety, or Evan's anger? Nope, you only *know* they're feeling these emotions, and knowledge is a poor substitute for feeling. The primary aim of fiction, it seems to me, is to make the readers experience what the characters experience; understanding that experience, if it happens at all, is only a byproduct of that primary aim. As E.L. Doctorow once said, "Good writing is supposed to evoke sensation in the reader—not the fact that it is raining, but the feeling of being rained upon." The three sentences I just quoted don't create the sensations of delight, anxiety, or anger because the abstract words *delighted, anxiety,* and *anger* can't convey the sensory feelings they label.

The problem with these examples is that they bypass the senses, and when you bypass the senses, you bypass the heart and go directly to the head, without passing Go. Undergraduate students aren't the only ones prone to writing such sentences, of course; even the best of us succumb to sensory bypasses in our weaker moments. Often, sensory bypasses star such words as *appear, seem, look, obvious, clear, visible* (and their variants), words that vainly attempt to give the illusion that the reader is actually witnessing the body language that conveys the emotions the author has labeled abstractly. Here are six examples, all but the last from writers I admire:

> Mr. Wilcox . . . glances at the couple, both visibly distressed . . .
> (Jhumpa Lahiri, *The Namesake*)

> The neighbor . . . was obviously a little confused at first . . .
> (Richard Bausch, "Wise Men at Their End")

> [I]t was clear that Miss Price was upset . . .
> (Richard Yates, "Doctor Jack-o'-Lantern")

> He appears nervous . . .
> (Adam Haslett, "Notes to My Biographer")

> Mary-Emma looked frightened.
> (Lorrie Moore, *A Gate at the Stairs*)

> He seemed genuinely sorry . . .
> (David Jauss, "Glossolalia")

Whenever I read the phrases *visibly upset* or *obviously pleased*—and I've read them and their first and second cousins literally thousands of times—I immediately want to know how the emotion is "visible" or "obvious." And since a given emotion can manifest itself in different ways at different times, I want to know what particular stage of the emotion is "visible" and "obvious." As Charles Darwin wrote in *The Expression of the Emotions in Man and Animals,* the first major study of nonverbal communication, "Persons suffering from excessive grief often seek relief by violent and often frantic movement . . . ; but when their suffering is somewhat mitigated, yet prolonged, they no longer wish for action, but remain motionless and passive . . ." So when we read the sentence "Hortense was obviously feeling grief," we may not know whether she's moving about frantically or sitting catatonically—or doing something else entirely. For sometimes people respond to grief—as to every other emotion—in unexpected ways. In *A Gate at the Stairs*, Lorrie Moore makes Bo Keltjin's grief visible through his unusual use of a handkerchief at his son's funeral. Instead of drying his eyes with it, as we might expect, he "presse[s] it completely over his face, like a barber's hot towel." With a sentence like that, we don't need the word *grief*; we witness it.

As the presence of words like *visible, appear,* and *look* in sensory bypasses might suggest, we often use the eyes as a shortcut to abstract statements of emotion. Besides opening, narrowing, closing, shifting, rolling, and tearing up, eyes do relatively little that is actually visible, yet they are the most overworked body parts in all of fiction. The main reason for this, I believe, is that mentioning the eyes gives us (if not the reader) the feeling that we're describing body language even when we're not. References to eyes almost always devolve into abstract statements, and as a result, sentences about eyes tend to fall into the category of sensory bypasses. Here are three examples, all taken from works by excellent writers to demonstrate that this is a weakness even the best of us are prone to.

> There was terror in the poor man's eyes.
> (Frederick Exley, *A Fan's Notes*)
>
> It almost embarrassed her to see his eyes so earnest and guilty . . .
> (Dan Chaon, *Await Your Reply*)
>
> The stiffly seated guests looked at me, some with anger in their eyes, some with cruel hilarity.
> (Rick DeMarinis, "Pagans")

As these examples should suggest, when it comes to conveying emotion, the eyes don't have it.

Glosses

As a mode of expressing emotion, a gloss is only marginally preferable to a sensory bypass. Whereas a sensory bypass might allude to body language but doesn't actually describe it, a gloss *does* describe body language—but then proceeds to interpret it for the reader. For example, when Stuart Dybek—one of my favorite writers, I hasten to add—says that a character's eyes "suddenly widened in horror," he's doing the reader's job of interpreting the emotion behind those widened eyes and thereby preventing the reader from fully participating in the process of discovering meaning. Glosses arise, I believe, when we fail to trust the reader to interpret correctly the body language we've described and the context in which it occurs.

Following are three examples of glosses by other exceptional writers. In the context in which each of these sentences appears, the reader should be able to ascertain the emotion through the body language without any additional prompting by the author:

> The mother's face contracted with disgust.
> (Katherine Vaz, "Math Bending Unto Angels")

> Indignation tensed the muscles of her face . . .
> (Lorrie Moore, *A Gate at the Stairs*)

> Sometimes his face swelled purple with anger, and he pounded on the door till he was sobbing with exertion.
> (Doris Lessing, *In Pursuit of the English*)

Butler, who argues that fiction should be an "omnisensual cinema" of the mind, uses the film *As Good As It Gets* to illustrate the problem with glosses:

> Consider how Jack Nicholson as a crotchety old bachelor in a movie looks at Helen Hunt. We see his face on the screen; he lifts an eyebrow; his lips curl. If the screen suddenly went blank and the word "wryly" came up, or "sarcasm," or "contempt," how would you react? You can imagine: with great discomfort. For readers

who know how to read, abstraction, generalization, analysis, and interpretation have the same deleterious effect.

That "deleterious effect" is the feeling of being condescended to by a writer who doesn't consider us bright enough to interpret the body language on our own. To me, glosses inevitably feel like authorial intrusions, the writer nudging us in the ribs to make sure we get the point. Often, the body language is little more than a feeble attempt to veil the author's reliance on the shortcut of abstraction. And sometimes the glosses take a related shortcut, the shortcut of scientific terminology. References to adrenaline "kicking in" are perhaps the most ubiquitous examples of this, although I've also come across references to dopamine, serotonin, oxytocin, and endorphins in many writers' work. Richard Powers at least has the excuse that his characters are scientists and so more are likely to think of biological reactions during moments of sexual passion. But that excuse doesn't make passages like the following any more effective at conveying his characters' passion:

> He surges on the dopamine, the spikes of endorphins . . . They flood each other, waves of oxytocin and a savage bonding . . .
> (*The Echo Maker*)

> Every program in his body, every enzyme, every gemule collaborates on synthesizing a single biophor: take this woman and kiss her . . .
> (*Gold Bug Variations*)

All of these allusions to chemicals have the effect of abstractions in that they don't actually describe a sensation or emotion but label it in non-sensory terms. What's worse, they take us out of the fiction and put us into a chemistry classroom.

It all comes down to this: glosses don't make us feel an emotion, they only make us *know* it. Still, interpreting or analyzing body language you describe is preferable to bypassing body language entirely and going directly to abstraction.

But now let's turn to more positive ways to convey emotion in our work.

3. Let's Get Physical: Body Language

Let me hear your body talk.
—Olivia Newton-John, "Physical"

Action Is Eloquence

Depending on which scientific study you most believe, 65% to 90% of all communication in life is conveyed through body language,[3] so it would stand to reason that fiction—at least the kind of fiction that attempts to replicate life—would have a similarly high proportion of body language. But even though body language is the principal way we experience and convey emotion in life, it is largely AWOL from our fiction. My best estimate is that body language accounts for less than a fourth—probably a good deal less—of the emotional communication in most contemporary fiction. Too many of us—myself included—neglect this all-important mode of communication.

But before we discuss this issue further, let's make sure we all understand what the term *body language* encompasses. As the scholar Barbara Korte says in *Body Language in Literature*, body language consists of "movements and postures, facial expression, glances and eye contact, automatic reactions, [and] spatial and touching behaviour." Most of these modes of body language are self-explanatory, but a couple might need some clarification. By "automatic reactions," Korte means such "physiological and physio-chemical reactions" as "trembling, change in skin colour, perspiration, etc." And by "spatial" behavior, she means the proximity of the characters, the way they "arrange themselves in relation to each other." For example, if a woman says "I love you" to a man while standing directly in front of him and gazing into his eyes, that sentence will mean something other than it would if she said it to him from across the room with her back turned to him.

The base function of body language is to reveal emotion in a sensory way. We don't need a gloss to understand what emotions the following characters are feeling:

> He let his eyes roam from my keggy thighs, to my hips, up to my stuffed blouse. As he looked,

his fine nostrils opened. I'm telling you he was breathing hard.
(Rick DeMarinis, "Culture Shocks")

Maples stabbed the ice in his drink with his straw.
(Anthony Doerr, "The Hunter's Wife")

When I open my arms to embrace him he takes a step backward.
(Adam Haslett, "Notes to My Biographer")

Nor do we need a gloss to know what the characters are feeling in this scene from Ian McEwan's *The Comfort of Strangers*:

> Colin had brought the joint indoors for Mary, and she had refused it—a quick murmur of "No thanks"—without turning in her seat. He lingered behind her, staring into the mirror with her, trying to catch her eye. But she looked straight ahead at herself and continued to brush her hair. He traced the line of her shoulder with his finger. Sooner or later, the silence would have to break. Colin turned to leave, and changed his mind. He cleared his throat, and rested his hand firmly on her shoulder . . . if he moved away now, having touched her, she might, conceivably at least, be offended . . . but then, she was continuing to brush her hair, long after it was necessary, and it seemed she was waiting for Colin to leave . . . Miserably, he ran his finger along the line of Mary's spine. She now held the handle of the brush in one hand and rested the bristles in the open palm of the other, and continued to stare ahead. Colin leaned forward and kissed her nape, and when she still did not acknowledge him, he crossed the room with a noisy sigh and returned to the balcony.

This passage contains virtually no dialogue, but its action is more eloquent than any dialogue could be. Even without the inclusion of Colin's gloss-like thoughts, we would know, from the body language alone, that he is trying, and failing miserably, to restore peace to their troubled relationship.

For many years, I've made the case for body language to my students by asking them to imagine the following scene: a woman gazing out a window while slowly tracing and retracing a circle in the dust on the windowsill with her fingertip. Then I ask them to tell me everything they know about this woman and what she's feeling. After the obligatory wisecrack "She's a lousy housekeeper," they say that she's sad, lonely, lethargic, bored, and pensive, and that she feels trapped in a repetitive, monotonous routine and wishes she could be elsewhere or that someone would come and rescue her from her dreary life. I then reveal that the woman I had in mind—and the woman they have described to a T—is none other than Emma Bovary.[4] And I also reveal that they have proved that Shakespeare was right when he said, "Action is eloquence, and the eyes of th' ignorant / More learned than the ears," for even the most ignorant of us hold PhDs in the interpretation of body language. And then, to indicate just how much more eloquent body language is to our learned eyes than abstract statements are to our ears, I "translate" my description of Emma into abstract summary, as follows:

> Emma was sad, lonely, lethargic, bored, and pensive, and she felt trapped in life's repetitive routines and wished she could be elsewhere or that someone would come and rescue her from her dreary life.

As this sentence should suggest, taking the shortcut to abstraction is like bypassing *Madame Bovary* and going directly to *Cliff's Notes*.

Body Language and Individuation

The best body language is not only revelatory but individuating, as when Bo Keltjin covers his face with a handkerchief "like a barber's hot towel" at his son's funeral in Lorrie Moore's *A Gate at the Stairs*. If Moore had written "He dabbed his eyes with the handkerchief," his body language would still have conveyed grief, but it would have been a generic grief, not the intense individual grief of this particular man. Elizabeth Strout is another writer who pays close attention to the individual ways her characters manifest their emotions. In her story "Tulips," both Olive and Henry Kittredge are devastated by some news their son has given them, but their devastation manifests itself in distinctly different ways, ways that reveal the differences in their characters:

> Henry spent the evening sitting in the living room with his head in his hands.
> "Come on. Snap out of it," Olive said. . . . But her hands were trembling, and she went and took everything out of the refrigerator and cleaned the inside and the racks with a sponge that she dipped into a bowl of cool water and baking soda. Then she put everything back into the refrigerator. Henry was still sitting with his head in his hands.

Great literature is full of examples of such individuated body language, but I'll content myself with just two examples. In *The Great Gatsby*, Fitzgerald conveys a plethora of Nick Carraway's individual qualities—his politeness, his sympathetic nature, his desire to save others from embarrassment, his concern for appearances, a physical fussiness that parallels his moral fussiness, and so forth—all through one small bit of body language. Early in the novel, Nick goes to a party at Mrs. Wilson's apartment in New York and meets Mr. McKee, a neighbor who, he says, "had just shaved, for there was a white spot of lather on his cheekbone." Nick doesn't mention this fleck of lather again until seven pages later, when he tells us that "Mr. McKee was asleep on a chair . . . Taking out my handkerchief I wiped from his cheek the remains of the spot of dried lather that had worried me all the afternoon." No one else at the party would have done what Nick did, and thus that act reveals his character in a non-generic, individualized way.

William Faulkner's "That Evening Sun" contains another brilliant example of individuated body language. In this story, a black servant named Nancy is terrified that her husband, Jesus, is going to kill her because she is pregnant with a white man's child. In an attempt to prevent her murder, she brings three children to her house and tries to entertain them. The children want to leave, so she tells them a story. They don't care for the story and they're about to leave, so Nancy tries again to keep them there. The body language that follows reveals her all-consuming fear of her husband far better than any direct abstract statement—or more typical body language like widened eyes and trembling hands—possibly could.

> "I know another story," Nancy said. . . . "It's better than the other one."
> "What's it about?" Caddy said. Nancy was standing by the lamp. Her hand was on the lamp, against the light, long and brown.
> "Your hand is on that hot globe," Caddy said. "Don't it feel hot to your hand?"
> Nancy looked at her hand on the lamp chimney. She took her hand away, slow. She stood there, looking at Caddy, wringing her long hand as though it were tied to her wrist with a string.

Mixing Body Language and Abstraction

As I mentioned earlier, mixing the abstract and the concrete can, despite the objections of Pound and Butler, be a valuable way to convey emotion. As proof, I offer one of Butler's own stories, the nearly novella-length "The American Couple," from his Pulitzer Prize-winning collection *A Good Scent from a Strange Mountain*. This story was clearly written before he descended from the mountain with the commandment to never name, explain, analyze, or interpret an emotion. Throughout the story, his narrator constantly interprets the body language of the people around her, and at one point she is even able to extrapolate the contents of a conversation between her husband and another man that she can't hear merely by witnessing their body language. The story not only uses a great deal of body language, it is in many ways *about* body language and what it communicates to us. The presence of abstraction in this story doesn't harm it; it complicates and enriches it. Indeed, if we stripped the abstract interpretations and analyses from the story, it would shrivel up and die.

What Butler's story reveals is that, sometimes, mixing the abstract and the concrete doesn't dilute the effect of the concrete, it *vivifies* the abstraction—in other words, by naming an emotion abstractly *and* conveying it sensorily, we can "import" physical sensation into the abstraction and make readers feel what they would otherwise only know. In some cases, then, linking an abstraction to body language goes beyond being a mere gloss and conveys what the body language and context alone could not possibly convey. Butler's story contains seventy-five pages of excellent examples; here is a typical—and typically wonderful—one:

> The wife lowered her book and her head angled slightly to the side and there was something around her eyes and mouth that was very hard to read. Like she loved this man and was distressed by him in such equal parts that there was only something very small and placid that she could ever show about him. Or maybe even feel.

If Butler had "gone in fear of abstractions," this passage would read, "The wife lowered her book and her head angled slightly to the side." How much of her emotion would this description of her body language allow you to feel? And how interested would you be in the story's first-person narrator if she didn't interpret the body language she witnesses? My guess is that your answer to both questions would be "Very little."

4. Getting Physical Through Metaphor

Mixing Body Language and Metaphor

The use of metaphor is another way writers "get physical." Metaphors are inherently sensory, after all, so they can complement and enrich body language. Diane Schoemperlen's story "Body Language" illustrates this use of metaphor superbly. As its title suggests, this story is, like Butler's "The American Couple," as much about body language as it is about its characters. The protagonist of the story suspects that his wife is having an affair but doesn't dare ask her, lest his suspicions be confirmed, so he spends the entire story attempting to understand, through her body language, what she is thinking and feeling. As Schoemperlen writes, "For now, as long as nobody speaks the words aloud, he can concentrate instead upon the language of her ankles, elbows, that small round bone protruding at the wrist . . . for now, he need listen only to her body . . ." But although the story focuses on body language, it also contains numerous metaphors that work with the body language to convey emotion. Here is my favorite example: "On a bad day she doesn't exactly push him away but turns, gracefully, out of his embrace like a ring once stuck on a finger magically removed with soap." What better way to convey his fear that his wife will leave him than to compare her body language to the removal of a ring?

In his story "Mission," Eric Puchner gives us another excellent example of a metaphor that works with body language to convey a feeling. "Later that night," he writes, "Nils woke from a dream, his heart clocking in his throat." Puchner doesn't need to say the word *panic*; the metaphor—the heart as a clock, the pulse of blood through veins as the clock's ticking—combines with the internal body language to convey not only the feeling of panic but the intensity of that feeling. Similarly, Julie Orringer conveys anxiety superbly in her story "Care" with her sentence "There's a hot fast clawing inside her chest"; Strout conveys confusion in "Incoming Tide" by saying "The inside of his head began to feel as choppy as the surf before him"; and Danielle Evans conveys shock and surprise in "Virgins" by saying, "It was like my whole body blinked." The work of our best writers is replete with similar examples.

Mixing Metaphor and Abstraction

Like body language, sensory metaphors can be used to vivify abstractions. Take this passage from *A Gate at the Stairs*, for example: "Here Sarah looked at me mischievously, her look a complicated room one might wander through, exploring for quite some time if there were any time." If Moore had merely said, "Here Sarah looked at me mischievously," she would have been guilty of writing a gloss and the emotion labeled by the abstract evaluation *mischievously* would have been dead on arrival. The metaphor complicates the gloss and brings the moment to life.

Here are some other sentences that successfully use sensory metaphors in conjunction with abstractions (and, sometimes, body language) to convey a variety of emotional states:

> The anger that had swarmed in his guts was gone . . .
> (Ehud Havazelet, "Like Never Before")

> The jolt of fear had burned all the red out of my blood.
> (Denis Johnson, "Two Men")

> Olive had almost spit, her fury's door flung open.
> (Elizabeth Strout, "Pharmacy")

> Rage consumed Elizabeth. She was a black flame.
> (Steven Millhauser, "A Protest Against the Sun")

> Guilt thick as tar bubbles in his gut . . .
> (Kirstin Valdez Quade, "The Five Wounds")

> Guilt and lust had grown in him like twin tumors.
> (Rick DeMarinis, "disneyland")

> Fear and sorrow flared up simultaneously like fires that put each other out.
> (Lorrie Moore, *A Gate at the Stairs*)

> Melanie waited for some dramatic feeling to wash over her. . . . Grief would be an embarrassing surrender, considering the new facts. Rage was inappropriate, given Michael's death. The two reactions had stalemated each other. She was an abandoned chessboard.
> (Rebecca Makkai, "The Museum of the Dearly Departed")

As these examples suggest, the principal advantage of using metaphor and/or body language in conjunction with an abstraction is to make the abstract idea become something we can perceive or feel. As Flannery O'Connor has said, "The fiction writer has to realize that he can't create compassion with compassion, or emotion with emotion, or thought with thought, or morality with morality. He has to provide these things with a body; he has to create a world with weight and extension." Fiction, she argues, is "an incarnational art," one that makes the abstract word become sensory flesh. But despite this argument against abstraction, and those by Pound and Butler (and yours truly), I believe mixing the abstract and the concrete is a technique that can, when used with care, enable that incarnation to take place.

Metaphor and Particularization

There is another important reason for using a metaphor in conjunction with an abstraction: just as body language can individuate a character, so metaphor can particularize an abstraction. One of the principal problems with abstractions is that they're one-size-fits-all; they are umbrella terms, as generic as possible, and so don't convey different gradations of an emotion. For example, the sentence "He felt despair" doesn't convey a particular kind or level of despair, much less how the despair felt. And adjectives and adverbs that convey the relative intensity of the emotion don't help much either, as when DeMarinis refers to a "small panic" or Moore describes a character as looking "fantastically sad." Good writers—and DeMarinis and Moore are of course among our best—are more successful when they particularize abstractions through the use of metaphors and/or body language.

Anthony Doerr obviously felt the need to distinguish between different kinds of joy when he wrote "a kind of joy splits his lips," but neither the word *kind* nor the lip-splitting smile can convey the particular kind of joy his character is feeling. Strout likewise acknowledges that there are different kinds of happiness when she writes, "He could not have said why this gave him the particular kind of happiness it did, like liquid gold being poured through him." Thanks to the use of this simile, however, she is better able to convey her character's particular kind of happiness than Doerr was able to convey his character's particular kind of joy. And Doerr himself does a better job of conveying a particular kind of joy in other stories, when he calls on metaphors to help him convey it. In "Mknondo," for example, he writes "joy founted up," and in "The Caretaker," he says, "Joy mounts in his chest; any moment his whole body could dissolve into light."

We can best see the particularizing function of metaphors when we compare different writers' descriptions of the "same" emotion. Here, for example, are two writers describing very different levels of "relief":

> Relief came... like a gentle lapping of the water's edge at low tide, a comforting quiescence.
> (Elizabeth Strout, "Incoming Tide")

> I feel a tidal wave of relief...
> (Jean Harfenist, "The Gift")

And here is a rough spectrum of seven different levels of panic:

> Panic, a sour tin flavor, came into my mouth.
> (Wells Tower, "Door in Your Eye")

> She can feel the rhythmic thwick of panic in her chest, the wingbeats of an insect.
> (Julie Orringer, "Care")

> ... adrenaline-soaked panic hummed like Muzak in the background of my brain.
> (Benjamin Percy, "The Woods")

> She felt panic rise up, her heart stammering.
> (Christine Sneed, "Quality of Life")

> I feel a wedge of something like panic being driven into my chest.
> (Damien Echols, unpublished death row journal)

> In moments of crisis, she has always managed to lose herself in a cyclone of panic.
> (Lydia Peelle, "Phantom Pain")

> The barks came up from the street with an urgency meant to induce panic. The Huns were at the gate, the tidal wave was almost here, the volcano was about to blow. Every night I fell out of bed in a running crouch, my heart looking for a way out of its cage.
> (Rick DeMarinis, "The Handgun")

Adam Haslett states the problem of adequately conveying "a certain register" of an emotion very clearly in his story "Devotion":

> It turned out Ben too had lost a parent at a young age. When Owen heard that, he understood why he'd been drawn to Ben: he seemed to comprehend a certain register of sadness intuitively. . . "I come up with lots of analogies for it [his sadness at his mother's death]," he could remember Ben saying. "Like I was burned and can't feel anything again until the flames get that hot. Or like people's lives are over and I'm just wandering through an abandoned house. None of them really work. But you have to think the problem somehow."

As this passage suggests, if we can't think of a way to convey the emotion solely through body language and/or metaphor—i.e., if we find it necessary to label an emotion abstractly—we should try to find a metaphor whose sensory connotations serve as an analogy for the abstraction and thereby help us "think the problem." Steven Millhauser finds just such a metaphor in his story "The Wizard of West Orange" when he refers to "an expression of alarm invading" a character's features. That metaphor works because an invasion is something that would indeed make us feel alarm. But abstractions tend to be even more effective when the metaphors we choose to express them are not only appropriate but *surprising*, as when Frederick Exley says, "For days I lived in a cocoon of rage" and Strout says, "Hope was a cancer inside him": it's a pleasant and instructive shock to realize that sometimes rage can be a comfort, and hope, which we normally think of as comforting, a torment.

The Pathetic Fallacy Isn't

There's one kind of metaphor that writers are commonly advised to avoid: one that attributes human emotion to natural and man-made objects. Back in 1856, John Ruskin threw a hissy fit about such metaphors, saying they were examples of what he called "the Pathetic Fallacy," which he defined as "a falseness in . . . our impressions of external things." The falseness, he argues, comes from being "under the influence of emotion, or contemplative fancy," and he says, "there is no greater baseness in literature than the habit of using these metaphorical expressions." What's more, he says such metaphors are "always the sign of a morbid state of mind." (*Always?* Really?) As an example of this morbid falsity he offers the following passage from an eighteenth-century poem in which a woman named Jessy, who has taken part in a "licentious amour" with a man who has betrayed and deserted her, says,

> If through the garden's flowery tribes I stray,
> Where bloom the jasmines that could once allure,
> "Hope not to find delight in us," they say,
> "For we are spotless, Jessy; we are pure."

Ruskin's response? "The flowers do not really reproach her. God meant them to comfort her, not to taunt her; they would do so if she saw them rightly."

Hmm. It's hard to disagree with someone who knows God's intentions as well as Mr. Ruskin, but it seems to me that a woman in Jessy's unhappy situation just might fail to take comfort in the flowers' spotless purity. And for someone critical of personifying nature, Mr. Ruskin seems more than willing to personify the flowers as sources of divine comfort—though of course he believes he's not imposing his response on the jasmines but rather "rightly" seeing God's intention in creating them. Rightly or (more likely) wrongly, Ruskin's full-frontal attack on personification has influenced generations of writers, scholars, and teachers, and as a result writers have been warned repeatedly to avoid the pathetic fallacy. Nancy Kress sums up the standard view about this "risky" technique:

> Sophisticated readers have rejected simple one-to-one correspondences between the facts

of nature and the emotions of man ever since Wordsworth and the other Romantics overused them. In fact, so widespread and derided was this technique that it earned its own critical designation: the Pathetic Fallacy.

Like any technique, the so-called pathetic fallacy can be misused, but I'm with James Wood, who says, "Ruskin's attack on personification of nature is as ridiculous as the Chinese government's 1931 banning of *Alice's Adventures in Wonderland* on the grounds that 'it was wrong for animals to speak human languages.'" And I second Ursula K. Le Guin's advice: "Work the pathetic fallacy for all it's worth. Focus on any item or detail that reveals the character."

Jolene McIlwain's story "The Steep Side" provides a superb example of the use of personification to reveal a character's emotion. In it, a boy hears screams as he rides a dirt bike up a remote pathway cut into a forest for a natural gas pipeline and discovers a young pregnant woman on the ground, her shirt pulled up over her bleeding belly, and an older woman crouched over her with a knife. The older woman quickly hides the knife and claims to be a nurse helping a friend but it's clear that she was attempting to steal the younger woman's baby. In a lesser writer's work, this could have been a moment of high melodrama, but McIlwain avoids the fallacious pathos of melodrama by doing precisely what Ruskin considered pathetic and false: she conveys the boy's response to his grisly discovery indirectly, by attributing his shock to the grass surrounding the pregnant woman:

> The older woman said to the boy, *We're good friends*. The pregnant woman on the ground didn't nod. She leaned on one elbow, kept her splayed hand on her full tight belly, which showed bare-naked above her partly pulled down shorts. A little strip of her bra was bright white next to her flowered shirt. The shirt, jam-packed with red and pink flowers, shocked all the green surrounding her body.

Here are some other examples of "pathetic fallacies" that successfully convey a character's state of mind, as the contexts in which they appear confirm:

> I see [West Egg] as a night scene by El Greco: a hundred houses, at once conventional and grotesque, crouching under a sullen, overhanging sky and a lusterless moon.
> (F. Scott Fitzgerald, *The Great Gatsby*)

> . . . only Miss Emily's house was left, lifting its stubborn and coquettish decay above the eyesores.
> (William Faulkner, "A Rose for Emily")

> Just before it was dark, as they passed a great island of Sargasso weed that heaved and swung in the light sea as though the ocean were making love with something under a yellow blanket, his small line was taken by a dolphin.
> (Ernest Hemingway, *The Old Man and the Sea*)

> There was a sense of black conspiracy . . . among these trees . . .
> (Malcolm Lowry, *Under the Volcano*)

> The east window happened to be agape in the living room, with the blind mercifully down, however; and behind it the damp black night of a sour New England spring had been breathlessly listening to us.
> (Vladimir Nabokov, *Lolita*)

> In fact, Ohio had been calling itself a state only seventy years when first one brother and then the next stuffed quilt packing into his hat, snatched up his shoes, and crept away from the lively spite the house felt for them.
> (Toni Morrison, *Beloved*)

He had a strange sensation that the place itself was judging him. Even the furniture seemed to watch him with critical eyes.
(Lydia Peelle, "Kidding Season")

I'd fish until it was neither day nor night, but balanced between. There never seemed to be a breeze, pond and shore equally smoothed. Just stillness, as though the world had taken a soft breath, and was holding it in, and even time had leveled out, moving neither forward nor back.
(Ron Rash, "The Woman at the Pond")

My advice: don't go in fear of pathetic fallacies either.

5. Conjoined Abstractions

Just as joining seemingly opposed abstractions and metaphors is often an effective way to convey emotion, so, too, is joining seemingly opposed abstractions. Obviously, saying "Rage comforted me" or "Hope tormented me" doesn't convey emotion as sensuously, and therefore as effectively, as comparing rage to a cocoon or hope to cancer, but it certainly conveys emotion more successfully than the sensory bypasses "I felt rage" and "I felt hope." It does so, of course, because the tension between the abstractions *particularizes* the emotion in a way that ordinary sensory bypasses or glosses cannot. Ideally, we should try to particularize an emotion through body language and/or metaphor, but there are some feelings that are too complex to be conveyed solely through sensory means, at least without extended, momentum-killing description. As a result, there are times when body language and even metaphor fail us, and that's when we need to turn to conjoined abstractions.

By revealing the complexity of an emotion, conjoined abstractions can elevate sensory bypasses into something that comes closer to conveying particular experience. The statement "I felt peaceful" is a run-of-the-mill sensory bypass, and so is the statement "I felt depressed." But Moore's sentence "I lay there in bed in a peaceful form of depression" is a sensory bypass of a much higher order, one that homes in on a complexity of feeling that cannot be captured by body language or metaphor, either solely or together. The same is true, I believe, of the following examples:

> A thrill of anxiety rose in Rebecca . . .
> (Elizabeth Strout, "Criminal")

> . . . a great unemotional happiness.
> (Alice Munro, "Dance of the Happy Shades")

> He got up from his desk, paced a little, and in a kind of frustrated joy spoke to his daughter . . .
> (John Williams, *Stoner*)

> He . . . walked to the dog in an agony of relief.
> (Thomas McGuane, "A Man in Louisiana")

> He felt for her an affectionate contempt.
> (Bernard Malamud, "God's Wrath")

> She resumes placing the dishes around the table, bored, apparently, by her own anger.
> (Kirstin Valdez Quade, *The Five Wounds*)

As with the other modes of conveying emotion we've discussed, this technique often works best in combination with other techniques. Haslett combines conjoined abstractions and body language to excellent effect when he says, in "The Beginnings of Grief," "I let out a moan of relief as the pain shot up my spine," and Moore combines them wittily with a simile when she says, in *A Gate at the Stairs*, "His face bore a look I'd seen before: it was one of bravado laced with doom, like fat in meat." And in *Roger's Version*, John Updike combines the abstractions *furious* and *tedium* with both body language and metaphor in the following passage, which, thanks to the multiplicity of techniques it employs, is one of the rare instances in fiction in which a description of eyes successfully conveys emotion.

> She looked up at me, my dear feminist manqué, and there was a glaze: a big-eyed white fish had swum up close to the green aquarium glass and let escape a flash of her furious tedium at going around and around in this tank every day.

I hope the examples I have given both here and earlier in this essay are sufficient evidence that abstractions, when handled wisely, can be highly effective means to convey emotion.

6. Some Caveats

As I've noted, there are many dangers involved in the use of abstractions, but there are also important and valuable ways around those dangers. It remains to point out the dangers involved in the use of body language and metaphor, for as essential as they are in conveying emotion, their misuse or misunderstanding can cause problems as serious as those caused by abstractions.

The principal danger involved in the use of metaphor is that we'll overdo it and the metaphor will swamp the emotion rather than buoy it up. Strout is usually masterful at conveying emotion through metaphors, but at times she goes overboard. Witness her cheesy—literally and metaphorically—description of Olive Kittredge's late-life sexual relationship with a man named Jack: "Olive pictured two slices of Swiss cheese pressed together, such holes they brought to this union—what pieces life took out of you."

We also need to keep in mind that metaphors have different meanings and effects in different cultures. An insulting metaphor in one culture can be laughable in another. It's hard, for example, for an American reader to respond with anything but laughter when the Chinese characters in Ha Jin's great story "Saboteur" angrily call people "Egg of a tortoise!" and "An arrogant son of a rabbit."

Body language is even less universal than metaphor, so we have to be aware that readers from another culture may misunderstand our characters' body language. As the scholar Otto Klineberg has noted, "The sentence 'Her eyes grew round and opened wide' would probably suggest to most of us surprise or fear; to the Chinese it usually means anger." And our eyes would probably widen with surprise to learn that the Chinese often express surprise by stretching out their tongues.

What's more, body language doesn't always mean the same thing within any given culture—witness the fact that, as Korte says, "there are tears of joy as well as tears of sadness." As a result, it is essential to consider the context, as well as culture, in which the body language occurs. And, of course, the meaning of body language within a given culture also changes over time, so we must take that fact into account as well. "In the Middle Ages and the Renaissance," Korte notes, "folded arms... were a common display of melancholy," but they no longer carry that connotation. And as Korte has also pointed out, to understand a key moment in Henry James's *The Portrait of a Lady*, we need to know a rule of propriety that is now obsolete: the rule that a man must stand in the presence of a standing lady unless he is in an intimate relationship with her. It is through the breach of this rule that Isabel Archer's husband Osmond inadvertently reveals to her that he has been having an affair with Madame Merle. James says little more than that "Madame Merle was standing on the rug, a little way from the fire; Osmond was in a deep chair, leaning back" and this seemingly minor bit of stage direction provokes a realization—"a sudden flicker of light"—that changes Isabel, and her life, significantly.

Perhaps the principal danger we face with body language is that it will seem cartoonishly exaggerated, like the overwrought gestures of actors in silent movies. In *Await Your Reply*, Dan Chaon turns this vice into a virtue in his depiction of John Russell, a character who expresses his surprise at seeing Miles, one of the book's three protagonists, for the first time in ten years by "put[ting] his palms against his cheeks, comically miming surprise." Chaon adds: "Miles had forgotten about John Russell's odd, nerdy gestures, as if he had learned about emotions from the anime cartoons and video games he used to love." The problem, of course, is that too many of us write body language as crudely as John Russell performs it.

Even if our body language is accurate and not cartoonishly exaggerated, there is the danger of overdoing it. The result is a boring naturalism, an attempt to do at length on the page what a film can do in an instant. Also, as Michael Irwin has said, "The exhaustive description... is false to the psychology of perception. We tend not to notice what is not exceptional." As a result, overdoing body language can destroy the very realism it intends to foster. And if we're too naturalistic, the forward momentum of the narrative is also compromised. Thomas Love Peacock mocks this naturalistic blow-by-blow approach to body language, and reveals its momentum-killing effects, in the following passage from *Nightmare Abbey*:

> The whole party followed, with the exception of Scythrop, who threw himself into his arm-chair, crossed his left foot over his right knee, placed the hollow of his left hand on the interior ankle of his left leg, rested his right elbow on the elbow of the chair, placed the ball of his right thumb against his right temple, curved the forefinger along the upper part of the forehead, rested the point of the middle finger on the bridge of his nose, and the points of the two others on the lower part of the palm, fixed his eyes intently on the veins in back of his left hand, and sat in this position like the immoveable Theseus . . . We hope the admirers of the *minutiae* in poetry and romance will appreciate this accurate description of a pensive attitude.

So does this mean we should just say "Scythrop looked pensive"? Butler would say no, in thunder, and I'd say no, too, only a little more quietly. But I'd also say, contra Butler and Pound, that abstractions *can* play a valid, and valuable, role in conveying emotion.

7. Other Considerations

So far we have discussed the most prevalent, and useful, means of conveying emotion—body language, metaphor, and, sometimes at least, abstraction—but these are hardly the only means by which we convey emotion in fiction. A fuller exploration of the subject would discuss the role of the sensory aspects of language itself—assonance, consonance, pitch, tempo, and rhythm—as well as such techniques as synesthesia, hyperbole, repetition, juxtaposition of images, and shifts in tense, person, and point of view. It would also address Gertrude Stein's assertion that "sentences are not emotional but paragraphs are." But these are subjects for another time. For now, I'll just say, All right, Ezra; let's go in fear of abstractions. But let's go forward, with our chins up, not turn and run away; let's master the fear, not give in to it. For scary though they be, abstractions can complement body language and metaphor and, sometimes, even take their place in ways that enrich the emotional experience of our readers.

The Art of Description

The analogy between the art of the painter and the art of the novelist is, so far as I am able to see, complete. Their inspiration is the same, their process (allowing for the different quality of the vehicle) is the same, their success is the same. They may learn from each other, they may explain and sustain each other.
—Henry James

I learn as much from painters about how to write as from writers.
—Ernest Hemingway

It is a commonplace for scholars and authors of creative writing textbooks to talk about description in literature as "painting with words," but that's usually where the analogy between the art of the painter and the art of the writer stops. They rarely go on to talk about what *kind* of painting a writer creates. And even when they do, it's rare that they explain what makes a given writer's description the literary equivalent of, say, an impressionist or an expressionist painting. Also, there's little agreement about how to categorize a writer's description. Most scholars refer to Hemingway's description as realist, for example, but Robert Paul Lamb argues that it's impressionist and Raymond S. Nelson says no, it's expressionist.[5] I think it's folly to label a writer's description according to any one of these terms for the simple reason that most writers use more than one approach to description—and sometimes even in the same sentence. So rather than try to place writers firmly in one of these categories, which seems to be the parlor game that scholars are playing, I decided to look at the actual practice of a variety of writers and see which techniques they use. To keep this essay to a manageable length, I'll discuss descriptive passages that are the literary equivalents of paintings from five of the most influential movements of art: realism, impressionism, expressionism, post-impressionism, and cubism. Let me stress, though, that there are virtually as many different ways to "paint with words" as there are art movements.

1. Realism

The goal of realism, in literature as in art, is to represent physical reality as accurately as possible. Behind the realist aesthetic is the assumption that the most objective and complete representation of reality is the most accurate. Hence a realist painting aims for something like the objectivity of a camera, which reproduces without embellishment everything the lens perceives. One of the greatest examples of this kind of painting is Johannes Vermeer's *The Music Lesson*,[6] which is so precisely and fully detailed that art historians have long theorized that Vermeer painted it with the aid of a camera obscura.

To test this theory, an inventor named Tim Jenison spent a year building an exact replica of the scene depicted in Vermeer's painting, then projected that scene onto a canvas with a camera obscura. He quickly realized that painting over the projected image made it impossible to match the colors accurately, so he placed a small mirror above the canvas at a forty-five-degree angle, thus allowing him to view parts of the projected image and the canvas simultaneously. Over the course of seven months, he meticulously produced a virtually identical copy of Vermeer's painting. Jenison's attempt to show how Vermeer created the illusion of reality was fittingly documented in the film *Tim's Vermeer* by the magicians Penn and Teller, who know a thing or two themselves about how to make an illusion look real.

Clearly, Vermeer's goal was to reproduce reality as accurately as possible, whether he actually used a camera obscura and a mirror or not. More recently, Ralph Goings, who has been called "the American Vermeer," and other so-called "photorealists" have used mechanical means to achieve the same goal. Rather than paint directly from reality, they first take a photograph of a person or scene, then mimic it so meticulously on canvas that the resulting painting is virtually indistinguishable from the photograph. If Goings's painting *Double Ketchup*[7] looks like a photograph, it's because it's a painting of a photograph, not an actual restaurant scene.

Most realist art and literature don't employ camera obscuras or photographs, of course, but they do aim at the same kind of photographic realism. When Hemingway began writing, he was just such a realist. In his view, the goal of description was to capture the facts, the observable truths of the world, and nothing more. As he says in *A Moveable Feast*, at this time in his life his writing mantra was "All you have to do is write one true sentence. Write the truest sentence you know." And it's clear that by *true* he meant *literally* true because he defines "one true sentence" as something "that I knew or had seen or had heard someone say."

An excellent example of this kind of realism appears in "Up in Michigan," a story he wrote in early 1922, before he fell under the influence of Gertrude Stein and, through her, Paul Cézanne. According to Constance Cappel Montgomery's *Hemingway in Michigan*, the town Hemingway calls Hortons Bay in the story is actually Petoskey, Michigan, where the Hemingway family's summer home was located, and he describes the town, she says, "with photographic realism." But beyond accuracy, there's not much to his description, and the setting plays no functional role in the story's plot or characterization, as the settings of his future stories would. The description is just "one true sentence" after another. It consists of facts for facts' sake. The description does contain one tantalizing detail that could—and would, in his later fiction—have symbolic significance, but it remains a mere fact in this story.

Here's his description of the town:

> Hortons Bay, the town, was only five houses on the main road between Boyne City and Charlevoix. There was the general store and post office with a high false front and maybe a wagon hitched out in front, Smith's house, Stroud's house, Dillworth's house, Horton's house and Van Hoosen's house. The houses were in a big grove of elm trees and the road was very sandy. There was farming country

and timber each way up the road. Up the road a ways was the Methodist church and down the road the other direction was the township school. The blacksmith shop was painted red and faced the school.

Hemingway's "photograph" of the town is almost entirely in black and white; the only overt exception is the red blacksmith shop, though we will of course see the road as the color of sand. In his later fiction, Hemingway pays much closer attention to color—and he also structures his descriptions so that the details appear in the order a character would naturally perceive them, a structure that, as we'll see, is a major characteristic of impressionist description. What he gives us in "Up in Michigan," however, is a *composite view* of the town, a portrait that could only be assembled in retrospect, not perceived in the order its details are listed. There's also very little concern with making any of the details vivid, much less detailed, or with conveying a character's impressions of the setting. The details are presented merely as facts. And the one potentially symbolic detail—the false front of the post office—goes for naught since none of the story's characters presents a false front to the others.

The same lack of concern for a character's impressions of a setting can be found in Alain Robbe-Grillet's descriptions. It may seem odd to offer as an example of realistic description a passage from the writer who is often called the first "cubist" novelist and who vehemently disparaged the realistic descriptions of Balzac, but in some ways Robbe-Grillet was the ultimate realist in that he emphasized descriptions of objects to an almost unprecedented level. He was what the French call a "chosist"—a "thing-ist"—a writer who is more interested in things than in characters, and his descriptions of them are minutely detailed.

In creative writing textbooks, we're often told that we should choose "significant details" when composing descriptions, but for Robbe-Grillet no detail has any more significance than any other, so his novels are packed with details that are, quite literally, insignificant in the conventional sense. What distinguishes his brand of realism from his predecessors' is that he believes that physical objects do not reflect or relate in any way to the character of the person who perceives them. As Andrew Gallix has said, in Robbe-Grillet's view, things are "neither significant nor absurd," they just "are," and humankind and the physical world are inexorably disconnected. For Robbe-Grillet, he continues, "The novelist's task . . . is to describe the material world, not to appropriate it or project himself onto it; to record the distance between human beings and things without interpreting this distance as a painful division." To emphasize the lack of connection between humankind and objects, Robbe-Grillet avoids similes and metaphors, which tend to anthropomorphize objects, and any adjectives that might seem to imply that the details have subjective or symbolic meaning. His descriptions are thus a highly impersonal and affectless list of facts. They tend to imitate the objectivity of a photograph or, as in the following example from his novel *The Voyeur*, the kind of 360-degree video of a room we might find on a hotel's website:

> Starting at the window and proceeding left (that is, counter-clockwise), were a chair, another chair, the dressing table (in the corner), a third chair, a cherrywood bed (placed lengthwise against the wall), a tiny pedestal table with a fourth chair in front of it, a commode (in the third corner), the door to the hallway, a kind of drop-leaf table that could be used as a desk when the sides were extended, and finally the . . . cupboard, standing diagonally across the fourth corner with the fifth and sixth chairs next to it.

I don't know about you, but when I enter a room, I don't survey its contents in such a methodical, unidirectional manner. My eye jumps around, taking in first this impression, then another. Only after gathering these scattered impressions could I reassemble them into the more logical, expository order that characterizes realist descriptions like this one. But now let's turn to descriptions that present impressions in the order in which they're actually perceived.

2. Impressionism

Impressionism, as a movement in art, was closely related to realism, at least in its beginning. Indeed, it started as a kind of "ultra"-realism. As the art historian Alfred Weaver has said, the impressionists strove for "the most scientific reproduction of the visible world" ever recorded in art; they wished "to record the sensations of the eye as faithfully as possible." Since the human eye can't take in the totality of a scene at once, the impressionists tried to capture the transitory instant of initial perception, before the objects they're perceiving can be fully processed and particularized. As Rebecca Solnit puts it, the impressionists were pursuing "the realism of what things look like rather than what they are." Whereas a realist painting is actually the result of prolonged and repeated observations of a person or scene that culminate in a fully detailed, composite depiction of those observations, an impressionist painting is intended to reproduce a vague, initial glimpse. Berthe Morisot's *English Seascape*[8] is an excellent example of the sketchy, incomplete nature of a transitory sight. And because, unlike the realists, the impressionists were committed to depicting the eye's *impression* of the objects rather than the specific objects themselves, they were particularly drawn to scenes in which perception was compromised by such things as darkness, artificial light, and fog, making the very objects of their perception difficult to identify. Witness, for example, Camille Pissarro's *The Boulevard Montmartre at Night*[9] and Claude Monet's *Waterloo Bridge, Sunlight in the Fog*.[10]

As Weaver argues, and as these paintings suggest, by trying to "record the sensations of the eye as faithfully as possible," the impressionists "dissolved nature into chromatic vibrancies, until at last they had dissolved form and lost it completely." By gaining one kind of verisimilitude, in short, they lost another. It was this loss that led to the focus on form rather than the act of perception that we will see in the work of the post-impressionists and cubists and their literary counterparts.

Ostensibly, the goal of impressionism was to record the artist's objective impressions, not to convey his or her emotional responses to or opinions about those impressions. It was merely to be an eye. Cézanne believed this was a mistaken goal, though he acknowledged that it led to some great art. ("Monet is nothing but an eye," he once said, "yet what an eye!") But artistic impressionism could never entirely avoid emotional or intellectual content, and literary impressionism never even tried to.

The central canon of literary impressionism, as Ford

Madox Ford noted, is Stephen Crane's dictum "You must render: never report"—in other words, you must convey what the character sees without explanation or comment. As the literary scholar James Nagel has said, "The fundamental method of Impressionism" is to "[render] direct sensory experience without expository intrusion, without authorial addition or correction" and thereby "[place] the reader in the same epistemological position in the scene as the character." Hemingway certainly agreed. He said that a writer should write "to be read by the eye" and "no explanations or dissertations should be necessary." As Hemingway's comment suggests, the whole purpose of rendering what the eye sees is to *imply*, rather than *report*, the character's emotional response to what he or she sees. The Hemingway scholar Robert Paul Lamb, from whose exceptional book *Art Matters* I am borrowing several of my points and examples, argues that T.S. Eliot's definition of an objective correlative is essentially a definition of the impressionist approach to writing, and I agree. Here's Eliot's definition:

> The only way of expressing emotion in the form of art is by finding an "objective correlative"; in other words, a set of objects, a situation, a chain of events which shall be the formula of that *particular* emotion, such that when the external facts, which must terminate in sensory experience, are given, the emotion is immediately evoked.

Essentially, an objective correlative is something objective, sensory, and external that correlates, or corresponds, to something subjective, abstract, and internal, and it is this correspondence that conveys the character's emotion. In *Death in the Afternoon*, Hemingway seconds Eliot, saying that writers should not describe an emotion but instead reproduce "the sequence of motion and fact which made the emotion."

A good example of an objective correlative occurs in Hemingway's "Soldier's Home." The main character, Harold Krebs, has just returned from the war with what we would now call PTSD. He spends his days sleeping late, reading, and shooting pool, and his mother is desperately trying to get him to return to his former self. At breakfast one morning, a month after his return from the war, she tries to convince him that "it's about time" he finds a job, saying, "God has some work for everyone to do. . . . There can be no idle hands in His Kingdom." Krebs responds, "I'm not in His Kingdom," and she replies, "We are all of us in His Kingdom," then proceeds to tell him that she prays for him "all day long." Here's the next sentence in the scene: "Krebs looked at the bacon fat hardening on his plate." Krebs doesn't respond to his mother, but he doesn't need to. Nor does Hemingway need to explain what Krebs is feeling at this moment. The image is an ideal objective correlative for his congealing resentment and anger at his mother and her religious harangues.

The objective correlative is the essence of Hemingway's aesthetic. As Lamb says,

> Rarely in the Hemingway canon does one encounter a narrator—first person or disembodied third person—stating emotions directly. . . . No other author . . . made the impressionist depiction of the objective into the aesthetic dogma that Hemingway did. Nor has any other writer ever put that principle into practice as rigorously. For Hemingway, the narrator's and characters' subjective feelings were the real omitted element of fiction, present in their absence, evoked by carefully selected details.

Hemingway's focus on details was such that his description is almost always concrete and only rarely figurative or abstract. In his demanding impressionist aesthetic, figurative and abstract description were considered "cheating" in that they explained what the concrete description should ideally convey by itself. "Hemingway rejected metaphors just as he rejected directly expressed emotions," Lamb says, "for when you employ a metaphor, however illuminating, you are not paying strict attention to the object you are supposed to be depicting." In a letter to the art historian Bernard Berenson, Hemingway wrote that similes "are like defective ammunition, the lowest thing I can think of . . ." (Whether he was aware of the irony of using a simile to criticize similes, we can only guess.)

Impressionism, then, is essentially a way of evoking internal emotion through external description. Its goal is to create and convey subtext. Hemingway's description of Hortons Bay in "Up in Michigan" merely provides factual information; it doesn't imply, much less provoke, emotion. There is no subtext; it's all text.

But Hemingway's "Big Two-Hearted River" is—literally and metaphorically—another story. As Jerome Lane has noted, "Hemingway . . . uses the setting and Nick's reactions to it as the primary means of revealing the subtext of the story, the war and Nick's avoidance of painful memories." "Big Two-Hearted River" is almost entirely subtext—as Hemingway himself said in a letter to Gertrude Stein, "nothing happens" on the surface of the story—and while it isn't solely impressionist in its approach to description—more on that later—impressionism plays a huge role in this story and in almost everything Hemingway ever wrote.

And as I mentioned earlier, a literary impressionist not only renders the details the character's eye sees but also the *order* in which the eye sees them, giving us a moment-by-moment series of individual perceptions rather than the kind of complete, retrospective, composite view that realists provide. There's a lengthy passage of description in Hemingway's "An Alpine Idyll" that illustrates this aspect of impressionism superbly, but for the sake of economy let's just consider the way it presents its opening details:

> The sun came through the open window and shone through the beer bottles on the table. The bottles were half full. There was a little froth on the beer in the bottles . . .

A writer less interested in presenting a character's impressions in the order they occur—that is to say, a realist—might have translated these sentences into a more economical and retrospective composite. Such a writer might have compressed the narrator's four separate observations—that the sun comes through the open window, that it shines through the beer bottles, that the bottles are half full, and that there's a little froth on the beer—into one sentence in which the perceptions might seem simultaneous: "The sun shone through the open window and the half full bottles of slightly frothy beer on the table."

This revision is certainly more concise; it not only condenses the three sentences into one, it also removes three of the four verbs and eliminates one repetition each of the words *through* and *beer* and two repetitions of the word *bottles*. But clearly Hemingway wanted to recreate the experience as his character perceived it moment by moment, not as he might reconstruct it later in memory. As Lamb points out, "impressionism . . . *always* depicts the moment as it is being experienced." It conveys a "series of immediate perceptions . . . as they impinge on the character's consciousness before being processed," not a single composite view constructed retrospectively. This is the principal difference between realist and impressionist description.

Another master of impressionist description is Joseph Conrad, who once said that the writer's task is "to make you see. That—and no more, and it is everything." Here's an example from *Lord Jim* that captures the moment-by-moment perceptions of his title character:

> The gale had freshened since noon, stopping the traffic on the river, and now blew with the strength of a hurricane . . . The rain slanted in sheets that flicked and subsided, and between whiles Jim had threatening glimpses of the tumbling tide, the small craft jumbled and tossing along the shore, the motionless buildings in the driving mist, the broad ferry-boats pitching ponderously at anchor, the vast landing-stages heaving up and down and smothered in sprays. The next gust seemed to blow all this away. The air was full of flying water.

There's only one word in this passage that departs from the impressionist credo of rendering rather than reporting. Did you notice it? It's the word *threatening*. That word tells us what the objective correlatives in the scene should imply. As the presence of this word suggests, even writers who are predominantly impressionist in their approach to description depart from that approach at times. Despite his edict "You must render: never report," Stephen Crane often did both. In the following passage from *The Red Badge of Courage*, the protagonist, Henry Fleming, has just come across the corpse of one of his comrades:

> He was being looked at by a dead man who was seated with his back against a columnlike tree. The corpse was dressed in a uniform that once had been blue, but was now faded to a melancholy shade of green. The eyes, staring at the youth, had changed to the dull hue to be seen on the side of a dead fish. The mouth was open. Its red had changed to an appalling yellow. Over the gray skin of the face ran little ants. One was trundling some sort of a bundle along the upper lip.

As Lamb comments, "Except for the phrase 'being looked at by a dead man' and the adjectives *melancholy* and *appalling*," this paragraph "is completely impressionist" because "Crane presents only the external data and refrains from depicting either the youth's or his own subjective responses." The mode of description we see in these three instances is what Lamb calls the literary equivalent of expressionism. Let's turn to that mode of description now.

3. Expressionism

According to Lamb, "Expressionism . . . was partially a revolt against impressionism. Rather than mimetically reproducing the impressions of the scene, expressionists sought to portray the emotions these impressions evoked in the artist." He goes on to say, "Although expressionists depicted the external world, the objects of that world were not accurate representations so much as they were externalized depictions of subjective states," and he concludes, "If impressionism in painting focused almost solely on the world-out-there, expressionism was mainly a depiction of the world-in-here." Edvard Munch's *The Scream*[11] is a classic example of the way expressionist paintings express the "world-in-here" via distorted, non-naturalistic depictions of the "world-out-there." It conveys intense angst through its exaggerated, swirling colors and its principal figure's howling skeletal face. Similarly, Otto Dix's *Trench*[12] conveys his horror at the bloody chaos of trench warfare in World War I through its garish colors and roiling jumble of fragmented body parts and anguished faces. And in *I and the City*,[13] Ludwig Meidner takes both top billing and center stage, and the skewed and fractured city in the painting's background seems almost to be exploding out of his tormented head.

Lamb's example of an expressionist fiction writer is Willa Cather. He says, "Cather and Hemingway are the yin and yang of American modernist minimalism. In depicting consciousness, they . . . both employ an aesthetics of omission and concision, but what one omits, the other features." Whereas Hemingway typically omits his characters' subjective responses and focuses on the physical details that evoke those responses, Cather typically omits the physical details and focuses on the characters' subjective responses. The principal difference between impressionist and expressionist description, then, is that in the former, the reader must infer from the external data the character's subjective response, and in the latter, the reader must infer the external data from the character's subjective response. Whereas the impressionist edict is "You must render: never report," the expressionist edict is, as Stéphane Mallarmé said, "Describe not the object itself, but the effect it produces."

Mark Doty agrees with Mallarmé's expressionist agenda. He says,

> What descriptions—or good ones, anyway— actually describe . . . is consciousness, the mind playing over the world of matter, finding there a glass various and lustrous enough to reflect back the complexities of the self that's doing the looking. . . . The eye looking at the world discovers itself.

If expressionists see themselves reflected in the mirror-like "world of matter," it's in part because, as Doty goes on to say, they project their emotions onto what they observe. The expressionist mode of description thus involves not only privileging subjective experience *over* objective reality but projecting subjective experience *onto* objective reality. We do this, Lyn Hejinian suggests, because "we long to join words to the world—to close the gap between ourselves and things." John Ruskin labeled the projection of human qualities onto nature the "pathetic fallacy," and virtually every literary critic since has seconded his distaste for the practice. Realist and impressionist writers likewise abhor this technique, especially Robbe-Grillet, whose studiously dull and affectless description is expressly designed to keep the gap between ourselves and things intact. Doty comes to the defense of the pathetic fallacy, however, arguing that, ultimately, there's nothing either pathetic or fallacious about it. He says,

> For literary describers, projection is not only no sin but our stock-in-trade, our method of operating, our modus operandi, a signature of our art. The insights of modern physics—that the observer changes the observed, the measurer influences what is measured—make what used to be called the "pathetic fallacy" seem a negative term for the inevitable perceptual work of the human.

For Cather, projection was so much her M.O. that she largely ignored the physical world on which her characters projected their emotions. In a 1922 essay, she argues that writers should focus on describing emotions, not objects. She complains that novelists have become little more than "interior decorators" who furnish every scene with superfluous physical details, and she urges her fellow writers to write what she calls "the novel *démeublé*," the unfurnished novel. Here's her expressionist advice:

> How wonderful it would be if we could throw all the furniture out of the window; and along with it, all the meaningless reiterations concerning physical sensations, all the tiresome old patterns, and leave the room . . . bare for the play of emotions, great and little . . .

The following passage from Cather's *My Ántonia* demonstrates how she throws virtually all of the furniture out the window and leaves the scene mostly bare for the narrator's emotions:

> There were none of the signs of spring for which I used to watch in Virginia, no budding woods or blooming gardens. There was only—spring itself; the throb of it, the light restlessness, the vital essence of it everywhere; in the sky, in the swift clouds, in the pale sunshine, and in the warm, high wind—rising suddenly, sinking suddenly, impulsive and playful like a big puppy that pawed you and then lay down to be petted. If I had been tossed down blindfold on that red prairie, I should have known that it was spring.

The conventional signs of spring—"budding woods" and "blooming gardens"—have been thrown out of the novel's window here, and the only external details that remain—"swift clouds," "pale sunshine," and "the warm, high wind"—are insignificant in comparison to the narrator's emotional response to the "spring-ness" of the moment, the indefinable "vital essence" that throbs through him and makes him feel such "light restlessness." Cather hasn't quite tossed us down "blindfold[ed]" on the prairie, but for the most part, the scene is bare of physical details and full of emotions, and, as Lamb says, "The reader must infer from the character's subjective response the external data producing it."

Note also that Cather's description of spring includes a simile, something Hemingway derided because it takes the reader's focus off the objective detail, which he believed should convey the emotion on its own. Whereas impressionist writers tend to focus on concrete description and downplay figurative and abstract description, expressionist writers tend to focus on figurative and abstract description and downplay concrete description. You'll never find Hemingway using a phrase like "vital essence," much less comparing the wind to a puppy.

Cather may be, as Lamb says, the yin to Hemingway's yang when it comes to American modernist minimalism, but Edgar Allan Poe's non-modernist and non-minimalist expressionism provides a much stronger contrast to Hemingway's impressionism. Poe throws out far more furniture than Cather and he clutters the bare scene that remains with a barrage of subjective responses, as the opening paragraph of "The Fall of the House of Usher" reveals:

> During the whole of a dull, dark, and soundless day in the autumn of the year, when the clouds hung oppressively low in the heavens, I had been passing alone, on horseback, through a singularly dreary tract of country; and at length found myself, as the shades of the evening drew on, within view of the melancholy House of Usher. I know not how it was—but, with the first glimpse of the building, a sense of insufferable gloom pervaded my spirit. I say insufferable; for the feeling was unrelieved by any of that half-pleasurable, because poetic, sentiment, with which the mind usually receives even the sternest natural images of the desolate or terrible. I looked upon the scene before me—upon the mere house, and the simple landscape features of the domain—upon the bleak walls—upon the vacant eye-like windows—upon a few rank sedges—and upon a few white trunks of decayed trees—with an utter depression of soul which I can compare to no earthly sensation more properly than to the after-dream of the reveler upon opium—the bitter lapse into everyday life—the hideous dropping off of the veil.

This paragraph contains a smattering of physical "furniture"—clouds, walls, windows, sedges, and trees—but mostly it consists of the narrator's overwrought emotional responses to things we cannot see. There's no external data that's sufficient to explain the narrator's emotions. We're merely told that things are *dull, oppressive, dreary, melancholy, insufferable, stern, desolate, terrible, bleak, bitter,* and *hideous,* and that the narrator feels *gloom* and *depression.*

Cather no doubt loathed Poe's manner of writing, but he's guilty only of taking her aesthetic to an extreme. By doing so, he points out what, for impressionist writers, is the principal problem of expressionism: if the external facts that cause a character's subjective response are absent, the emotional response will almost invariably seem out of proportion. Of course, a disproportionate response is appropriate for a narrator who, like so many of Poe's, is both barking mad and a little too familiar with the effects of opium.

Lamb argues that some predominantly expressionist writers like F. Scott Fitzgerald "made a place for impressionism" in their work, but that "Hemingway was tenacious in his commitment to just the one mode." However, I'd argue that Hemingway wasn't as tenaciously committed to impressionism as Lamb suggests. In addition to occasional moments of realism and expressionism, another mode of description, one related to the post-impressionist work of Paul Cézanne, appears in much of his fiction. Let's turn to post-impressionism now.

4. Post-Impressionism

Realism and impressionism focus on factual accuracy, either to the external world or the viewer's perception of it, but early in his writing life, Hemingway discovered a kind of description that departs from fact, a kind of description very different from that of Vermeer and Monet and their literary counterparts. This kind of description is so different, in fact, that Hemingway stopped calling it description.

In an interview in *The Paris Review*, he says, "A writer, if he is any good, does not describe. He invents or *makes*," and he adds, "You make something through your invention that is not a representation but a whole new thing truer than anything, true and alive . . ." This new conception of description—and truth—was the result of his discovery of the paintings of the post-impressionist Paul Cézanne. As he says in *A Moveable Feast*, "I was learning something from the painting of Cézanne that made writing simple true sentences far from enough to make the stories have the dimensions I was trying to put in them." As this suggests, after discovering Cézanne, he abandoned his conception of description as photographic realism composed of "one true sentence" after another and, like Thomas Hudson, the painter protagonist of his novel *Islands in the Stream*, he set out to "paint [life] truer than a photograph."

Between 1922 and 1924, there were forty-three Cézanne paintings on exhibit within walking distance of Hemingway's Paris apartment, and he went to see some of them nearly every day. In 1949, during a visit to the Metropolitan Museum of Art that Lillian Ross recounts in her book *Portrait of Hemingway*, he spent several minutes looking at Cézanne's *Rocks at Fontainebleau*[14] and said, "Cézanne is my painter. . . . I learned how to make a landscape from Mr. Paul Cézanne by walking through the Luxembourg Museum a thousand times with an empty gut."

So what did Hemingway learn from these paintings that allowed him to create stories with the "dimensions" he wanted?

One thing he learned was the necessity of altering literal reality in order to capture the essential emotional truth of his subject. "Painting from nature is not copying the object," Cézanne said. "It is materializing one's sensations." As the art historian Richard Murphy explains, for Cézanne, "A picture was not an impression of nature or a bit of social commentary or an illustrated story or a piece of decoration. It was an expression of the emotion evoked in the artist by the enduring forms and colors of the natural world." In his attempts to "materialize the sensations" a particular scene conveyed, Cézanne departed significantly from the actual landscapes he observed. Both Erle Loran's *Cézanne's Composition* and Pavel Machotka's *Cézanne: Landscape into Art* present his paintings side by side with roughly contemporaneous photographs of the scenes they depict and the differences reveal that Cézanne was anything but a photographic realist. He regularly eliminated some objects or replaced them with other objects, altered the arrangement of objects, and added objects that didn't exist in fact. As Murphy notes, he might "use a single bush or perhaps a house to express a volume that in nature was expressed by a mass of trees." He also downplayed or exaggerated elements of a scene and would often "move some objects forward in space and others backward" and alter the physical arrangement of a landscape so that the plane of a roof line, say, might parallel the plane of a road on the other side of the painting.

But perhaps the most consistent way Cézanne altered reality was in his use of color. He "might put orange in the trunk of a tree," Murphy says, "or give the blue sky some of the greens of the trees." By doing this, he would create an interrelationship between elements of the scene that would help him "materialize his sensations." As Cézanne himself said, "It is all a question of putting in as much interrelation as possible." Significantly, these interrelations tend to link things we would normally see as opposites, such as something physical, like a forest, and something ethereal, like the sky. The interrelation of opposites is something that invigorates not only painting but literary description. As Doty has said,

> To yoke, within a single figure, the vegetal and the made, or the hard and the soft, or the tiny and the immense, is a means of bringing energy into language through the unexpected collision of elements that seem to meet only in the mind, in the framing field of thinking.

Cézanne creates this same sort of "unexpected collision of elements" in his paintings. His painting *Mont Sainte Victoire Seen from Les Lauves*[15] is an excellent example of his unrealistic use of color to create interrelations that allow him to manifest the sensations the scene provoked in him. Clearly, the sky didn't literally contain splotches of green the day Cézanne sat down to paint this scene, nor did the forest contain patches of the sky's blue, but adding these colors to these elements links them and conveys the sense that Cézanne's response to the forest colors his view of the sky and vice versa. Also, using color this way allows him to "yoke" together not only the physical and the ethereal but also the near and the far and thus helps him convey the unity of the scene's impact on him.

But Cézanne not only added, replaced, distorted, or rearranged objects and colors in his paintings, he also omitted them. As Murphy notes, he "would leave out a great deal, including colors he felt were not expressive of the country" and sometimes even "intentionally leave small areas of canvas blank." In his various paintings of Gardanne, for example, he consistently omits foliage and buildings that appear in photographs of the town,[16] and in one, *The Village of Gardanne*,[17] he leaves nearly a fourth of the canvas blank. To many of his contemporaries, this painting and others like it looked unfinished, but Cézanne adamantly insisted that they were complete and that the blank spaces were intentional. As the Hemingway scholar Ron Berman concludes, "Implicit [in Cézanne's use of blank spaces] is the idea that a painting is not simply exposition. It concerns information withheld." The parallel to Hemingway's famous theory of omission should be obvious.

In 1924, Hemingway began to incorporate the things he was learning from Cézanne's paintings and, as a result, began to "make" instead of "describe." In August of that year, he wrote to Gertrude Stein about a new story he was writing called "Big Two-Hearted River," saying, "I'm trying to do the country like Cézanne and having a hell of a time and getting it a little bit. It is about 100 pages long and nothing happens and the country is swell. I made it all up, so I see it all . . ."

As his letter suggests, his description of the story's setting—Seney, Michigan, and its surroundings—is "made up," not a description composed of "one true sentence" after another. In his effort to convey the essence of his protagonist, Nick Adams, he altered the facts of his setting dramatically. Here's how Hemingway describes Seney, where the story opens:

> There was no town, nothing but the rails and the burned-over country. The thirteen saloons that had lined the one street of Seney had not left a trace. The foundations of the Mansion House Hotel stuck up above the ground. The stone was chipped and split by the fire. It was all that was left of the town of Seney. Even the surface had been burned off the ground.

Seney was indeed razed by fire—but in 1894, five years before Hemingway was born. When Hemingway and two friends took the train to Seney in 1919 for a weeklong fishing trip, the town was considerably smaller than it had been in its heyday—just a few buildings—but only one building had been burned and not as a result of a forest fire. And the land around Seney was "flat as a table top" so all those steep hills that Nick Adams hikes up and down are made, not described, too. Also, Hemingway and his friends fished on the Fox River, not the Big Two-Hearted River, which is forty-five miles northeast of Seney—not exactly within easy hiking distance. Hemingway changed the name of the river, he said, "not from ignorance nor carelessness but because [the name] Big Two-Hearted River is poetry."

And what about those "big islands of pine" he describes? Well, they were long gone by 1919, not to mention 1924, thanks to excessive logging, not a forest fire—and as Meyly Chin Hagemann has noted, the grove of arching pine trees where Nick lies down and rests resembles a Cézanne landscape, *The Lane of Chestnut Trees at the Jas de Bouffan*,[18] that was on exhibit at the Bernheim Gallery while Hemingway was writing "Big Two-Hearted River."

Speaking of the Bernheim Gallery, in an early draft of the story, Hemingway mentions the Cézanne paintings that Nick had "seen every day at the loan exhibit at Bernheim's," then says the following about their influence on Nick's literary ambitions:

> He wanted to write like Cézanne painted. Cézanne started with all the tricks. Then he broke the whole thing down and built the real thing. . . . He, Nick, wanted to write about country so it would be there like Cézanne had done it in painting. You had to do it from inside yourself. There wasn't any trick. Nobody had ever written about country like that. He felt almost holy about it. It was deadly serious. You could do it if you would fight it out. If you'd lived right with your eyes.

Like Cézanne, Hemingway "broke the whole [landscape] down and built the real thing" by omitting details that actually existed—the entire town of Seney, for starters—and by adding details that didn't exist anywhere near Seney—the burned-out countryside, the steep hills, the islands of pines, the Big Two-Hearted River—and thereby created a landscape of devastation that corresponds to his character's state of mind after returning from World War I. And Hemingway doesn't just omit the town of Seney; he also omits any reference to war. The story is about Nick's attempt to come to terms with his war experiences, but the war is entirely AWOL. As Hemingway says in *A Moveable Feast*, he began omitting key facts and details in his fiction because "the omitted part would strengthen the story and make people feel something more than they understood." Like the blank spaces on a Cézanne painting, the absence of references to the war makes us all the more acutely aware that something is being withheld, that there's a subtext pulsing under the surface of every detail Nick observes.

In addition to omitting and adding details, there's another way that I believe Hemingway "built the real thing" in his description of the landscape in "Big Two-Hearted River": by using words in much the same way, and for the same reason, that Cézanne used colors. Just as Cézanne created interrelations by repeating colors, Hemingway creates interrelations by repeating words. Many readers have noted Hemingway's heavy use of repetition—and, often, criticized and even parodied it—but I think it serves an important symbolic purpose. For example, at one point in the story, the repetition of the word *tightened* serves as what Theodore L. Gaillard, Jr. calls "a metaphoric spot of color" linking Nick and a trout. Nick notices several trout "keeping themselves steady in the current with wavering fins," then watches one "float down the stream with the current, unresisting, to his post under the bridge where he tightened facing up into the current," then, Hemingway tells us, "Nick's heart tightened as the trout moved." By interrelating Nick and the trout, Hemingway leads us to realize that Nick, too, needs to learn how to keep himself *steady*—a word Hemingway repeats four times in his descriptions of the trout—despite the current of memories that threaten to overcome him.

Throughout the story, natural facts—the burned landscape, the trout, the blackened grasshoppers, the swamp—serve as both literal and symbolic elements in Hemingway's description. The literal (albeit invented) fire-scarred terrain of Seney parallels both the destruction Nick witnessed during the war and also the effect of that destruction on his psyche. The external world thus correlates to and conveys Nick's inner world. To an extent, then, the external world is an objective correlative of Nick's internal world—and the story is impressionist in nature—but the objective details don't correlate only to Nick's subjective emotions; they also correlate to *ideas*—and these ideas are not necessarily Nick's; indeed, they seem more like the author's. Another thing Hemingway learned from Cézanne, then, is how to go beyond realism and impressionism to communicate symbolically while still avoiding the overt authorial commentary that impressionists deplore. In this story, the interrelations created by repetitions of words enable Hemingway to comment indirectly, through symbolic detail, rather than directly, through statement.

The subtlety, unity, symbolism, and narrative effectiveness of Hemingway's landscapes greatly increased as he absorbed the lessons of Cézanne and moved beyond the photographic realism that characterized his depiction of Hortons Bay in "Up in Michigan." And the more he practiced what he learned from Cézanne, the more adept he became at composing landscape descriptions that read like Cézanne paintings. He may have been able to "do the country" like Cézanne only "a little bit" in his 1924 "Big Two-Hearted River," but he became more expert at it in the coming years. Witness, for example, the opening of his 1930 story "Wine of Wyoming":

> It was a hot afternoon in Wyoming; the mountains were a long way away and you could see snow on their tops, but they made no shadow, and in the valley, the grain-fields were yellow, the road was dusty with cars passing, and all the small wooden houses at the edge of town were baking in the sun. There was a tree made shade over Fontan's back porch and I sat there at a table and Madame Fontan brought up cold beer from the cellar.

Like many of Hemingway's descriptions, this one may at first seem simple, but when we look at it closely, we see its considerable complexity. The first half of the first sentence gives us the narrator's initial overall experience of the scene, then the eye moves from high and far away to low and near, creating various planes along the way à la a Cézanne painting. In a mere two sentences, Hemingway creates five distinct planes: those marked by the mountains, the grain-fields, the road, the houses, and the tree that shades the porch. And like Cézanne, he interrelates the far and the near, using the words *shadow* and *shade* as verbal equivalents of spots of color, and he further interrelates both far and near and high and low through references to coldness—*snow on the high, distant mountain; the cold beer from the nearby cellar.* The passage also yokes together the very opposites that Doty mentions—the vegetal and the made (*the grain-fields and tree; the cars and houses*), the hard and the soft (*mountains; dust*), and the tiny and the immense (*the bottle of beer; the mountains*)—plus several others, including the inanimate and the human, hot and cold, sunlight and shade, and motion and stillness. As two-sentence post-impressionist paintings go, it'd be hard to beat this one.

Now let's turn to cubism, a movement inspired in large part by Cézanne because of his rejection of pictorial realism, his use of multiple perspectives on a single object, and his belief that "natural forms all tend to the sphere, the cone and the cylinder."

5. Cubism

According to art historian Robert W. Greene, "Cubism as an aesthetic arose out of the growing awareness . . . of the tremendous gap that separates the artistic representation of an object from its actual structure." He goes on to say,

> For the Cubists . . . representation and structure conflict. Since the solidity of things can never be totally reconciled with the picture plane, any attempt to render objective reality through imitation is doomed to failure. . . . The Cubists . . . thus began painting objects not as they saw them but as they conceived of them.

Or, as Gertrude Stein put it, the cubists didn't imitate reality, they "analyzed it."

Stein was of course an early proponent of cubism, and she applied many of its principles to her own work. "Pablo was doing abstract portraits in painting," she said. "I am trying to do abstract portraits in my medium, *words*." She even referred to her work as paintings, saying "my middle writing was painting." Between 1913 and 1932, her "middle" years, she wrote many examples of literary cubism. Her 1913 book *Tender Buttons* is her first, and perhaps her best, example of this mode of description. The book consists of verbal equivalents of cubist still lifes. As Stein said, "I used to take objects on a table, like a tumbler or any kind of object and try to get the picture of it clear and separate in my mind and create a word relationship between the word and the things seen." Needless to say, her words are as non-representational as the cubists' paintings, for she was analyzing reality, not imitating it.

The following prose poem from *Tender Buttons* does in words what Picasso's *Still Life with Liqueur Bottle*[19] does in paint: it breaks down a common glass object in order to explore its significance.

A CARAFE, THAT IS A BLIND GLASS.

> A kind in glass and a cousin, a spectacle and nothing strange a single hurt color and an arrangement in a system to pointing. All this and not ordinary, not unordered in not resembling. The difference is spreading.

In this verbal still life Stein defines the carafe as a blind glass because unlike the other kind of glass—the kind that helps us see—we don't wear carafes as spectacles. Hence her joke that it is a "kind in glass"—*kind* being etymologically related to the word *kin*—and a "cousin" to eyeglasses. While the carafe is a spectacle, she says, it is not specta*cles*. And while there's nothing strange about this blind glass, it is also not ordinary, for nothing seen in a new way is ordinary. As for the color of the glass, perhaps it seems hurt because the carafe contains wine the color of blood (or, possibly, because the glass is colorless, all of its blood-like wine bled out?). Finally, the entire carafe is—like a painting—an arrangement, and its arrangement is designed to culminate in a point—the point from which the contents of the carafe are poured. This point is the carafe's point, its reason for existing. The carafe doesn't exist to resemble its cousin, the unblind spectacles; it exists for itself, its own order, and the more we look at it, the more the difference between the two kinds of glass, the two different kinds of spectacles, spreads.

"A Carafe, That Is a Blind Glass" replicates the analytic process behind cubism, but there is another, more accessible kind of cubist description, one that simply describes a scene as if it were a cubist painting. Although many of Robbe-Grillet's descriptions are ultra-realistic, as we discussed earlier, he merits being called the first "cubist" novelist not only because he fragments time and structure and presents descriptions and events from multiple perspectives, but also because he often describes scenes as if they were the verbal equivalents of cubist paintings. The following passage from *The Voyeur* illustrates this approach to description:

> At the end of the jetty the structure grew more elaborate; the pier divided into two parts: on

the parapet side, a narrow passageway leading to a beacon light, and on the left the landing slip sloping down into the water. It was this latter inclined rectangle, seen obliquely, that attracted notice; slashed diagonally by the shadow of the embankment it skirted, it showed up as one dark triangle and one bright. All other surfaces were blurred. The water in the harbor was not calm enough for the reflection of the pier harbor to be distinguished. Similarly the shadow of the pier appeared only as a vague strip constantly broken by surface undulations. The shadow of the parapet on the jetty tended to blend into the vertical surface which cast it.

Notice the way Robbe-Grillet breaks the scene down into an inclined rectangle slashed diagonally into two triangles by a shadow, and also notice the way he stresses how difficult it is to distinguish the blurred surfaces of the water and the pier and to ascertain what is the parapet and what is merely its shadow. The thought process we undergo reading this paragraph is not significantly different from the thought process we undergo looking at a cubist painting: we recognize, obliquely, the actual entities being portrayed, but our focus is on their geometric structures and their intersections. Like the cubists, Robbe-Grillet is "painting" objects not as they appear in everyday reality but as they are structured. His focus is on the objects' inherent forms, not on the viewer's act of perception.

As I hope I've shown, writing and painting are indeed, as Henry James said, analogous arts, and as Hemingway suggested, we can learn as much from painters as we can from writers. In this essay I've discussed five kinds of literary description that parallel visual art, but there are of course other parallels, most obviously, perhaps, between symbolist, surrealist, and magic realist literature and paintings. But even art movements that were lesser-known and/or short-lived have influenced literary description, and I encourage you to seek out examples of their influence. And I further encourage you to try your hand at some of these modes of description. If you do, you just may find a new way of looking at the world and at your work.

"What We See With":
Redefining Plot

I dislike the word *plot*. Not only does it make me think of a cemetery plot, in common usage the word has meanings that are at best unhelpful and at worst misleading for fiction writers. When people say a novel has a good plot, they usually mean it has a lot of exciting action, not that those events are organized in a particular way. The word is also used pejoratively, as a way to distinguish action-driven genre fiction from character-driven literary fiction—witness William H. Gass's wisecrack that plot is "That which is extracted from a novel to make a movie." And the word is also commonly used to mean a *plan*, as in "There was a plot to assassinate the president," and as a result, perhaps, beginning writers often think of plot as something that precedes the actual writing of the story, not something they discover as they write, and since *plot* in this sense usually refers to a *nefarious* plan, they sometimes also associate literary plots with something distasteful, sneaky, even devious. Ideally, a plot is not what we begin with, it's what we end with; it's a goal, not a preconception. And the process of creating one is a process of learning to see what it is. No wonder, then, that Eudora Welty said, "Plots are what we see with."

What I dislike most about the word *plot*, however, is that authors of fiction writing guides, and therefore teachers and students of writing, almost universally use it to refer to a single, monolithic organizing principle, one characterized by a focus on causality and character change. For example, Robie Macauley and George Lanning say, "A plot . . . is a pattern of cause and effect that is always in process of change. One event causes another to occur . . ." and John McNally says, "Plot should be about causation: this happens *because* that happened. One scene should grow organically out of the previous scene." Likewise, Madison Smartt Bell says plot is "a sequence of causes and effects, like a string of dominoes falling" and adds that plot and causality are "inextricably intertwined." Similarly, Norman Friedman and virtually all other writers on the subject assert that a plot depicts a "completed process of change" in the protagonist. Janet Burroway speaks for the vast majority when she says that "Every story presents some sort of journey, literal or psychological or both, that results in a change in the central character." And although writers sometimes use different terminology to name the principal parts of a plot, they concur that a plot consists of a conflict, complications, a climax, and a resolution.[20]

The consensus definition of a plot, then, is essentially this: *A sequence of causally linked events that effect a completed process of change in a character by forcing him or her to deal with a conflict that gets progressively more complicated and intense until it finally reaches a climax and then is resolved.* I don't understand why we persist in suggesting that all works of fiction should follow this definition when so many acknowledged masterpieces depart from it. This definition accurately describes the kind of plot many—maybe most—writers and readers tend to prefer, but character change is not essential—the climax of many stories is a character's failure to change—nor is causality the only organizational principle available to writers of fiction. E.M. Forster famously insisted that causality was the essence of a plot—according to him, "The king died and then the queen died" is a mere "narrative of events arranged in their time-sequence," but "The king died and then the queen died of grief" is a plot since it reveals the causal relationship between the two events—but even he felt restricted by this definition of plot. "The plot is exciting and may be beautiful," he said, "yet is it not a fetish, borrowed from the drama, from the spatial limitations of the stage? Cannot fiction devise a framework that is not so logical yet more suitable to its genius?" And he concludes his discussion of plot by praising "modern writers" for their "constructive attempt to put something in the place of a plot." I second that praise, though I'd argue that what they put in place of a plot is nothing more than other kinds of plot—and, in most cases, kinds of plot that have already existed for centuries.

More recently, writers have criticized the structure of the standard causal plot as inherently sexist. Whereas Robert Scholes blithely and approvingly asserted that "The archetype of all fiction is the sexual act" since it echoes "the fundamental orgastic rhythm of tumescence and detumescence," Jane Alison says, "Something that swells and tautens until climax, then collapses? Bit masculo-sexual, no?" And paraphrasing the poet Eloise Klein Healy, Diane Lefer points out that a chronological sequence of events that moves from conflict to rising action to climax to denouement "sounds suspiciously like male sexual response," which, she adds, "is not . . . the only way to satisfy a reader." Lefer goes on to postulate the kind of story structure that would "illustrate female textual/sexual response": one "that peaks again and again" and "in which waves of excitement and satisfaction are diffused throughout the text instead of being focused on a single moment near the end." Similarly, Alison advises us to look for less masculo-sexual patterns:

> So many other patterns run through nature, tracing other deep motions in life. Why not draw on them, too? . . . Energy in narrative might also flow in smaller waves, wavelets. Dispersed patterning, a sense of ripple or oscillation, little ups and downs, might be more true to human experience than a single crashing wave.

Even if we prefer the standard causal plot, we should be aware that there are other organizing principles besides causality, character change, and masculo-sexual structure that can help us see the meaning of our characters and their actions—and thus there are other kinds of plot. Focusing on just one kind of plot implies there is only one valid way to organize a story, and as a result too many craft books and teachers approach the subject of plot in a prescriptive manner. I believe that all commentary about literary technique should be descriptive, not prescriptive; it should focus on what can and has been done, so we can learn about the wide range of techniques available to us as fiction writers.

Because we tend to define plot so narrowly, works of fiction that eschew causality and/or character change—and there are many, especially in twentieth- and twenty-first-century literature—are regularly dismissed as "plotless." The scholar Clare Hanson goes so far as to distinguish between "short stories," which have a plot, and "short prose fictions," which lack one. (Needless to say, she rates the former more highly than she does the latter.) Personally, I think it makes more sense to consider short fiction as one genre with multiple forms of plot rather than as two separate genres, one causally plotted and the other not. In any case, defining plot so narrowly forces us to put all stories into a mere two categories—plotted and plotless—and that's as unhelpful as describing coffee merely as caffeinated or decaffeinated. Also, many so-called "plotless" stories employ non-causal organizing principles that deserve to be recognized. If teachers and scholars are aware of these non-causal organizing principles, however, they almost universally fail to mention them.

John Gardner's *The Art of Fiction* is the only craft book I know that discusses specific non-causal ways to organize a work of fiction and unfortunately it does so in what is essentially no more than a brief aside. While Gardner clearly prefers causal plots, he acknowledges that "causal sequence . . . is not the only possible means" to organize a novel, and he argues that "Successful novel-length fictions can be organized" episodically, by stringing together non-causally related incidents; "juxtapositionally," by putting the novel's parts in "symbolic or thematic relationship"; and "lyrically," by "some essentially musical principle" as in "the novels of Marcel Proust or Virginia Woolf." In a lyrical novel, he adds, "What carries the reader forward is . . . some form of rhythmic repetition: a key image or cluster of images . . . ; a key event or group of events . . . ; or some central idea or cluster of ideas." He also says, "A story or novel may develop argumentatively, leading the reader point by point to some conclusion. In this case events occur not to justify later events but to dramatize logical positions; thus event *a* does not cause event *b* but stands in some logical relation to it."

In addition to causality, then, Gardner identifies four other organizing principles for works of fiction—and therefore, to my way of thinking at least, four other kinds of plot. These four plot forms are: episodic, juxtapositional, lyrical, and argumentative. I'd argue that there are at least two other forms of plot Gardner doesn't mention: expository and associative.

Gardner is talking about novels, of course, but in my opinion his definitions apply even more to short fiction. Of these non-causal modes of organization, only the episodic is less common in short stories than in novels, and the reason is obvious: most stories are simply too short to include many episodes. The other non-causal modes are far more prevalent in short stories than in novels. This makes sense, given that stories are less concerned with the *evolution* of character—i.e., the causally linked events and circumstances that change a person—than with the *revelation* of character.[21] As David Harris Ebenbach has said, "For the most part, stories do not explore characters' ability to change; they explore who characters already are." As a result, stories don't always have the same conflict/complication/climax/resolution plot structure that we often find in novels. Generally, stories tend to deal with an incident that leads the character and/or the reader to realize something significant about his or her nature, but rarely does the character go through the sort of completed process of change that we typically find in novels. Instead of causally linked events, short stories often present events that relate to each other episodically, juxtapositionally, argumentatively, expositorily, associatively, and/or lyrically, and I'd like to see us acknowledge these ways to organize a work of fiction as valuable options available to writers.

In short, I'd like to replace the monolithic notion of *a* plot with the concept of *plots*, plural. Literary scholars have done this in terms of fiction's *content*—in his essay "Forms of the Plot," Norman Friedman talks about tragic, sentimental, punitive, and disillusionment plots, for example—but to my knowledge no one has done this in any comprehensive and cohesive way in terms of fiction's *form*. I suggest we define the various plot forms according to the principles that organize them: *causal, episodic, juxtapositional, argumentative, expository, associative,* and *lyrical.*

But before I proceed to discuss these plot forms, two cautionary notes:

First, identifying a particular work's plot requires close and careful reading. One reason it can be difficult to categorize a story's plot is that its structure can disguise the nature of its plot. A causal plot is of necessity linear and chronological—first *a* happens, which causes *b* to happen, which causes *c* to happen, and so forth—but its structure need not be linear and chronological. Sometimes a story that appears to be non-causal in form is in fact a standard causal plot with a non-standard—i.e., non-chronological—structure, and we have to assemble the linear causal relationships between events as we read. (Tim O'Brien's "The Things They Carried," which we'll discuss later, is one example.) Also, the characteristics of different plot forms often overlap. For example, all plot forms—including causal—involve juxtaposition of characters and incidents for thematic and/or symbolic purposes, so it's necessary to determine which organizing principle is the primary one a given work employs—causality or juxtaposition. Similarly, all non-causal plots are episodic to some degree since the events don't comprise a chain of cause and effect, but often their episodic nature is clearly subordinate to some other organizing principle.

Second, just as there are works of fiction that are hybrids of more than one genre—witness *Don Quixote* and *Moby-Dick*, both of which, as Northrop Frye notes in *Anatomy of Criticism*, incorporate elements of the novel, the romance, and the anatomy—so, I believe, there are works of fiction that have hybrid plots, and we should acknowledge them as well. While hybrid plots are most often created by combining two or more non-causal plot forms, sometimes writers combine a causal plot with a non-causal plot. So even if we want our fiction to be causal in nature, non-causal plot forms provide a way to approach plot and structure in a more complex, varied, and original way. Indeed, we can argue that creating hybrid plots by combining plot forms—be they causal or non-causal—is a major way that fiction writers have lived up to Ezra Pound's injunction to "Make it new." As we'll see, several of the works discussed below achieve their originality by bringing together two or more plot forms.

Now let's explore the seven alternate plot forms in more detail.

THE EPISODIC PLOT

An episodic plot consists of a series of discrete incidents unified by little more than the fact that they are all experienced by the protagonist. An individual episode may contain causal elements, but it does not cause the next episode. Most if not all of the episodes could be rearranged (and some could be eliminated and others added) without substantially altering the work's overall meaning or effect.

The episodic plot is an ancient—and persistent—plot form. Homer's *The Odyssey*, written in the eighth century B.C.E., is essentially an episodic plot, and Petronius' *Satyricon*, which dates to the first century C.E., is the forerunner of the later, more dominant form of the episodic plot known as the picaresque novel, which arose in the sixteenth century with the anonymous publication of *The Life of Lazarillo de Tormes*. We see its influence in such varied works as Thomas Nashe's *The Unfortunate Traveller*, Cervantes's *Don Quixote*, Voltaire's *Candide*, Henry Fielding's *Tom Jones*, Laurence Sterne's *Tristram Shandy*, William Makepeace Thackeray's *Vanity Fair*, Charles Dickens's *The Pickwick Papers*, Mark Twain's *Huckleberry Finn*, Virginia Woolf's *Orlando*, and Saul Bellow's *The Adventures of Augie March*.

While there are many novels influenced by the episodic picaresque tradition, there are comparatively few episodic short stories—at least outside of Introduction to Creative Writing classes, where episodic plots of the "A Day in the Life of ___" variety are common. But rare as they are, episodic short stories do exist. Perhaps the purest example is Nikolai Gogol's "The Nose." It's what E.M. Forster would call a mere "narrative of events arranged in their time-sequence," not in their causal relationship. Virtually nothing in this wonderfully absurd story makes even the remotest causal sense—and that's precisely the point. The story satirizes the very notion of causality. Throughout, its characters respond rationally to absurd events, hoping to cause the effects they desire, but their actions fail to have any effect at all.

The story opens with a barber named Ivan discovering a nose in a loaf of bread his wife has just baked and recognizing it as belonging to Major Kovalyov, one of his customers. Although it makes no sense to Ivan (or us), he concludes that he must have cut the nose off Kovalyov (apparently without either of them noticing) and that it somehow wound up in his wife's bread. To get rid of what might be considered incriminating evidence, he wraps the nose in a rag and tosses it into a river. At that very moment, Kovalyov wakes up across town and discovers his nose is missing—the place where it belongs, Gogol tells us, is a "perfectly smooth surface" that is as flat as "a pancake fresh off the griddle"—and so he quite logically sets off in search of his nose. Although very little time has passed since Ivan tossed the nose into the river, Kovalyov quickly encounters his nose—which is now, inexplicably, as large as a human being and wearing a gold-embroidered uniform and a plumed hat that indicates it holds the rank of state councilor. Kovalyov then makes a series of perfectly rational efforts to resolve his irrational situation: he confronts the Nose and demands (unsuccessfully) that he return his nose; he attempts to report the theft to the chief of police (who isn't home) and the district police inspector (who refuses to pursue the matter because he just ate a big meal and needs a nap); and then he tries to place an ad about his missing nose in a newspaper (the clerk rejects the ad but kindly offers Kovalyov a pinch of snuff, which, lacking a nose, he is of course unable to use). After Kovalyov returns home, a man he's never met abruptly arrives and gives him his nose, which he says he found boarding a stagecoach to leave the city. But Kovalyov's problem isn't resolved by its return. The nose is once again of normal size, but try as he might, Kovalyov is unable to make it stick to his face. So he does what any rational human being would do when faced with such a problem: he calls for a doctor. But the doctor also fails to attach the nose. Even though Kovalyov retains possession of the nose, in the days that follow, people see the Nose strolling in various parts of the city and shopping in a pastry store. And then one morning Kovalyov wakes up, looks in the mirror, and finds his nose has been magically restored, and his life returns to normal.

At this point, Gogol's narrator says he realizes that "there is much that is improbable" in his story but he insists that "Whatever anyone says, such things happen in this world; rarely, but they do." I suppose the Freudians among us could argue that the story has a kind of dream logic, and is about Kovalyov's fear of losing an appendage farther south than his nose, but whatever causality we might find in the story would have to be imposed on it from without, not discovered from within. If the story is about anything, it's about the utter folly of assuming causality exists. There are no discernible causes for the nose's disappearance, transformations, and reappearance, and everything Ivan, Kovalyov, and the doctor try to do—hide the evidence, confront the thief, report the crime to the police, advertise the loss in the newspaper, and attach the nose—fails to achieve the effect it attempts to cause. Ultimately, the most absurd thing in this very absurd story just may be the fact that, despite all the evidence to the contrary, the characters continue to believe life is logical and events are causally related.

Perhaps the best-known and most-anthologized example of a contemporary episodic plot is Susan Minot's "Lust," which recounts in fifty-four brief episodes the protagonist's sexual history with various men. Since there's no causal or chronological link between the episodes, all but the first few and last episodes could be placed elsewhere in the sequence without affecting the story's meaning or impact. And virtually any of them could be cut—and others added—without any significant change in the story's effect.

It should be noted, though, that the story doesn't entirely eschew the notion of causality. Some episodic plots differ from causal plots not in the total absence of causation—indeed, their events *do* cause the story's climax and resolution—but in a lack of causal connection between episodes. Whereas each episode in a causal plot is a chronological link in a chain of cause and effect, in an episodic plot the episodes don't cause each other, but rather they *accumulate* and the resulting pressure they put on the protagonist leads to the climactic revelation of his or her character. "Lust" is an excellent example of this looser, accumulative kind of causality, for it conveys how the episodes add up to motivate the narrator's climactic feeling that her sexual experiences have filled her "finally and absolutely with death" and made her "disappear."

Carmen Maria Machado's "Inventory" resembles Minot's story both in subject matter and, to an extent, structure. It consists of twenty episodes from its protagonist's sexual history, and as in "Lust," the episodes have no causal connection between them but they nonetheless accumulate in a way that motivates the narrator's climactic recognition of the relationship between sex and death. However, Machado does something that Minot doesn't do: she juxtaposes her episodic plot to a second plot, one that symbolically parallels the episodic plot. So although the story may at first seem purely episodic on the surface, it also contains a juxtapositional plot, and I'll discuss the reasons for this categorization a little later.

Dorothy Allison's "River of Names" is yet another example of an episodic story with an accumulative kind of causality. As the title suggests, the story is flooded with named characters—there are twenty-seven in ten pages—plus innumerable characters identified only as grandparents, parents, stepfathers, uncles, and so many cousins that they "were without number"—and it is a litany of the many violent acts that she and her family members suffered or committed. "Almost always," the narrator says, "we were raped, my cousins and I," and one cousin murdered his wife and their three children, and many of her relatives died by suicide, murder, drowning, car accident, fire, and so forth, while others were beaten or blinded by family members. The story makes no attempt to explain what caused all of this violence, much less how any one violent act might have caused another. They're just "things that happened." The list is overwhelming, several novels' worth of drama and trauma crammed into a space far too small to allow room to investigate causal connections. Nonetheless, the story's episodes are causal in the sense that, together, they allow the narrator to explain to her lover Jesse (and perhaps to herself) why she is obsessed with violence and doesn't want to have children.

Most episodic plots eschew even the loose, accumulative kind of causality we see in "Lust," "Inventory," and "River of Names," however. Caroline Gordon's "Summer Dust" is one example. Written in four sections, each of which contains a separate episode from the life of Sally Ellis, the child protagonist, this story recounts such unrelated events as walking down a dusty road, riding a horse through the woods, visiting a sick old lady, and so forth—and the episodes have no causal connection and could be rearranged without any significant change in effect. (Indeed, a previously published version of the story was called "Four Tales of Summer Dust," the very title of which suggests the lack of causal connection between its episodes.)

Also, the protagonist undergoes no change. Rather, the story is a static portrait of Southern life in the early twentieth century from the perspective of an innocent child. Outside of the fact that all four episodes concern very short trips Sally makes in her rural neighborhood via foot, horse, or buggy, there is no apparent connection between the episodes. Flannery O'Connor acknowledged as much when she said the story "is actually much closer in form to life than a story that follows a narrative sequence of events." O'Connor went on to compare the story to an impressionistic painting that "comes into focus" only when we see it from "the right distance."

Episodic plots have been compared not only to impressionistic paintings but to collages. "Lust" has been called a "collage" story, for example, and Donald Barthelme, who has said that "the principle of collage is one of the central principles of art in this century," has written many collage stories. But Barthelme's episodic collage stories generally lack even the loose, accumulative kind of causality. Instead, they tend to eschew causality entirely. Even those stories that adopt some of the plot conventions of nineteenth-century narratives—for example, the sections in "Views of My Father Weeping" devoted to the narrator's detective-like search for the aristocrat whose coach ran down and killed his father—do so only in order to call attention to the fact that the causal chain of events leads to no climax or resolution. Furthermore, Barthelme fragments the narrative by inserting several sections describing his father weeping on a bed, but when this scene took place, if it ever did, isn't clear: sometimes it seems to have happened in the past, and sometimes it seems to be happening now, after the father's death. Barthelme also inserts other fragmentary sections into the semi-cogent narrative of the search for the narrator's father's killer. In these sections, his father pretends to be an outlaw with a red bandana over his face and a water pistol in his hand, throws a ball of orange yarn into the air, sticks his thumb in pink cupcakes, rides a large dog, writes on the wall with crayons, puts pepper in the sugar bowl, knocks over doll furniture in a doll house, and attends a class on good behavior. When these episodes took place in relation to the others is never established, nor is there any causal relationship between them. And, most important, they do not add up to cause anything like a climactic change in the protagonist. The final section of the story makes it clear that his conflict will continue unchanged forever. The section reads, in its entirety, "Etc."

Robert Coover is another author who has written collage-like fiction. His story "The Elevator" strikes me as a metafictional updating of the ancient episodic journey plot, and given that it repeats one event—the protagonist's daily elevator ride to his office—with variation, it is a lyrical plot as well as an episodic one. It consists of fifteen separate episodes, all but a few utterly independent of the others. These episodes present different, often contradictory, and often absurd, takes on a single event, and the majority of them could be placed elsewhere in the sequence with little significant effect on the story as a whole. Similarly, many of the 107 episodes of his story "The Babysitter" contain diametrically opposed scenarios, implying that one so-called "cause" could have different, even contradictory, effects. The episodes are mostly chronological, but they are not causally linked. Ultimately, both of these stories reject, in both form and theme, the notion that there's a necessary causal connection between any two events. As such, they illustrate the belief that, as Gass has said, *"from any given body of fictional text, nothing necessarily follows, and anything plausibly may."* In Coover's hands, both in these stories and in his more recent "choose-your-own-adventure"-style novels, the episodic plot serves to overturn the conventional belief in causality, both in life and in art.

The episodic plot form works best, I believe, when the story is about the protagonist's repression of her conflict rather her resolution of it. Elizabeth Bishop's "In the Village" is a superb example. The retrospective narrator—who sometimes speaks of herself in third person as "the child"—recounts her mother's return home to Nova Scotia from a Boston sanitarium, where she has been since suffering a nervous breakdown after the death of her husband. The story opens with a scene in which her mother is getting fitted for a dress—her first dress in years that isn't black—when all of a sudden, and for no apparent reason, she screams. Her daughter escapes the horrifying scream by running to the blacksmith's shop, where she finds comfort in the clanging sound of the blacksmith making shoes for a horse.

Over the course of the story, there are only two more very brief scenes involving the girl's mother, and the scream is mentioned again only five times, for a total of fifty words, in the story's sixteen pages. Every time the little girl starts to think about the scream, she immediately turns her focus to something else: her grandmother and aunts, her cow Nelly, the pasture where Nelly grazes, the villagers, the village's various shops, etc. In fiction workshops, we're often told that a story should only include "essential" events—i.e., ones that intensify and complicate the story's central conflict and lead it toward resolution—but virtually every event in this story could be replaced with any other mundane event typical of village life in that time and place without lessening the story's impact in the least. The story's power derives precisely from what prevents it from being a standard causal plot—the child's attempt to escape her conflict by repressing it rather than by facing and overcoming it in some climactic moment that changes her forever. And it's clear she hasn't escaped it and never will: the story opens with the words "A scream, the echo of a scream, hangs over that Nova Scotia village" and "it hangs there forever." Instead of conflict, complication, climax, and resolution we get a conflict that is never faced and never resolved. And we leave the story with that terrible scream still echoing in our ears, too.

The Juxtapositional Plot

Although the episodic plot dominates ancient literature, one could make a case that the earliest kind of non-causal plot is the juxtapositional plot, a plot that, as Clare Hanson says of Modernist short stories, organizes its events "according to the law of similarity" rather than causality. The oldest-known collection of stories—the Egyptian *Tales of the Magicians*, which was written around 2,000 B.C.E.—consists of a king asking his three sons to tell tales on one subject—magic—and they oblige and vie for his approval. (And we thought poetry slams were something new!) We see this same organizing principle in such longer works as Boccaccio's fourteenth-century *The Decameron*, which juxtaposes ten tales on a given theme for each of the ten days it covers, and Charles Baxter's *The Feast of Love*, which follows Boccaccio's lead, though Baxter's 2000 novel covers one night, not ten days, and only one theme—love.

The juxtapositional plot is most prevalent in short fiction, however, both old and new. And, as Gardner notes, it comes in two varieties, thematic and symbolic. A thematic juxapositonal plot juxtaposes characters and incidents that relate to each other thematically rather than causally. All stories have a theme, of course, but in a symbolic juxtapositional plot the theme is primarily expressed through analogy rather than through thematically related characters and incidents.

Thematic Juxtaposition

Tolstoy's "Three Deaths" is an excellent example of a juxtapositional plot that organizes itself thematically. As the title indicates, the story recounts three deaths: those of an aristocratic lady, a poor peasant, and—wait for it, wait for it—a tree. The only thing that connects these three storylines is the character Sergey, who is the driver of the lady's coach, the nephew of the dead peasant, and the person who chops down the tree. Sergey is not affected in any discernible way, much less "changed," by any of the deaths. As these facts suggest, he is not the story's protagonist; he is merely a device to connect the three juxtaposed, thematically related storylines.

The story's real "protagonist," so to speak, is the theme of death. As Mikhail Bakhtin notes, Tolstoy "juxtaposes, contrasts, and evaluates all three lives and all three deaths," which "illuminate each other" despite the fact that no single character, including Sergey, is aware of them all. The events are chosen not because they're causally linked and lead a character to some change but because they allow Tolstoy to compare and contrast these deaths and, through his imagery (and an occasional aside to the reader), convey his ideas about death.

Each of the story's sections reveals that the living either don't care about the one dying or forget her, him, or it very soon and go on about their lives. Even as the lady lies dying, Tolstoy says, "There was joy and youth everywhere in the sky, on the earth, and in the hearts of men." The story ends with the death of the tree, to which the trees around it respond by "flaunt[ing] the beauty of their motionless branches still more joyously in the newly cleared space" and by "rustl[ing] slowly and majestically over the dead and prostrate tree."

The trees, like the people surrounding the dead lady and peasant, not only continue to live but live joyously. But rather than attribute this joy to a deplorable indifference and selfishness in human beings and, indeed, in nature itself, Tolstoy suggests that the joy is due to our intuitive recognition that death is the means by which the Lord "renewest the face of the earth" and reveals that His "glory . . . shall endure forever." We do not mourn the death of anyone or anything for long, Tolstoy suggests, because death ultimately leads to new life, and because our mortality has the beneficial effect of making us more aware of the Lord's glorious immortality. (Whether we'll one day share in His immortality isn't mentioned, though I suspect Tolstoy had his hopes.)

With its three-part structure, Tolstoy's story is the literary equivalent of a triptych panel painting in that it paints three separate pictures of one subject and each of the pictures informs and expands the meaning and effect of the others. William Faulkner's "Dry September" is another triptych-like story that employs thematic juxtaposition. While it contains the nominal outline of a causal plot (a black man falsely accused of raping a white woman is hunted down and murdered offstage), that plot only serves as background for the principal plot, which juxtaposes three different white characters' perspectives on race: those of McLendon, the man who leads the mob that kills the innocent black man; Hawkshaw, the barber who vainly tries to stop the mob; and Miss Minnie, the lonely spinster who fabricated the whole story in order to bring some drama and excitement into her life. None of these characters is the protagonist of either the causal or the juxtapositional plot; each exists only to provide Faulkner a different angle of vision on his story's principal theme, which is the irrationality of racism. In Faulkner's view, the capacity to reason, not skin color, is what truly distinguishes one human being from another. When McLendon irrationally says to the men gathered in the town's barbershop, "Are you going to let the black sons get away with it until one really does it?" Hawkshaw reasonably responds, "Find out the facts first, boys. . . . Let's get the sheriff and do this thing right." Then McLendon turns his "furious, rigid face" on Hawkshaw, who stares back, refusing to be intimidated, and the omniscient narrator comments, "They looked like men of different races." Miss Minnie shares McLendon's irrational fury: as the narrator notes, her eyes betray the "bafflement of furious repudiation of truth." But while McLendon is merely (merely!) an irrational man, a man who beats his wife after ostensibly killing an innocent black man in order to protect white women, Miss Minnie is out-and-out insane, as her breakdown at the picture show in section four reveals.

 The three juxtaposed characters and plotlines of this story, then, serve a thematic purpose, and whatever causal connections exist between the characters and incidents is subordinate to the theme the juxtapositional plot serves to illustrate.

 Yuri Olesha's "Lyompa" is another triptych-like example of thematic juxtaposition. The action of the story is minimal: a sick old man named Ponomarev lies on his deathbed while his adolescent grandson Alexander builds a model plane and another much younger grandson toddles around. Ponomarev certainly goes through a "completed process of change"—he dies at the end of the story—but no one would consider the story conventionally plotted. I've heard it described as a "slice of life," a "vignette," and a "set piece," but none of these terms recognizes what unifies and organizes the story: the juxtaposition of three characters, and three stages of life, and their attitudes toward the material world.

When the story opens, young Alexander is in the kitchen, planing wood for a model airplane he's making, and while he works, he revels in the beauty of the multitude of ordinary things that surround him: the "burst of splendor" of the stove's orange flame, a glass glistening on the window sill as the sun begins to set, the "magnificent dusk." To him, even the scabs from cuts on his fingers are "beautiful."

Meanwhile, his grandfather is lying in his bed and nearing death. When Ponomorev first learned he was critically ill, Olesha tells us, he realized

> how huge and varied was the world of things and how few were the things that remained to him. Every day fewer of these things were left. A familiar object like a railroad ticket was already irretrievably remote. First, the number of things on the periphery, far away from him, decreased; then this depletion grew closer to the center, reaching deeper and deeper, toward the courtyard, the house, the corridor, the room, his heart.

Now, the only things in his life are some medicine, a spoon, the light, and the room's wallpaper.

Shortly before the old man dies, his toddler grandson enters the room. Olesha says, "The little boy had just learned to recognize things" and "Each second gave him a new thing." At the end of the story Ponomarev gets a new thing, too, though it comes too late and is therefore laden with irony. The story concludes with the little boy exclaiming the good news: "Grandpa! Grandpa! They've brought you a coffin." It is the juxtaposition of these three contrasting characters and their differing relationship to the things of the world that creates the story's meaning, not any action or series of actions.

Dorothy Canfield Fisher's "Sex Education" is another story that juxtaposes three perspectives but in this case, they are the perspectives not of three different characters but of a single character, the protagonist Aunt Minnie, at three different periods of her life. Each time she tells the story of a frightening event that occurred in a cornfield when she was a teenager, she has a new understanding of it—and of herself. Initially, she tells the story to warn the narrator—one of Minnie's nieces—about the dangers of sex, but by the time Minnie is old, the story has become one about her devastating realization that she, not the man she encountered in the cornfield, was at fault and that her youthful reaction to him ruined his life. In short, what starts out as a typical sex education lesson for her nieces becomes an account of her own dark and sorrowful education about sex.

Whereas "Sex Education" conveys its theme by juxtaposing different versions of a single event, other stories convey their themes by juxtaposing different events that reveal a repeated pattern in a character's life. Any story that involves what Gardner calls "rhythmic repetition" of "a key event or group of events" is to an extent a lyrical plot, but most often the repetition exists less for lyricism's sake than for the purpose of thematic juxtaposition. Gustave Flaubert's "A Simple Heart" is an excellent example of a story that repeats one central dramatic action with variation in order to establish its theme. Basically, each repetition reads like an abbreviated causal plot, one in which his protagonist Félicité, a housemaid, falls in love with someone or something, achieves happiness with him, her, or it, and then loses him, her, or it. While the individual episodes are causal in nature, there's no cause-and-effect relationship between the episodes. In short, the story follows Gardner's definition of a novella as a form that moves "through a series of increasingly intense climaxes"—a structure whose sexuality, I suspect, both Jane Alison and I would consider more "femino" than "masculo."

In the course of the novella, Félicité falls in love with and loses (usually through death) a young man she wants to marry; Virginie, the daughter of Madame Aubain, for whom she works as a housemaid; her nephew Victor; Madame Aubain herself; and a parrot named Loulou, which she not only loves but venerates as a descendent of the Holy Ghost. ("God the Father could not have chosen a dove as a means of expressing Himself," she argues, since, unlike parrots, "doves cannot talk," so God must have chosen "one of Loulou's ancestors" to represent Himself.) After Loulou dies, Félicité has the parrot stuffed, and until she's near death, she treats it as the object of her love, hugging and kissing it despite its worm-eaten condition.

This summary might suggest that the story is a satiric portrait of Félicité's pathetic, even obsessive need to love someone or something, but the story is anything but. Flaubert considered the story to be a "modern saint's tale," and its ending echoes that of "The Legend of St. Julian Hospitator," which follows "A Simple Heart" in his collection *Three Tales*. Both stories end with the heavens opening as their protagonists die and a lowly creature each has treated with love and reverence (a leper in St. Julian's case, Loulou in Félicité's) transforming into a divine being (Jesus Christ and the Holy Ghost, respectively) that bears them up to heaven.

Novellas often repeat a single plotline with variation and thereby reveal a pattern that helps define their protagonist. But as Chekhov's "The Darling" reveals, that formal structure can be achieved in far fewer pages than we normally find in novellas. The story, which is quite probably a response to Flaubert's story, follows exactly the same pattern, albeit in a much more condensed manner and with a far darker theme. Like Flaubert's Félicité, Chekhov's Olenka "was always fond of someone, and could not exist without loving," but whereas Flaubert sees Félicité's love as saintly, Chekhov sees Olenka's love as parasitic.

In Russian, the story's title is "Dushenka," a term of endearment that translates literally as "Little Soul," and that's Olenka's problem: she has very little soul, or self. She adopts the opinions and beliefs of whomever she loves and echoes everything they say. When she was married to her first husband, the manager of a theatre, she told everyone that "the theatre was the chief and most important thing in life, and that it was only through the drama that one could derive true enjoyment and become cultivated and humane," but after he dies and she marries a man who works for a timber merchant, all she can talk or think about is timber, and when a friend suggests she go to the theatre, she says she and her husband "have no time for nonsense. What's the use of these theatres?" And after her second husband dies, she has an affair with a veterinary surgeon who is separated from his wife and she begins to think and talk only about such things as cattle and foot-and-mouth disease. After the veterinary surgeon is transferred to Siberia and she is left alone, Olenka endures a long, melancholy period of emptiness in which she "thought of nothing, wished for nothing" and "worst of all, she had no opinions of any sort . . . and did not know what to talk about."

When the veterinary surgeon eventually returns, now reconciled with his wife, Olenka's love descends upon his ten-year-old son Sasha. And now, Chekhov says, with more than a little irony, "she had opinions of her own" once again, but they are of course the opinions of Sasha—opinions about how difficult school lessons are and so forth. She becomes the nineteenth-century equivalent of a "helicopter mother" to this boy who is someone else's son. She even follows him to school, despite the fact that he repeatedly tells her to leave him alone. The story ends with Sasha crying out in his sleep, "I'll give it to you. Go away! Shut up!"—words clearly directed at the woman who hovers over him as oppressively as Flaubert's parrot hovered over Félicité joyfully. Whereas Félicité's selfless love is rewarded with eternal life in heaven, Olenka's selfish love is punished with rejection by someone she loves.

While both "A Simple Heart" and "The Darling" consist of a series of miniature causal plots, the individual episodes aren't causally connected, and hence each story communicates its theme primarily through thematic juxtaposition. And importantly, the otherwise omniscient third-person narrator of "The Darling" explicitly denies any understanding of what causes Olenka to feel and act as she does. This is how he describes her love of Sasha: "For this little boy with the dimple in his cheek and the big school cap, she would have given her whole life, she would have given it with joy and tears of tenderness. Why? Who can tell why?"

Chekhov has another story that creates its meaning through thematic juxtaposition without any causal connection, and the lack of understandable causality is again the story's point—and also the reason the story is called "A Story Without an End": there's no way to predict how the character and his life will change in the future, nor any way to understand why it changed in the past. The story juxtaposes two very different scenes. In the first, the narrator—who is not-so-coincidentally a doctor and a writer of short stories like Chekhov himself—is called to a neighbor's house where he discovers that a lodger has shot himself in the chest and is bleeding profusely, the result of his attempt to commit suicide out of grief over the death of his wife. "In the big eyes which he lifted upon me," the narrator says, "I read unutterable terror, pain, and entreaty." And what he's entreating the doctor to do is to shoot him. But of course the doctor ignores his entreaty and tends to his wound.

In the second scene, which takes place a year later, the once-suicidal lodger is now in the doctor's drawing-room, "playing on the piano and showing the ladies how provincial misses sing sentimental songs," and he and the ladies are laughing. The narrator calls him into his study and asks him to read the story he wrote about the night he attempted suicide. The man goes pale while reading it and when he finishes, the narrator asks him, "How does it end?" The lodger answers,

> "I have had burdens to bear that would have broken an elephant's back; the devil knows what I have suffered—no one could have suffered more, I think, and where are the traces? It's astonishing. One would have thought the imprint made on a man by his agonies would have been everlasting, never to be effaced or eradicated. And yet that imprint wears out as easily as a pair of cheap boots. . . . Everything in the world is transitory, and that transitoriness is absurd!"

The ladies then call for the lodger to return to them, and the narrator says, "I see him, entering into his habitual rôle of intellectual chatterer, prepare to show off his idle theories, such as the transmutation of substances . . . and at the same time I recall him sitting on the floor in a pool of blood with his sick imploring eyes." He then asks himself (and us) the question he asked the lodger: "How will it end?" He has no answer. Clearly, people undergo transmutation too, and who we are one day does not necessarily determine who we will be in the future.

Symbolic Juxtaposition

In a symbolic juxtapositional plot, the theme is primarily expressed through analogy rather than through thematically related characters and incidents. As I mentioned earlier, Carmen Maria Machado's "Inventory" seems, on the surface, to be an episodic plot like Susan Minot's "Lust," but its meaning ultimately depends on symbolic juxtaposition. The story's episodic plot, the inventory of the narrator's sexual history, is juxtaposed with a second plot that, as the story progresses, gradually intersects with the episodic plot in a way that creates a symbolic analogy. The second plot, which involves the spread of a deadly virus across the country, initially seems largely unrelated to the main plot—and even relatively unimportant. It's mentioned briefly, and sometimes obliquely, in only half of the episodes, and it takes place entirely offstage, in the story's background, until the final episode, in which the protagonist has sex with a woman who is infected. In this episode, the plot about disease merges with the plot about sex, and we see how the two plots are symbolically related: just as one plot traces the effects of the virus as it spreads from person to person, the other plot traces the effects of the protagonist's sexual experiences with person after person. The implied theme, then, like that of "Lust," is that sex, which we normally associate with birth, can lead to a kind of death, be it metaphorical or literal. By linking a plot that focuses on sex with a plot that focuses on disease, death, and even the extinction of the human race, Machado not only symbolically links sex and death, she gives her story a stronger sense of unity than we normally find in an episodic story, a kind of unity that is symbolic, not literal.

Kevin Brockmeier's "The Ceiling" has a similar kind of symbolic unity. Like "Inventory," it juxtaposes an episodic plot with a plot that symbolically parallels it, and again like "Inventory," the plot that symbolically parallels the episodic plot is dark and ominous. The story consists of a sequence of events that have no causal connection; even the narrator's climactic discovery that his wife is having an affair with their neighbor is a matter of pure chance, something that happens only because "a whim" leads him near the restaurant where he discovers them together. Interspersed into this plot is a second plot in which a square, black object—dubbed "the ceiling" by local newspapers—suddenly appears in the sky and over a period of months progressively descends and expands in size, blotting out the stars, the moon, and the sun and crushing water towers, buildings, and streetlamps until the ceiling is "no higher than a coffee table" above the ground and the narrator is lying next to his wife, unable to do anything but wait "until the earth and the sky met and locked and the distance between them closed forever."

But whereas the literal epidemic in Machado's story parallels the deadly metaphorical sickness that results from her narrator's sexual experiences, in Brockmeier's story the metaphorical descent of the square black object parallels the literal darkening of his narrator's emotional state as his marriage collapses. And ultimately the cause of the failure of his marriage is as unclear and mysterious as the cause of the ceiling's descent.

Chekhov is the master of symbolic juxtapositional plots (and many other kinds of plots). His regrettably little-known "Fortune," one of his personal favorites, is an outstanding example. (For a discussion of this story, see pages 138-139 of "Returning Characters to Life.") His much better-known "Gooseberries" is another outstanding example. On the surface, little of significance seems to happen in the story—two friends, Burkin and Ivan, are hiking through the countryside when it starts to rain, so they seek shelter at their friend Alekhin's nearby home, where Ivan joyfully swims in the river despite the rain and later that night tells his two friends an impassioned story about his brother's obsession with gooseberries and the illusions and self-deceptions on which human happiness is based. Burkin and Alekhin are bored by his story. As Chekhov explains,

> It was not interesting to listen to the story of a poor clerk who ate gooseberries, when from the walls generals and fine ladies, who seemed to come to life in the dark, were looking down from their gilded frames. It would have been much more interesting to hear about elegant people, lovely women.

The men then retire for the night. The story ends with Burkin lying in bed, unable to sleep, and listening to the rain tapping on the windowpanes. The continual tapping of the rain symbolically echoes the tapping of the hammer that Ivan spoke of earlier:

> "Apparently those who are happy can only enjoy themselves because the unhappy bear their burdens in silence, and but for this silence happiness would be impossible. It is a kind of universal hypnosis. There ought to be a man with a hammer behind the door of every happy

man, to remind him by his constant knocks that there are unhappy people, and that happy as he himself may be, life will sooner or later show him its claws, catastrophe will overtake him—sickness, poverty, loss—and nobody will see it, just as he now neither sees nor hears the misfortunes of others. But there is no man with a hammer, the happy man goes on living and the petty vicissitudes of life touch him only lightly, like the wind in an aspen tree, and all is well."

Burkin blames his inability to sleep on the strong smell of stale tobacco from Ivan's pipe, but we suspect that what is truly keeping him awake is the gradually growing awareness that his own happiness is based on his refusal to face the misery of his fellow human beings, and we further suspect that, before long, he will be overcome with the same kind of "sadness bordering on desperation" that Ivan says often keeps him awake at night. For Burkin, then, there *is* somebody with a hammer, and that somebody is Ivan, and his hammer is his story, which hammers away at Burkin's complacency just as Chekhov's story hammers away at ours. Through the implied analogy between the rain and the hammer, we experience the climactic insight that Burkin will experience, if ever, only after the story's ending. And through this analogy, a story that has seemed to be solely a complex investigation of the pros and cons of happiness becomes also a story about the power of a story to haunt and change us.

It's hard to imagine two stories that are more different on the surface than Chekhov's "Gooseberries" and John Barth's "Lost in the Funhouse," yet both employ symbolic juxtapositional plots. Barth's metafictional story braids together two plotlines, one about a boy named Ambrose who gets lost in a literal funhouse in Ocean Springs, Maryland, and another about the author/narrator, who gets lost in the metaphorical funhouse of the creative process while writing Ambrose's story. Without the symbolic plotline, the story would be merely a straightforward, realistic story about a young boy discovering his vocation as—you guessed it—a maker of funhouses, just like Barth himself.

Frame stories, like "Gooseberries" and "Lost in the Funhouse," frequently employ symbolic juxtaposition. Joseph Conrad's *Heart of Darkness* is a classic example of this combination. In it, an unnamed frame narrator tells us the story Marlow told him and their fellow shipmates, and Marlow frames his story of his journey to the heart of darkness in the Congo with accounts of two other symbolic journeys he's taken to the heart of darkness—one to Belgium and one to England. Just as there are three stages in Marlow's literal journey in the Congo—to the Outer Station, the Central Station, and the Inner Station—there are three stages in Marlow's symbolic journey to the heart of darkness—the first to "the door of Darkness," the Belgian headquarters of the company responsible for the atrocities Kurtz and others commit in the Congo; the second, to the Congo and Kurtz; and the third, to Kurtz's "Intended" in London. As the fact that the novella repeats several journeys to the heart of darkness (and obsessively repeats the words *heart* and *darkness* and their relatives) suggests, it fulfills Gardner's definition of a lyrical plot. However, as with Flaubert's "A Simple Heart" and Chekhov's "The Darling," the rhythmic repetition-with-variation of one storyline exists primarily to establish theme, albeit in a manner that is more symbolic than in those thematic juxtapositional stories.

I'll focus here on the final stage of Marlow's symbolic journey to the heart of darkness, his visit to Kurtz's fiancée, whom he calls his "Intended." As Conrad's imagery makes clear, this stage of Marlow's journey leads him to understand that the "horror" Kurtz glimpses in his epiphanic dying moment is in the heart of every human being, even the most seemingly "civilized." When Marlow enters the Intended's house, he says he feels "the heart of a conquering darkness." And when the Intended enters the room, he notes that "The room seemed to have grown darker," and his sense of time becomes distorted in a symbolically significant way. "For her," he says,

> "[Kurtz] had died only yesterday. And, by Jove! The impression was so powerful that for me too he seemed to have died only yesterday—nay, this very minute. I saw her and him in the same instant of time—his death and her sorrow—I saw her sorrow in the very moment of his death."

At this point, he turns to his shipmates and says, "Do you understand? I saw them together—I *heard* them together" (emphasis mine). Obviously, the Intended wasn't literally with

Kurtz when he died, but the fact that Marlow not only "sees" them together at the moment of his death but imagines hearing her say, along with Kurtz, the words he spoke at that moment—"The horror, the horror"—subtly suggests that Conrad is drawing a symbolic parallel between the Intended and Kurtz.

Later in the scene Conrad overtly draws a parallel between the Intended and Kurtz's African mistress, the "savage and superb, wild-eyed and magnificent" woman he describes as "the image of [the jungle's] soul." Marlow says the way the Intended "put out her arms as if after a retreating figure, stretching them back and with clasped pale hands across the fading and narrow sheen of the window" made him recall Kurtz's mistress "bedecked with powerless charms, stretching bare brown arms over the glitter of the infernal stream, the stream of darkness." I find the fact that Marlow compares the Intended to the woman who embodies the heart of darkness yet another sign that he believes that, despite her "veneer" of civilization, she, too, has a heart of darkness. If Conrad wanted to establish the Intended as the opposite of Kurtz's savage mistress—the "hope of civilization," as scholars generally argue—I think he would have gone on to point out that she resembles her only in her gesture and her love for Kurtz, but he doesn't. Instead, when the Intended says, in the very next sentence, "He died as he lived," Marlow reacts with a "lie" that tells the truth: "'His end,' said I, with dull anger stirring in me, 'was in every way worthy of his life.'" Without directly contradicting her faith that Kurtz lived and died nobly, he nonetheless expresses his belief that he didn't.

Conrad has been preparing us for this literally false but symbolically true "lie" since early in the novella, when Marlow tells his shipmates,

> "You know I hate, detest, and can't bear a *lie*, not because I am straighter than the rest of us, but simply because it appalls me. There is a taint of death, a flavour of mortality in lies—which is exactly what I hate and detest in the world—what I want to forget. It makes me miserable and sick, like biting something rotten would do."

But, he goes on to admit, he once went "near enough" to a lie by not correcting a young man's assumption that he had influential friends in Europe. That earlier "near lie" prepares us not only for the first near lie he tells the Intended about Kurtz's death being worthy of his life, but also for a second, even more powerful half-lie/half-truth. As Marlow and the Intended continue to talk, the darkness of the room deepens, until finally she asks him what Kurtz's last words were. To tell her the straightforward truth about Kurtz's final words, Marlow says, "would have been too dark—too dark altogether," so in order to preserve "the faith that was in her, . . . that great and saving *illusion* that shone with an unearthly glow in the darkness" (emphasis mine) without literally lying, he tells her a metaphorical truth. And when he says that Kurtz's last words were her name, he's telling the men listening to his tale (and by extension, all of us reading it) that her name (and *everyone's* name) is "The horror, the horror." In short, the "lie" he tells her is also the most horrible truth: that even she—the most innocent, faithful, loving, and civilized of human beings—is also "the horror."

The fact that none of the men on the ship calls Marlow on his deceptive answer to the Intended's question suggests that they recognize that it's another "near lie" and that it is symbolically true. In any case, it's clear that at least the novella's frame narrator has gotten the message that the heart of darkness is not just in the Congo but in all people everywhere. Before Marlow told his story the frame narrator was rhapsodizing about the glories of English colonialism, calling his countrymen "bearers of a spark from the sacred fire" who spread civilization to the savage places in the world, but at the end of the novella he sees the whole world, including his own country, as "the heart of an immense darkness." Marlow certainly did deceive the Intended with his "near lie," but it's clear the frame narrator, and most likely his shipmates, saw the truth behind it. And thanks to the novella's use of the symbolic juxtapositional plot, we see it too.

The Argumentative Plot

An argumentative plot resembles a causal plot, although the conflict is between ideas more than between characters and the action consists of arguments instead of events. There is a conflict, then, and it gets complicated, but given the risk of coming across as dogmatic, authors rarely resolve the conflict, and when they do, it's usually in an indirect, ironic way.

Langston Hughes's 1957 story "Radioactive Red Caps" is an example of an argumentative plot that resolves its conflict both indirectly and ironically. In it, Hughes's narrator, Ananias Boyd, debates current race relations with his bar buddy Jesse B. Semple—aka Simple. The story opens with Boyd naively exclaiming, "How wonderful that Negroes are being rapidly integrated into every phase of American life," but Simple— and, clearly, Hughes—argues that nothing has changed. Boyd counters by saying, "Look at the ever greater number of Negroes in high places," and Simple responds, "Name one making an atom bomb." He then goes on to say the atom bomb isn't "an integrated bomb" and whites "don't want no Negroes nowhere near no bomb that can kill a whole state full of folks. . . . Just think what would happen to Mississippi." Boyd asks Simple if he wants to fight another Civil War, and Simple says not "without an atom bomb."

Boyd then warns Simple that the atomic bomb would make him radioactive, and Simple responds, "That will worry white folks. Just suppose all the Negroes down South got atomized, charged up like hot garbage, who would serve the white folks' tables, nurse their children, Red Cap their bags, and make up their Pullman berths?" And, he adds, "Atoms, they tell me, is catching," so whites will become radioactive too.

Boyd counters that Simple will be annihilated along with the white folks, but Simple objects, saying, "Negroes are very hard to annihilate. I'm a Negro—so I figure I would live to radiate and, believe me, once charged I will take charge." He concludes the argument by saying, "If Negroes can survive white folks in Mississippi, we can survive anything."

Simple may be simple, but in this argument, he clearly bests his more "intelligent" friend. There's no indication, however, that Boyd is convinced by Simple's hilariously irrational but nonetheless convincing arguments.

More often than not, though, it's not clear who is the victor of an argumentative plot—or if victory is even possible. In Chekhov's "Lights," which I discuss in more detail in "Returning Characters to Life" (see page 135), a philosophical debate between an old man and a young student leads the narrator to conclude that "there's no understanding anything in this world!" and that the only possible "resolution" of the argument is the realization that no resolution is possible. Isaac

Bashevis Singer's "The Boarder" is similar. In it, a devout, observant Jew and his boarder, an irreligious Holocaust survivor, sit at a table eating their lunch and arguing over whether God is a merciful deity "who feedest the whole world with . . . Goodness, with Grace, with Loving Kindness" or "a Nazi to end all Nazis" who "tortures everybody." They also argue over whether there's a heaven, and whether people are virtuous or nothing but "filth." There is no resolution to their argument; neither character changes his opinion. The entire plot consists of nothing but the argument, and as in Chekhov's story, we're left without any resolution of the issues Singer's characters have raised.

Grace Paley's "A Conversation with My Father" is yet another story that consists almost entirely of an argument between two characters. Its narrator (who, though named Faith, not Grace, just happens to have written one of Grace's stories, "Faith in a Tree") and her father argue, very appropriately, about the role of plot in stories. As in "Lights" and "The Boarder," there is no climactic moment at which the argument is won. And even if there were, Paley suggests, it wouldn't necessarily be the real end. As Faith/Grace argues, even if a story ends with the words *the end*, "it is not necessarily the end"; like Chekhov in "A Story Without an End," she believes characters and lives can change in unforeseen and inexplicable ways. As she explains, she's "always despised" the "absolute line between two points" that constitutes plot because plot "takes all hope away. Everyone, real or invented, deserves the open destiny of life." Fittingly, then, her argument with her father about how to tell a story ends without closure: neither character changes his or her position—though the possibility that they might remains, thanks to the "open destiny of life."

The Expository Plot

Like the argumentative plot, the expository plot focuses more on ideas than on characters and events. The conflict, to the extent that one exists, is between someone who doesn't understand something and someone who does. The organizing principle, then, is explanation, and the story takes the form of either an informative essay or a conversation between two characters, one of whom enlightens the other.

Not surprisingly, a great many fictional expository plots take as their subject—what else?—fiction. Jorge Luis Borges's satire on literary criticism, "Pierre Menard, Author of *Don Quixote*," is an excellent example. Like a scholarly article, it consists of a discussion of a literary work, quotations from various texts, footnotes, and the refutation of another scholar's opinion, but in this case, the author—Pierre Menard—and the scholar—Henri Bachelier—are fictional. And while the story does refer to many actual writers—Edgar Allan Poe, Stéphane Mallarmé, and Paul Valéry, among them—it also refers to invented writers and books and to such nonexistent scholarly publications as *The Journal for the Suppression of Reality*.

The story describes how Menard "resolved to outstrip that vanity which awaits all the woes of mankind" by undertaking "a task that was complex in the extreme and futile from the outset. He dedicated his conscience and nightly studies to the repetition of a pre-existing book in a foreign tongue." Borges's pedantic narrator argues that Menard's version of *Don Quixote* is "almost infinitely richer" than Cervantes's not in spite of the fact that their texts are "verbally identical" but *because* they are identical. He argues that the fact that a twentieth-century Frenchman wrote an identical version of a seventeenth-century Spaniard's novel makes the text more subtle, meaningful, and complex and constitutes "a new approach to the historical novel," one that embraces "deliberate anachronisms."

While this story is the best-known of Borges's fictional "essays" on nonexistent authors and works, he wrote many others, including an entire book of them. *The Chronicles of Bustos Domecq*, which he wrote with his friend and collaborator Adolfo Bioy-Casares, skewers both literary critics—Bustos Domecq is every bit as pompous and idiotic as the narrator of "Pierre Menard"—as well as various aesthetic fads of twentieth-century literature.

Some expository plots do more than address the way we read fiction, however; they instruct readers on how to *write* it. Margaret Atwood's much-anthologized "Happy Endings" is perhaps the best-known example of this kind of an expository plot and it, like Paley's "A Conversation with My Father," takes plot as its subject matter. It opens "John and Mary meet. What happens next?" then offers six possible plotlines, before concluding that "the endings are all the same however you slice it": "The only authentic ending is . . . *John and Mary die. John and Mary die. John and Mary die.*" This, she tells us, is "all that can be said for plots, which anyway are just one thing after another, a what and a what and a what." Her final advice to us is to forget what happens and focus on "How and Why."

Essentially, then, the story is an expository "essay" that raises a question ("What happens next?"), gives us six alternative answers, then concludes with its thesis statement. Since the story juxtaposes six plotlines, it also contains a thematic juxtapositional plot, but its primary organizing principle is exposition, not juxtaposition, since its main point is that all six alternative plotlines ultimately end the same way.

Like "Happy Endings," Tim O'Brien's "How to Tell a True War Story" takes the form of an expository essay that includes examples that illustrate its points. "A true war story," he says, "is never moral. It does not instruct, nor encourage virtue, nor suggest models of proper human behavior, nor restrain men from doing things men have always done. If a story seems moral, do not believe it." He also says, "you can tell a true war story" by its "absolute and uncompromising allegiance to obscenity and evil" and by the fact that "it embarrasses you." He goes on to say that, in a true war story, "Often the crazy stuff is true and the normal stuff isn't, because the normal stuff is necessary to make you believe the truly incredible craziness," and he adds that "Like a killer forest fire, like cancer under a microscope, any battle or bombing raid or artillery barrage has the aesthetic purity of absolute moral indifference—a powerful, implacable beauty—and a true war story will tell the truth about this though the truth is ugly."

O'Brien supports these claims by telling us four separate war stories, and he tells one of those stories—about the death of a soldier named Lemon—four times, each time making it both stranger and truer. And at the end he tells us that his entire story—including all of the ostensibly "true" stories it tells—is "all made up. Every goddamn detail. . . . None of it happened. *None* of it." Just as Atwood says the only legitimate ending is death of the characters, so O'Brien says the only true war story is a lie. "A thing may happen and be a total lie," he says, and "another thing may not happen and be truer than the truth."

As its title suggests, Lucia Berlin's "Point of View" is an expository exploration of the role point of view plays in writing fiction. It opens with a discussion of Chekhov's choice of third person for his story "Grief" (also translated as "Misery" and "Heartache"), which is about a St. Petersburg cab driver whose son has just died, and she says that we would feel "embarrassed, uncomfortable, even bored"—just like the passengers in the cab—if the cab driver told his story in first person, then she explains why she has followed Chekhov's lead and chosen third person for a story she's working on about a pathetic, lonely woman named Henrietta and her inexplicable and unreciprocated love for the doctor she works for. If she tells Henrietta's story in first person, she says, we'll be bored and stop reading. But if she tells the story in third person, she argues, "You'll listen to all the compulsive, obsessive boring little details of . . . Henrietta's life" because "You'll feel, hell if the narrator thinks there is something in this dreary creature worth writing about there must be. I'll read on and see what happens."

The narrator then goes on to summarize, in third person, the compulsive, obsessive, and boring details of Henrietta's sad life. But why, we'll wonder, did Berlin create a first-person narrator to tell Henrietta's story in third person? Why didn't she just tell the entire story in third person? As the story proceeds, we'll suspect—rightly, it turns out—that the story is more about the narrator than Henrietta, though we can't yet be sure why. Our question about Berlin's choice of point of view will hover in the back of our minds throughout the story and won't be fully resolved until the story's final sentences.

It will soon be clear, however, that Berlin's subject is not just Henrietta and her pathetic life but the craft of fiction, and the story exists to teach us how characters are created and stories are written. While most of the story consists of her third-person summary of Henrietta's pathetic life, the narrator continues to talk about herself in first person, and significantly she talks about her role in creating Henrietta's character. She points out that "Most writers use props and scenery from their own lives," then tells us that she, like her character, eats her dinner every night "on a blue place mat, using exquisite Italian stainless cutlery." She also reveals that the doctor in her story is based on one she once worked for and that Henrietta is based on a nurse named Shirley who also worked for him.

But this is where the "facts" stop and fiction starts: whereas Shirley loved the doctor, despite his "disdain" for her and his "mocking and cruel" behavior, the narrator hated him. The story has thus become, in part at least, about the central act of fiction writing: the attempt to imagine our way into the mind and heart of someone different from ourselves.

The narrator admits that she's "having a hard time writing" about the sad and boring details of Henrietta's life, especially conveying "the long hollow feeling of Sundays" and "the hopelessness" and loneliness that her character feels. But eventually she imagines a scene that succeeds. Here's how the story ends:

> She turns off the TV and sips her tea, listening to cars pulling in and out of the Arco station across the street. Sometimes a car stops with a screech at the telephone booth. A car door slams and soon the car speeds away.
>
> She hears someone drive up slowly to the phones. Loud jazz music comes from the car. Henrietta turns off the light, raises the blind by her bed, just a little. The window is steamed. The car radio plays Lester Young. The man talking on the phone holds it with his chin. He wipes his forehead with a handkerchief. I lean against the cool windowsill and watch him. I listen to the sweet saxophone play "Polka Dots and Moonbeams." In the steam of the glass I write a word. What? My name? A man's name? Henrietta? Love? Whatever it is I erase it quickly before anyone can see.

How do we know that the narrator has succeeded in imagining what Henrietta is feeling at this moment? By the fact that she shifts from third person to first. She is now experiencing what her character—and its factual inspiration, Shirley—experienced. Berlin doesn't present this moment as a huge *Eureka!* moment in which all of the difficulties of creating a character and a story are resolved; she's too smart to think it happens all at once. Hence the story ends with her uncertain what word Henrietta would write—and certain only that whatever word it is, she would erase it.

So a story that begins with a first-person narrator assuming she should tell the story in third person ends with her becoming her character—and a first-person narrator—if only for a moment.

Rick DeMarinis's "Rudderless Fiction: Lesson One" is another "instructional manual" of sorts that takes fiction writing as its subject—but instead of focusing on a single aspect of fiction, like the stories we've just examined, it covers a plethora of essential aspects of the craft of fiction, and it does so in a hilarious scatter-fire way that fits with the narrator's off-kilter persona. (The narrator is the crazed director of a correspondence school for writers, and the entire expository plot is cast in the form of an extended advertisement for the school.) But scattered and funny as it is, the advice is dead-on smart. Like Atwood and O'Brien, DeMarinis illustrates his points with snippets of various unrelated plotlines. For instance, to illustrate his point that a story should "Hit the Ground Running" by establishing the protagonist's conflict immediately, he says,

> Say Don's life is a mess. Say his wife just walked out, preferring a young buck with artistic sensibility named Stu. Or say Barb's husband, Helmut, decides to move into his secretary's apartment, and then, a week later, Barb's sweet retriever, Love Me Do, dies of a twisted intestine. You get the idea. We call this 'The Rack.' (Lesson 2).

The expository plot of Donald Barthelme's "The Balloon" isn't about *how* to write fiction; it's about *why* some writers write fiction. The first-person narrator of the story describes in expository fashion an art installation he created—a balloon that covers forty-five blocks of Midtown Manhattan—and goes on to discuss it in terms we use to talk about fiction. He calls it "a rough draft," for example, and says that it's wrong to think of the balloon as "implying sets of circumstances leading to some resolution, some escape of tension"—in other words, we shouldn't think of it as functioning like a standard causal plot—and he says, "There was a certain amount of initial argumentation about the 'meaning' of the balloon" and "Critical opinion was divided." Many people were vexed by the "apparent purposeless of the balloon" but would have approved of it if he'd painted an advertisement on its side, he says, but others saw it as an "imposture, something inferior to the sky that had formerly been there"—i.e., insufficiently realistic—and others wished "to lose themselves in the balloon" the way some people desire to escape into fiction.

He also says that people began to "locate themselves in relation to aspects of the balloon," referring to where the balloon intersected with a certain street or building, and the narrator notes that "Each intersection was crucial, meeting of balloon and building, meeting of balloon and man, meeting of balloon and balloon," a comment that suggests that a work of art's relationship to physical reality, human beings, and other works of art needs to be taken into account when considering its meaning or purpose. Furthermore, he argues, the balloon was designed to offer "the possibility, in its randomness, of *mis*location of the self, in contradistinction to the grid of precise, rectangular pathways under our feet" (emphasis mine).

But although he says the meaning of the balloon is too complex to be "limited, or defined," the reason for its existence turns out to be relatively simple—and downright Freudian. In the final paragraph, the narrator meets his girlfriend, who has been in Norway for twenty-two days, and he tells her that "The balloon . . . is a spontaneous autobiographical disclosure, having to do with the unease I felt at your absence, and with sexual deprivation, but now that your visit to Bergen has been terminated, it is no longer necessary or appropriate." The story ends with him having the balloon deflated and stored away in case of some "other time of unhappiness, some time, perhaps, when we are angry with one another."

Like Barthelme's balloon, the museum that Steven Millhauser describes in his story "The Barnum Museum" is an expository metaphor for fiction. There is an actual Barnum Museum in Bridgeport, Connecticut, but it's nothing like Millhauser's. His story gives us a twenty-five-section tour of a fantastic, labyrinthine museum that contains innumerable rooms (some of which have as many as fourteen doors that open on to more rooms and doorways), a forest, a city in a lake, and three subterranean levels, and it is replete with such marvels as magic carpet rides, a griffen, a unicorn, a winged horse, a talking horse, a lorax, a transparent man, a giant, mermaids, and leprechauns. Mentally replace each reference to the museum in the following passage with the word *fiction* and you'll see the point Millhauser is making:

> It has been said . . . that our museum is a form of escape. In a superficial sense, this is certainly true. When we enter the Barnum Museum we are physically free of all that binds us to the outer world, to the realm of sunlight and death; and sometimes we seek relief from suffering and sorrow in the halls of the Barnum Museum. But it is a mistake to imagine that we flee into our museum in order to forget the hardships of life outside. . . . In the branching halls of the Barnum Museum we are never forgetful of the ordinary world, for it is precisely our awareness of that world which permits us to enjoy the wonders of the halls. Indeed I would argue that we are most sharply aware of our town when we leave it to enter the Barnum Museum; without our museum, we would pass through life as in a daze or dream.

And in the final section of the story, Millhauser adds, "If the Barnum Museum were to disappear, we would continue to live our lives much as before, but we know we would experience a terrible sense of diminishment."

While Millhauser's story gives us an expository tour of an imaginary museum, Michael Martone's *The Blue Guide to Indiana* gives us a similarly expository tour of his home state. Following the format of the factual *Blue Guides* published by W.W. Norton, Martone provides brief descriptions of such imaginary—and hilarious—tourist attractions as the Tomb of Orville Redenbacher, the Trans-Indiana Mayonnaise Pipeline, the Musée de Bob Ross, the Site of the First Observed Human Female Orgasm in America, and the State Hair Dump, where all the hair cut in barber shops and hair salons across the state is collected. Believe it or not, as Ripley would say, some excerpts from the book were initially published as news items in Indiana newspapers.

The works I've discussed so far all take the form of exposition addressed to the reader, but sometimes, as with the argumentative plot, the story takes the form of a dialogue, but instead of two characters arguing, one is explaining something to the other. One example of such a plot is Poe's "The Power of Words." It consists entirely of a conversation between two angels, Oinos, who is a "new-fledged" spirit, and Agathos, who has been an angel for three hundred years and thus has much to teach Oinos.

Oinos is surprised to discover that he has not become, as he expected, "at once cognizant of all things, and thus . . . happy" now that he has passed into immortal life. Agathos responds that "not in knowledge is happiness, but in the acquisition of knowledge!" and for the rest of the story he helps Oinos acquire knowledge. Agathos teaches Oinos some surprising things, including the fact that "the Deity does not create"—or, rather, that He created "In the beginning only," and since then everything that has sprung into being is only "the mediate or indirect" result of God's initial act of creation. Invoking a concept similar to the "butterfly effect," Agathos explains that every word spoken creates a vibration that affects "every particle of the earth's air . . . forever" and that every "impulse given the air, must, in the end, impress every individual thing that exists within the universe."

Agathos concludes by explaining "the physical power of words": since every word is "an impulse on the air," every word creates part of the universe. In the beginning was the Word, in short, but since then, all of creation is due to *our* words. In the story's final paragraph, Agathos points to a star the two angels are passing and says, "This wild star—it is now three centuries since, with clasped hands, and with streaming eyes, at the feet of my beloved—I spoke it—with a few passionate sentences—into birth." And with this climactic revelation, Poe's expository plot concludes.

The Associative Plot

An associative plot is minimally causal in that one thought triggers another, but its focus is not on the movement from conflict to climax and resolution that dominates the causal plot; rather, it is concerned with revealing a different kind of order, an interior order rather than an external one, and hence there is generally little external action in an associative plot—a fact that probably explains why associative plots appear far more commonly in short stories or individual chapters (for example, the final chapter of Joyce's *Ulysses*, the so-called "soliloquy" of Molly Bloom) than in entire novels.

In her essay "Modern Fiction," Virginia Woolf advocates for the associative plot, saying, "Let us record the atoms as they fall upon the mind in the order in which they fall, let us trace the pattern, *however disconnected and incoherent in appearance*, which each sight or incident scores upon the consciousness" (emphasis mine). As she acknowledges, such an organizing principle will appear "disconnected and incoherent" to a reader accustomed to a traditional causal plot, but she asserts that the associative movement of the mind is "the proper stuff of fiction."

Woolf's story "Moments of Being: 'Slater's Pins Have No Points'" is a classic example of an associative plot. There is a cause-and-effect relationship between the story's main "events"—as Julia Craye strikes the last chord of a Bach fugue on her piano, Fanny Wilmot loses a pin that had been holding a rose on her dress, then she looks for it, finds it, and uses it to pin a carnation on Julia's dress—but Woolf is not the least bit interested—nor should we be—in how these trivial events relate to each other causally. Rather, she's interested in the associative movement of Fanny's thoughts while searching for the pin.

Julia's comment about Slater's pins having no points leads Fanny to imagine Julia, "who lived, it seemed, in the cool, glassy world of Bach fugues," waiting in line at the counter of Slater's store "like anybody else," and that leads her to remember something the principal of a local music college said about the death of Julia's brother, and that leads her to think about the fact that none of the Crayes ever married, and that leads her to remember something Julia said about "the use of men" and so forth until eventually all of these thoughts lead her to a new understanding of Julia, an understanding that allows her to see "the very fountain of her being," to recognize that she had always been true to her own spirit, "obstinately adhering, whatever people might say, in choosing her pleasures for herself," and to witness her blaze, "in a moment of ecstasy," "like a dead white star."

There is slightly more external action in Tillie Olsen's powerful story about motherhood "I Stand Here Ironing" than there is in Woolf's story, but not much. For virtually all of the story, the only action is, as the title advertises, the narrator ironing. As she irons, though, we follow the "tormented" associative movement of her thoughts about her daughter and the difficulties she's experienced raising her, thoughts triggered by an offstage phone call from one of her daughter's teachers. She stops ironing only twice, once to change her son's diaper and once for a very brief conversation with her daughter. These two events take up half a page, whereas her thoughts take up eleven pages. Clearly, Olsen, at least in this story, is following Woolf's advice to "record the atoms as they fall upon the mind in the order in which they fall."

Stuart Dybek's "Pet Milk" is another story that records the atoms as they fall. The story's surface action is almost ludicrously minimal: the narrator merely drinks instant coffee and Pet milk on a winter day. But inside that seemingly trivial moment, there's a lot of passion and drama, for the way the Pet milk swirls in the coffee triggers some swirling memories in the narrator. First, he remembers that his grandmother, who always drank Pet milk in her coffee, referred to it as "cream," and he recalls listening to the yellow plastic radio on her kitchen table "on winter afternoons after school, as I sat by her table watching the Pet milk swirl and cloud in the steaming coffee, and noticing, outside her window, the sky doing the same thing above the railroad yard across the street."

The swirling sky leads him to remember "seeing the same swirling sky in tiny liqueur glasses containing a drink called a King Alphonse: the crème de cacao rising like smoke in repeated explosions, blooming in kaleidoscopic clouds through the layer of heavy cream," and this leads him to recall his girlfriend Kate and the little Czech restaurant that he took her to, at which a waiter named Rudi would make each of them a King Alphonse at their table. He remembers talking with Kate about their future plans—he intended to go into the Peace Corps and she wanted to go to graduate school in Europe—and how these talks made him feel like he was "missing someone I was still with."

These general memories lead to a more specific memory, a vivid recollection of his twenty-second birthday, which he and Kate celebrated at the Czech restaurant with champagne and oysters and more talk of their futures, then, their passion fueled by the sense that they would soon be separated, perhaps forever, they left and, on the L train to Kate's place to make love, they stood and kissed and rocked their bodies together to "the rhythm of the ride." The sound of their "quick breathing," the narrator remembers, "was louder than the clatter of tracks." Then the train slowed down as it reached a local station, and he looked up and saw what the story's final words describe:

> A high school kid in shirt sleeves, maybe sixteen, with books tucked under one arm and a cigarette in his mouth, caught sight of us, and in the instant before he disappeared he grinned and started to wave. Then he was gone, and I turned from the window, back to Kate, forgetting everything—the passing stations, the glowing late sky, even the sense of missing her—but that arrested wave stayed with me. It was as if I were standing on that platform, with my schoolbooks and a smoke, on one of those endlessly accumulated afternoons after school when I stood almost out of time simply waiting for a train, and I thought how much I'd have loved seeing someone like us streaming by.

Beginning with the simple act of pouring Pet milk into a cup of coffee, the story takes us on a journey through time to a timeless moment, a moment in which the narrator recognizes both the beauty and transitory nature of love and how what's lost nonetheless remains, arrested in memory.

Claire-Louise Bennett is another writer who employs associative plots. As Meghan O'Rourke has noted, Bennett's stories "shun conventional narrative devices (like plot), instead dramatizing the associative movement of the narrator's 'mind in motion.'" Her story "Morning, Noon & Night" is a good example of this approach to plot. Whereas "Pet Milk" traces associations triggered by coffee and Pet milk, her narrator's story starts with coffee and a banana and proceeds to move associatively through a wide variety of seemingly innocuous topics—everything from gardening to placemats to en-suite bathrooms to Japanese tapestries—all the while subtly revealing, seemingly against her will, the devastating effect a failed relationship has had on her.

The story opens "Sometimes a banana with coffee is nice," then proceeds to warn us that bananas, unlike apples, don't "take well to being forgotten about" and can easily "wizen and stink of putrid and go almost black." She then talks about other breakfast foods: oatcakes, pears, and porridge with black jam and blanched almond slices. Noting that almond slices look like fingernails leads her to think about her own fingernails, which leads her to talk about how her hands "look like the hands of someone very charming and refined who has had to dig themselves out of some dank and wretched spot they really shouldn't have fallen into."

And that associative thought leads her to a series of memories about a metaphoric "dank and wretched spot" she fell into, memories that, like rotten bananas, get increasingly dark. She recalls speaking at a "very eminent university" about "the essential brutality of love." Her talk "attempted to show that in the whole history of literature love is quite routinely depicted as an engulfing process of ecstatic suffering which finally, mercifully, obliterates us and delivers us to oblivion." The gist of her argument, she says, "was simply that love is indeed a vicious and divine disintegration of selfhood." The lover's "desire to come apart irrevocably," she says, is "*As deep as ink and black, black as the deepest sea.*"

The image of a blackened banana has led her to this thought, and this thought leads her to the memory of her "ill-starred liaison" with a man whose loss "unhinged" her and led her to feel so "pathetic and irrelevant" that her life came to a literal standstill: after leaving a shop where she bought cigarettes, she was unable to decide for half an hour whether to turn right or left. "I was left standing absolutely and purposely alone," she says. As soon as she faces this moment of the disintegration of her own selfhood, she retreats to talk about her mundane daily tasks—gardening, feeding birds, fetching mail, etc.—in an apparent attempt to avoid facing the blackness of her vision and the obliteration of her self. Then she says, "Everything: every plant, every flower, every bird, every insect, just getting on with it." And that, of course, is what she's trying—not very successfully—to do herself.

The story ends with her incessantly chopping vegetables in "a kind of contracted stupor, morning, noon and night" and "trying not to pay any heed to [her] reflection in the mirror." Structurally, then, the narrative vacillates between the associative movement of her mind, which leads her to see herself with frightening clarity, and her desperate attempts to repress her memories, to "change the subject" to something that will make her seem—to herself as much as to us, her imagined audience—still whole, still "getting on with it," not forgotten, not obliterated.

THE LYRICAL PLOT

As Gardner notes, the organizing principle of a lyrical plot is "rhythmic repetition" of "a key image or cluster of images," "a key event or group of events," or "some central idea or cluster of ideas" that "increasingly deepens and redefines" their meaning. Of course, repetition of key images, events, and ideas appears in causal and other kinds of plots as well, but Gardner is talking about rhythmic repetition as the principal structural device that conveys the work's meaning. Several of the works we've already discussed repeat with variation a single dramatic event—an elevator ride in Coover's "The Elevator," four trips a young girl takes in Gordon's "Summer Dust," various journeys to the "heart of darkness" in Conrad's novella, the serial loss of loved ones in Flaubert's "A Simple Heart" and Chekhov's "The Darling," and a hauntingly misunderstood encounter from the past in Fisher's "Sex Education"—but in each case the lyrical plot is subordinate to another kind of plot. The plot of Woolf's "Moments of Being: 'Slater's Pins Have No Points'" is primarily associative, but it also contains the fugue-like series of repeated images, ideas, and words that is characteristic of a lyrical plot. In a mere five pages, Woolf repeats eighteen key words and phrases (or variants of them)—most notably *pin, glass, flower, never married, music, bright,* and *odd*—no less than 123 times. And in its concluding paragraphs, Woolf braids together thirty-one repetitions of those words and phrases. Eileen Baldeshwiler says that the "plotline" of a lyrical story consists of "tracing complex emotions to a closing cadence utterly unlike the reasoned resolution of the conventional cause-and-effect narrative," and I think that's an excellent description of Woolf's "closing cadence." Indeed, I would argue that the story's sense of closure derives almost as much from this crescendo of interrelated and repeated motifs as from Fanny's association-driven epiphany about Julia.

For the most part, lyrical plots play supporting roles in fiction, but there are some stories that rely so much on musical, rhythmic repetition that they are primarily or even solely lyrical. Rick Moody's "Boys" is one example. The story is an episodic narrative of the lives of twin boys from the time they first enter their parents' house after their birth until, boys no longer, they exit the house after the death of their father. The events are chronological but not causally connected. What organizes and unifies the story is its litany-like repetition of the sentence "Boys enter the house." In the course of six pages, this sentence is repeated verbatim thirty-two times and the phrase "enter the house," without "boys" immediately preceding it, appears an additional fifteen times, for a total of forty-seven repetitions—an average of nearly eight per page. What's more, the word *boys* (or variants thereof) is repeated 104 times, an average of seventeen repetitions per page. Even more than Woolf's story, "Boys" gets its emotional impact from its rhythmic repetitions.

John O'Brien's brilliant but largely unknown story "Birds" has even less of a narrative arc than "Boys," and it relies on lyrical repetition far more than Moody's story. In just eight pages, O'Brien uses the word *bird* or *birds* fifty-two times and mentions specific species of birds—everything from parakeets to puffins—another ninety-nine times for a total of 151 bird references, an average of nearly nineteen per page. Unlike Woolf's story, which has at least minimally causal action and associative movement of thought, or Moody's story, which is structured chronologically, the twenty-nine brief mosaic-like sections of O'Brien's story have no causal or associative relationships and range backward and forward throughout the narrator's lifetime with no concern for chronology or a narrative "arc." It is unified almost solely by the obsessive, musical repetition of its imagery.

Another story that fulfills Gardner's definition of the lyrical organizing principle is Larry Brown's "The Rich." The story is essentially a character study of Mr. Pellisher, who works at a travel agency, via his attitudes toward his wealthy clients. In its six pages, Brown repeats the phrase *the rich* 124 times, *rich* seventeen times, and *richening* and *richly* once each, for a total of 143 repetitions—an average of nearly twenty-four per page. The story consists almost entirely of a cluster of rhythmic repetitions of its key words and phrases and is thus the purest example of a lyrical story I have encountered so far.

The Hybrid Plot

In my opinion, one of the most effective ways that writers can achieve originality is by combining two or more plot forms. As I've suggested above, in most hybrid plots, one plot form is primary and another is secondary. However, some hybrid plots combine plot forms in such equal measure that it's difficult to say that any one dominates. Here are three examples:

Amy Hempel's "The Harvest" opens with a standard causal plot about a disfiguring motorcycle accident and its effect on the narrator's relationship with a married man, but the story doesn't end with the climax and resolution of the causal plot; what follows is an expository plot in which she tells us all of the things she left out, exaggerated, or invented in the process of telling the story—and, much like O'Brien in "How to Tell a True War Story," explains why she needed to alter the truth to make the story feel "true" to the reader. Both plots are equally important to the success of the story, and hence it is an excellent example of a hybrid plot.

Lucia Berlin's "A Manual for Cleaning Women" is another superb example. It weaves together three different plot forms: the episodic, the expository, and the causal. The story is an episodic and non-chronological account of the narrator's bus rides to work, conversations with other cleaning women, and snippets of scenes with the various people whose houses she cleans, but as the title suggests, Berlin's narrator Maggie regularly departs from the episodic account of her job to pass along expository advice to cleaning women, typically in parenthetical "asides" of sorts.

But the expository plot is not the only one that interrupts the episodic plot; there's also a causal plot about Maggie and her grief over her husband's death. Like the expository "advice" plot, the causal plot is woven into the episodic plot in bits and pieces, creating a kind of contrapuntal rhythm to the action of the episodic plotline. All told, the references to her husband add up to barely more than one of the story's thirteen pages, but as James Joyce once said, "Absence is the highest form of presence," and her husband's relative absence from the story makes us feel that Maggie is doing everything she can to repress her grief. Then, in the final two pages, the episodic plot and the causal plot intersect: we get a scene with Maggie and her client

Mrs. Johansen, an eighty-year-old woman whose husband died six months before and who distracts herself from her grief by working on picture puzzles. There's a piece missing from one of the puzzles and Maggie finds it for her, and Mrs. Johansen is almost as happy as if she found what she's really missing—her husband. Only after Maggie's encounter with another grieving widow do we get the climactic moment of the causal plot, and the story's last sentence: "I finally weep."

All told, only three of the story's thirteen pages directly address the causal plot, and it would have been an emotionally thin story if Berlin had given us only those three pages' worth of material. In order to convey Maggie's repressed grief she had to do something like Bishop does in her story "In the Village"—show her character distracting herself by focusing on things unrelated to what she's feeling. So, brief as it is, the causal plot is as essential to the story's success as the foregrounded episodic and expository plots.

Tim O'Brien's "The Things They Carried" is another stellar example of a hybrid plot. As Sarah Stone and Ron Nyren have said, the story consists of a "regular, alternating pattern of storytelling and lists"—in other words, of a causal narrative and non-causal lists—that is unified "because the theme of carrying extends through the storytelling segments as well [as the lists]." They further note that the story uses "repetition and image as an organizing principle" and that the story is "full of recurring imagery, as repetitive and jumbled as the men's traumatic memories." Although Stone and Nyren do not use the terms *causal, thematic juxtapositional,* and *lyrical,* their description of O'Brien's story clearly conveys the fact that the story is a hybrid of these three plot forms.

Although "The Things They Carried" is anything but chronological, it is relatively easy to recognize that it has a conventional causal plot at its heart.[22] The conflict that drives the story is Lieutenant Jimmy Cross's love for Martha, a woman he fears doesn't return his feelings. This conflict is complicated when one of his men, Ted Lavender, is killed by a Viet Cong sniper. Cross blames himself for Lavender's death because he was thinking about Martha at the time, not about his men. Throughout the story, he grapples with this feeling of blame and his love for Martha until he makes the climactic decision to burn her letters and photographs, "dispense with love" and "perform his duties firmly and without negligence." The story ends with him preparing to lead his men into further conflict.

The plot is chronological, but the story certainly isn't. Its thirteen sections leap backward and forward in time, and from generalized events to specific ones, in a dizzyingly fragmented and repetitive fashion.[23] The story's plot and structure are strategically, and meaningfully, divorced from each other. If O'Brien had structured his story more or less chronologically, its causal plot would be front and center: we'd see how Cross's love for Martha causes—at least in Cross's mind—the death of Lavender and leads, ultimately, to his climactic decision to give up all thoughts of love and devote himself to becoming a perfect soldier. But O'Brien was less concerned with the causal nature of the plot than he was with conveying Cross's mental disorientation and the way he obsessively relives the moment of Lavender's death. In the course of the story, O'Brien returns to Lavender's death no less than fifteen times.

The repetitive return to Lavender's death not only conveys the nature of post-traumatic memory, it also conveys Cross's attempt to recover from the trauma of Lavender's death and achieve the kind of mental balance that will allow him to proceed. As the story reveals, repetition and recovery are intimately related: the soldiers repeat the same phrases over and over, O'Brien says, "as if the repetition itself were an act of poise, a balance between crazy and almost crazy." Note that the balance Cross and his fellow soldiers aim to achieve through their litany-like repetition isn't between totally crazy and totally sane; "almost crazy" is the best one can hope for in a war as insane as the Vietnam War. And just as total sanity is not possible for the soldiers, a clear, reasonable, straightforward account of what happened is not possible for an author who wants to convey the truth of that war and its impact on those who fought it.

Hence the story not only repeats the fact of Lavender's death fifteen times but the word *dead* (or *die* or *died*) thirty-one times—and other key words and phrases, including *love* (or *loved*) twenty-eight times and *moral* seven times. But the most repeated word, of course, is *carried* (or variants thereof), which appears no less than 122 times, and there are sixty-six additional repetitions of words related to carrying—words like *hump, weighed, pounds, ounces,* and their variants—so the story contains a whopping 188 words related to "the things they carried" in twenty pages, an average of more than nine per page.

By presenting what would otherwise be a fairly straightforward causal plot via a fragmented, looping, repetitive structure, O'Brien forces us to do what Cross must do: assemble order and meaning out of the chaos of post-traumatic memory. And by repeatedly fracturing the narrative with contrapuntal lists of the things, literal and metaphorical, that Cross and the other men carried, O'Brien further forces us to do what the soldiers must do: find a balance between a crazy and an "almost crazy" account of the insanity of war.

Because the causal, thematic juxtapositional, and lyrical plot forms bear relatively equal weight in the story, I consider "The Things They Carried" a true hybrid plot rather than, say, a causal plot with secondary lyrical and juxtapositional plots. In this story, then, O'Brien does exactly what Tom Bailey says all good story-writers should do: shape the story "to its own demands." And the story also illustrates how combining different plot forms can create a highly original and powerful story.

Despite the fact that the majority of literature and creative writing textbooks suggest otherwise, not all works of fiction employ a causal plot. This is especially true in the twentieth and twenty-first centuries, and since plots are "what we see with," as Welty said, the movement away from causal plots suggests that we have changed the way we see both life and fiction. As Macauley and Lanning have said,

> Plot . . . could be accepted in an age that took a relatively simple view of human personality. . . . The vast, gradual shift in the basic assumption of fiction came not so much through a boredom with stale plots and worn-out devices as through new ideas of how men and women can be known and understood.

They also note that "The tendency to minimize plot in favor of other values can be seen early in the stories of Sherwood Anderson, Katherine Mansfield, and Ernest Hemingway and in such novelists as Virginia Woolf and James Joyce," but I would point out that this tendency has a much longer pedigree. We see it, as I've noted, in *The Decameron*, picaresque novels, Tolstoy's "Three Deaths," and innumerable stories by Chekhov, the writer who more than anyone else challenged the conventional causal plot and invented alternatives to it.

An even earlier nineteenth-century writer, Gustave Flaubert, also wished to minimize plot, although that wish remained more desire than accomplishment. Flaubert lamented the necessity of a plot, saying,

> The story, the plot of a novel is of no interest to me. When I write a novel I aim at rendering a color, a shade. For instance, in my Carthaginian novel [*Salammbô*], I want to do something purple. The rest, the characters, the plot, is a mere detail. In *Madame Bovary*, all I wanted to do was render a gray color, the moldy color of a wood louse's existence.

Flaubert not only regretted the need for a plot, he wished he could write a book without a theme or, even, a subject. As he said,

> What seems beautiful to me, what I should like to write, is a book about nothing, a book dependent on nothing external, which would be held together by the strength of its style, just as the earth, suspended in the void, depends on nothing external for its support.

Even E.M. Forster, who believed a causal plot was "the fundamental aspect without which [a novel] could not exist," bemoaned its necessity and wished novels could be structured according to "something different—melody, or perception of the truth, not this low atavistic form."

Neither Flaubert nor Forster ever wrote a book that was wholly independent of a causal plot, of course, though several later writers have certainly made an effort, chief among them, perhaps, Alain Robbe-Grillet, who, like Flaubert, claimed to be more concerned with style than with plot and character, which he called "obsolete notions." He rebelled against the "ready-made idea of reality" implicit in a traditional plot, saying the "unconditional adoption of chronological development, linear plots, . . . etc." tends to "impose the image of a stable, coherent, continuous, unequivocal, entirely decipherable universe." Now that that image of the universe has been rejected, he says, "To tell a story has become strictly impossible."

Plot and character are not obsolete notions to me—far from it—but I can understand why Flaubert and Robbe-Grillet felt inhibited by the conventions that dominated the fiction that came before them. Clearly, many writers have felt similarly inhibited and as a result have found new ways to organize their fiction. They may have abandoned conventional causal plots that lead a character to a climactic change, but they didn't abandon the idea that a work of fiction needs some organizing principle to give it form and unity. And some writers have found original and experimental ways to tell a story without entirely abandoning the conventional causal plot. Witness the fiction of Kurt Vonnegut, who has argued that "no modern story scheme . . . will give a reader genuine satisfaction, unless one of those old-fashioned plots is smuggled in somewhere. I don't praise plots as accurate representations of life, but as ways to keep readers reading."

Ideally, though, *all* of the plot forms I've discussed here are ways to keep readers reading. More important, they are different ways to see our fellow human beings and the world around us, and without them, we would see not only less but less well.

Returning Characters to Life: What Chekhov Teaches Us about Endings

In one of his letters, Chekhov wrote, "When I am finished with my characters, I like to return them to life." By returning his characters to life, he meant, I believe, something like what David Chase did in the controversial ending of the HBO series *The Sopranos*: instead of conclusively ending the series by "whacking" Tony, or shipping him off to prison for life, or having him see the error of his ways and turn state's evidence against his fellow mobsters, Chase simply returned him to his daily routine, essentially as unchanged as the world in which he lives. A great number of Chekhov's stories end similarly, saying implicitly what the ending of one story says explicitly: "And after that life went on as before." Whereas previous (and most subsequent) fiction focuses on a climactic change, Chekhov's stories are frequently less about change than they are about the failure to change. Indeed, as the poet, translator, and scholar Anne Frydman has said, his stories "provide an exhaustive investigation into the reasons for changelessness in human life." And even when his characters *do* change, Chekhov's endings often reveal that their changes either fail to last, merely complicate the existing conflict, or create a new and often greater conflict. In short, Chekhov tends to end his stories by returning his characters to life and the problems created either by their change or their failure to change. As a result, his endings don't just conclude, they also open up; they are, to borrow Stanley Kunitz's description of the best kind of ending for a poem, "both a door and a window."

Before Chekhov, stories did not typically end in these ways. The traditional Aristotelian plot was—and remains—little more than a machine engineered to create change and closure: the protagonist finds herself faced with a conflict that gets complicated and intensified until it reaches a climactic moment in which it is resolved and her life is forever altered. But Chekhov was deeply skeptical about the possibility of change, especially if that change was presented as permanent and positive, as it so often is in pre-Chekhovian fiction. Readers who expected his stories to end with such conclusive resolutions were disappointed and criticized his stories as "incomplete."[24] (In this they resemble far too many of today's readers, alas.) In response to such criticism, perhaps, he titled one of his stories "A Story Without an End." But for all of their apparent inconclusiveness, his stories *do* have endings; they're just not the kinds of endings favored by previous writers—or by the average viewer of *The Sopranos*. They are subversive endings, endings designed to undercut our expectations and, thereby, force us to examine our conceptions about life and human nature. They are, I would argue, the kinds of endings that much of contemporary fiction lacks, and needs.

Clearly, Chekhov was aware relatively early in his writing life that new kinds of endings were necessary in literature. While writing *Ivanov*, his first full-length play, he wrote to his publisher about the conventional endings of plays—"Either the hero gets married or shoots himself," he complained—and he concluded, "Whoever discovers new endings for plays will open up a new era." And that is exactly what Chekhov did, both for plays and for short stories. Even now, more than a hundred years after his death, we are still very much in the era Chekhov opened up. Chekhovian endings have been adopted, and adapted, not only by the usual suspects—Katherine Mansfield, Virginia Woolf, Sherwood Anderson, Ernest Hemingway, John Cheever, Eudora Welty, Raymond Carver, Andre Dubus, Richard Bausch, and Tobias Wolff—but also by such otherwise un-Chekhovian writers as Donald Barthelme and John Barth.[25] But while a few of Chekhov's innovative strategies for closure (or anti-closure, as the case may be) are now relatively commonplace, others have been largely overlooked or ignored.

Many of today's writers seem to write as if unaware of most of the possibilities Chekhov opened up and thus end their stories in predictable and conventional ways. For these reasons, I believe it is time for us to take a close look at Chekhov's strategies for closure. I hope that an examination of his innovations will lead to further innovations in our own endings, and perhaps even to another new era.

In this essay I will discuss the principal ways Chekhov subverted traditional short story endings to "return his characters to life" and its inconclusive conclusions. For convenience's sake, I will discuss these strategies for the most part as if they occur in isolation, but I would urge the reader to keep in mind that they often appear in combination.

1. Anti-Epilogues

One way Chekhov returned his characters to life is by subverting the convention of epilogues, which tie up all of a work's loose ends and so are the epitome of conclusiveness. Chekhov's attitude toward epilogues was much like that of Henry James, who complained about their vapid "distribution . . . of prizes, pensions, husbands, wives, babies, millions, appended paragraphs, and cheerful remarks." Chekhov wrote more than five hundred stories in his short life, and not one of them ends with anything approximating a conventional epilogue. Several, however, end with what we can call anti-epilogues, for they deny the very premise of an epilogue: the possibility of knowing what the future might hold. Instead of giving us a pat account of how everything will turn out, he typically returns the character, and us, to the uncertainty of life, leaving us wondering what will happen next.

"The Steppe," for example, ends with Egorushka, who has just completed an arduous journey across the steppe, slumping wearily onto a bench and greeting "the new, unknown life that was now beginning for him . . ." Rather than tell us what will happen in this unknown life, Chekhov merely echoes the question Egorushka is asking himself: "What sort of life would it be?" Similarly, "Three Years" ends with its protagonist, Laptev, asking the kind of questions that are usually answered in epilogues—and with Chekhov refusing to answer them:

> ... maybe he was to live another thirteen or thirty years ... And what were they to live through in that time? What does the future hold for us?
> And he thought:
> "Time will tell."

The fact that these endings leave his characters' future fates open suggests that, although Chekhov was generally pessimistic about the possibility of change, he was also aware that sometimes lives change in dramatic and unpredictable ways. Chekhov makes this point explicitly in "A Story Without an End." The narrator of this story presents two portraits of his neighbor, the first showing him as he was a year before, after his wife died and he attempted suicide in response, and the second showing him now, playing the piano and singing and laughing with a group of ladies in the narrator's drawing-room. Witnessing this change, which he compares to "the transmutation of substances," leads the narrator to realize the impossibility of predicting what his neighbor's future life will be like. Thus, this story without an end ends with the unanswered question, "How will it end?"

2. Reverse Epilogues

Whereas Chekhov's anti-epilogues return the characters to what Grace Paley has called "the open destiny of life," most of his endings close off, rather than open up, the protagonist's possibilities for future change. This tendency is apparent in another way he subverts the conventional epilogue: by shifting into the past at the very moment we expect the story to move into the future. Instead of telling us what *will* happen, a reverse epilogue tells us what *has* happened—and thereby implies, as Frydman notes, that nothing will change in the character's future.

"The Chorus Girl" exemplifies this mode of closure. In this story, a chorus girl named Pasha is confronted by the wife of a man with whom she's been sleeping. While the husband listens in the next room, the wife badgers Pasha into giving her some pieces of jewelry that she wrongly believes her husband gave to Pasha. After the wife leaves, the husband returns and says, "My God, a decent, proud, pure being like that was even prepared to kneel down before this ... this whore! And I brought her to it! I let it happen!" He then shoves Pasha roughly aside, calls her "trash," and leaves. At this point, Pasha starts to sob. Conditioned as we are by conventional fiction, we might naturally expect Pasha's humiliation to lead her to change her life. But instead of showing, or even implying, a future change, Chekhov abruptly segues into her past. The final sentence reads, "She remembered how three years ago, for no rhyme or reason, a merchant had given her a beating, and sobbed even louder." By revealing that Pasha has undergone even worse mistreatment in the past without learning any life-changing lessons, the ending implies that her life will continue unchanged in the future. Thus, the reverse epilogue serves to return Pasha to life and its continuing humiliations and sorrows.

3. Echo Endings

Another way Chekhov returns his characters to life—and conveys the essential changelessness of those lives—is by echoing in the ending the events, imagery, and/or language of the story's opening. These echoes create the sense that either nothing has changed or whatever temporary change has occurred has been undone. As Frydman notes, such endings paradoxically evoke "endlessness."

The conclusion of "In a Strange Land" is an excellent example of this kind of endless ending. The story opens and closes with Nikolai, a bigoted landowner, holding forth on the folly of the French to Champoun, his children's tutor. Champoun would like to escape his master's bigotry and return to his native France, but he has lost his passport. As a result, he is forced to endure Nikolai's endless series of diatribes. The story ends with the sentence, "The same performance begins over again, and Champoun's sufferings have no end."

"Anyuta" also ends as it begins, though its ending follows the protagonist's temporary change. It opens with a medical student named Stepan using his girlfriend Anyuta's naked chest as a "study guide" for an upcoming exam. Oblivious to the fact that she has "turned blue with cold," he marks her ribs with charcoal, then reads these words from his textbook: "The right lung consists of three sections . . . The upper section reaches the fourth or fifth rib on the front wall of the chest, the fourth rib at the side . . . the *spina scapulae* in the back . . ." Then an art student arrives and asks Stepan if he can use Anyuta as a model—ironically, he's painting a portrait of Psyche, who had significantly more success at winning the love of Eros than Anyuta has at winning the love of the utterly unerotic Stepan—and, although Anyuta protests mildly, Stepan orders her to go "for the sake of art." While she's gone, serving art as she has shortly before been serving science, Stepan begins to imagine his future, when he will become a successful doctor and have a "respectable" wife, not someone like "homely, slovenly, pitiful" Anyuta, and he makes the seemingly climactic decision "to separate from her, at once, whatever the cost." But later, when he tells her to leave, her tears cause him to decide to let her stay—though only, he tells himself, for one more week. Relieved, Anyuta returns to the sewing work she's been doing to support her ungrateful boyfriend, and Stepan picks up his textbook and reads again the words, "The right lung consists of three sections . . . The upper section reaches the fourth or fifth rib on the front wall of the chest . . ." In short, everything returns to the way it was. Stepan's conflict is resolved, but the resolution is retracted almost immediately, leaving him once again facing the same conflict. By echoing the beginning, Chekhov's ending suggests that the cyclical pattern we've just witnessed will continue to repeat itself in the future.

Chekhov's echo endings are rarely as overt as that of "Anyuta," however. The ending of "Gusev" is typical of the subtlety that usually marks his handling of this form of closure. The story opens with Gusev telling Pavel, another soldier in the ship's infirmary, a story about a ship that "bumped into a big fish and smashed a hole in its bottom," and it ends with a big fish—a shark—tearing a hole in the bottom of the sailcloth that contains Gusev's body after his burial at sea. There is an even subtler echo here, too. After the shark rips the bottom of the sailcloth, one of the gridirons that were sewn inside to weight Gusev's body down drops out and falls to the bottom of the sea, a detail that echoes the fact that, after Gusev tells the story about the big fish, a jug falls to the infirmary floor. The ending of "Gusev" also returns—as I will discuss later, in a different context—to the opening's personification of nature, an echo that bears significantly on the story's meaning.

4. Chiastic Endings

Sometimes an echo ending repeats the words and/or actions of the opening in reverse order, creating a kind of inverted symmetry. Cathy Popkin compares such endings to the rhetorical device chiasmus, in which the order of words in two otherwise parallel phrases are reversed, as in Lord Byron's famous line "Pleasure's a sin, and sometimes sin's a pleasure." As Popkin notes, "The House with the Mezzanine," a story about an idle, deluded artist's thwarted love for a young woman named Zhenya, ends "chiastically," with the protagonist-narrator, Monsieur X, "retreating along the same path by which he had originally approached [Zhenya's home], describing the fir trees, lime trees, orchard, gate, courtyard, and willows in reverse order from the original description." But this inversion is not just variation for variation's sake; rather, it points us toward another inversion, one that leads us to the story's meaning—the inversion of the opening's principal image. Whereas the story opens with the "frightening" image of the "ten big windows" of Monsieur X's manor-house "suddenly lit up by lightning," it ends with his "sudden" memory of Zhenya's family's farmhouse and the one window of her room lit by a dim green light. The contrast between the frightening light of the opening and the melancholy light of the ending is poignant, but the poignancy is laced with our sense that Monsieur X did not truly deserve Zhenya. It is also laced with our realization that he needs the kind of enlightenment described in the opening, but is too afraid to see himself clearly and so has remained essentially blind, seeing only by the dimmest of lights.

5. False Climaxes

Some of Chekhov's stories conclude with what appears to be a climax but in fact is not one, for the conflict remains unresolved and the character is ultimately unchanged. "Misery" is an excellent example of this way to achieve a sense of closure while still acknowledging the inconclusiveness of life. In this story, a St. Petersburg cab driver named Iona attempts to tell a series of passengers, a passerby, and a fellow cab driver about the recent death of his son, but everyone responds with indifference. Looking at the crowds of people on the street, he laments that he cannot "find among those thousands someone who will listen to him." At the end, he is reduced to telling his sorrow to the horse who draws his cab. Chekhov writes: "The little mare munches, listens, and breathes on her master's hands. Iona is carried away and tells her all about it." At first, this seems like a climactic resolution—finally, he has found an audience for his grief—but the problem the story poses—the indifference of his fellow human beings to his suffering—remains unresolved. As Frydman concludes, "the relief at the end is a false relief . . . [for] the horse [is] a poor substitute for a sympathetic human listener."

6. Omitted Climaxes

Given Chekhov's skepticism about the possibility of change, it should be no surprise that many of his stories lack the very thing that fiction typically seems to exist for—a climax. Whereas some stories, like "Misery," employ a false climax to imply the absence of a true one, these stories omit any kind of climax whatsoever. They consist solely of the "rising action" of a plot—the exposition and complication of a conflict—and therefore come to what may seem to be a premature conclusion. As Conrad Aiken observed, these stories "do not . . . conclude at all—they merely stop." But the conclusions are not actually premature, for the point of these stories is that no conclusion is possible: the conflict will continue and nothing will ever be resolved. To adapt a term Frydman uses for a variety of Chekhov's endings, we can call these "dead end" stories, for they come to an abrupt stop just when we expect to reach a destination that, we now discover, does not exist.

"The Witch" is a good example of a "dead end" story. In it, Chekhov describes an escalating argument between a subdeacon and his wife that takes place during a blizzard. The subdeacon irrationally believes that his wife is a witch who creates storms in order to lure male travelers to seek shelter in their home. At first the wife laughs off this charge, but as the story progresses, she grows increasingly angry, especially at his threat to tell the local priest that she is a witch, and at the end she hits him in the nose. This act makes the reader expect him to report her to the priest and/or to beat or possibly even kill her. Instead, Chekhov ends the story by stating, simply,

"The pain in his nose soon passed but his torment continued." Just when we are expecting a dramatic and conclusive climax, Chekhov stops short. As a result, the ending hits the reader like a punch in the nose.

Chekhov often uses the "dead end" conclusion in stories whose expected climax is an epiphany. In "Lights," an engineer named Ananyev attempts to convince a young student named Von Schtenberg that "thoughts of the transitoriness, the insignificance and the aimlessness of life, of the inevitability of death, of the shadows of the grave, and so on . . . are good and natural in old age when they come as the product of years of inner travail," but "for a youthful brain on the threshold of real life they are simply a calamity!" Ananyev tells the student and the story's narrator that he himself had similar beliefs when he was the student's age, and he relates the events that led to his realization of his error. His attempts to persuade Von Schtenberg fail; the student does not duplicate his would-be teacher's epiphany. Nor is the philosophical debate resolved in the narrator's mind either. At the end of the story, he says, "I carried away with me no answer to any question," and he concludes, "There's no understanding anything in this world!" In short, the intellectual conflict between Ananyev and Von Schtenberg gets complicated and intensified, but just when we expect it to be resolved one way or the other, Chekhov gives us the metaphysical equivalent of "The Witch"'s literal punch in the nose: he suggests that the only possible "resolution" is the realization that no resolution is possible.

Ironically, Chekhov's "dead end" conclusions frequently occur in death scenes, where readers of the time were accustomed to encounter dramatic soul-saving epiphanies. Two of Chekhov's greatest contemporaries—Turgenev and Tolstoy—were noted for such deathbed epiphanies. But, as Frydman observes, "Chekhov rejected the 'deathbed revelation' as a dramatic device." Tolstoy's "The Death of Ivan Ilych" is a typical example of this convention. Just before Ivan dies, Tolstoy tells us that he "caught sight of the light, and it was revealed to him that though his life had not been what it should have been, this could still be rectified." And by asking forgiveness of all those he has sinned against, he does indeed rectify his life, and so when he dies, "In place of death there was light."

Witness, by contrast, the account of the protagonist's death in Chekhov's "Ward No. 6":

> Andrei Yefimych understood that his end had come and remembered that . . . millions of people believed in immortality. And what if it was so? But he did not want immortality, and he thought of it for only a moment. A herd of deer, extraordinarily beautiful and graceful, which he read about the day before, ran past him; then a peasant woman reached out to him with a certified letter . . . Mikhail Averyanych said something. Then everything vanished and Andrei Yefimych lost consciousness forever.

In a sense, Andrei's life "flashes" before his eyes via these images. The first is the image of the beautiful deer he recently read about, an image that suggests the importance of nature, reading, and beauty in his life. The second image—the certified letter—suggests how much value he placed on true communication (communication important enough to be sent via certified mail), as opposed to empty small talk, and this refers to the great stock he put in his conversations with his friend Gromov. These images are certainly positive, but hardly indicative of any epiphanic transformation. The last image before Andrei sinks into oblivion is, however, a decidedly negative one—"Mikhail Averyanych said something." As we know all too excruciatingly well by this point in the story, there is nothing Andrei hated more than listening to the pompous, dull, nonstop yakking of Mikhail. This final image suggests that everything that was important and beautiful in Andrei's life has been, both during his life and now at its end, undercut by the banal and trivial. Just when we expect a conventional deathbed epiphany, Chekhov pulls the rug out from under those expectations. There is no Tolstoyan revelation at the moment of Andrei's death to "rectify" his life. Rather, his life ends, as his friend Gromov said all lives end, "not with a reward for suffering, not with an apotheosis, as in the opera," but with the cold, hard, physical facts of death: "peasants will come and drag your dead body by the arms and the legs to the basement."

In "Gusev," Chekhov omits not only the conventional

deathbed epiphany but also the protagonist's death. What would normally be the climax of such a story—the death of its protagonist—is not even summarized, much less presented. Chekhov writes: "He sleeps for two days and on the third at noon two sailors come down and carry him out of the infirmary." At the beginning of this sentence Gusev is asleep, and at the end, three days later, he is dead and being brought topside in preparation for burial at sea. Instead of showing Gusev confront his mortality in some climactic way, Chekhov merely describes his burial and its aftermath. By doing so, he returns us, if not his character, to life, which continues as if Gusev had never existed at all, leaving us to realize the ultimate insignificance of human life in the vastness of nature and time.

7. External Climaxes

As the ending of "Gusev" may suggest, Chekhov sometimes omits climaxes in order to make the reader have an epiphany his protagonist fails to have. A character may reach a "dead end," in short, but the reader sometimes continues the journey in the character's stead. In such stories, the climax is an external one—it occurs outside the story, within the reader, not inside the story, within a character. I suspect that behind this kind of ending, which we find most frequently in Chekhov's later work, is the belief that an epiphany is more powerful if the reader experiences it personally rather than merely witnesses a character experience it, and that therefore the best epiphanies take place in the blank space that follows a story.

One way Chekhov creates an external climax is through the use of an unreliable narrator, one who fails to see what his story reveals about him. In "The Little Joke," for example, the narrator recounts a "joke" he played on a woman who loved him, a joke he cannot understand—but we can, and do. He tells of going tobogganing with this woman and how, as they roared down the hill with the wind in their faces, he would whisper, "I love you" into her ear, then pretend he had said nothing, so she couldn't be sure if what she heard was real or imagined. She was terrified of tobogganing, yet kept on doing it—and even once went by herself—to see if she would hear those words again. The story ends: "And now that I am older, I cannot understand why I said those words, why I played that joke on her . . ." Although he achieves no climactic understanding, the reader does. The reader realizes that he actually did love the woman and that, despite his refusal to face the facts of his own emotions, he regrets playing the joke and losing his one chance at love. And the reader also realizes that the joke was ultimately a big one, not a little one, and that it was on him, not her.

The principal way Chekhov triggers an epiphany in the reader, however, is through the use of implied analogies. Such analogies appear at the ends of many of his stories, but their use is most dramatic and powerful, I believe, in those relatively or completely plot-less stories in which, as Frydman says, "Inertia emerges . . . as the law that determines lives." (One of the characters in Chekhov's "Aborigines" makes a similar point when he observes that "Russian inertia is unique on the terrestrial globe.") Stories of this sort are often sketch-like in their stasis, but though the characters may not change, our perception of them, and perhaps of ourselves, does, and the result is a conclusion as satisfying as that of any overtly plotted story.

The regrettably little-known "Fortune," one of Chekhov's personal favorites, is such a study of stasis that it is virtually a verbal still life. In it, two shepherds, one old and one young, do little more than watch their flocks and talk briefly about buried treasure to each other and a ranger who stops to light his pipe. The sheep, too, are static—they stand "as if rooted to the spot"—and so is the world around them: "nothing stirred in the bluish distance," Chekhov says, then describes the Scythian burial mounds which tower "here and there above the horizon and the endless steppe," watching over the three men with the same sort of "mute immobility" and "complete indifference" with which the men watch over the sheep.

As morning approaches, movement briefly enters this still, suspended world. Some solitary rooks fly overhead, and Chekhov comments that "There was no obvious point to the lazy flight of these long-lived birds, nor to the morning which repeated itself punctually every day." Then, shortly after sunrise, the sheep "suddenly become jittery" and charge off "in some inexplicable terror." The young shepherd momentarily feels the same "animal terror," but he returns to calm "somnolence" as quickly as the sheep. The story ends with the two shepherds standing, "without moving," at opposite ends of the motionless flock. "Wrapped up in their own lives," Chekhov says, "they were already oblivious of each other." And here is where he slips in, almost as if it were an afterthought, his subtle yet devastating analogy: "The sheep were also lost in thought."

By comparing the shepherds—and the ranger, who has three times earlier been described as "lost in thought"—to the sheep, Chekhov creates a quiet detonation: we feel an epiphany of sorts, one denied the shepherds themselves, the epiphany that they—and perhaps all of us—are "sheep" who do everything we can to avoid facing our animal terror at the fact that there is no more point to our long-lived lives than there is to the rooks'. And, further, the ending implies that we avoid facing this terror by being as immobile and indifferent to others, and therefore as "lifeless," as those burial mounds, and that our fortune will not be to unearth buried treasure but to be buried ourselves, both literally after death and metaphorically during our lives.

"Gooseberries" is another great story that concludes with a subtle analogy that allows the reader to understand what the character has not recognized, at least not fully. (For a discussion of this story, see pages 100-101 of "'What We See With': Redefining Plot.")

8. Temporary Climaxes

So far we have been focusing mostly on stories about changelessness, but in many of Chekhov's stories, a character does undergo a climactic change. However, as in "Anyuta," the change doesn't last: the character quickly relapses into old beliefs and behavior. Like the echo ending, a relapse ending shows the protagonist back where he or she began, facing—or, more accurately, *failing* to face—the same conflict. Because the relapse plot is perhaps Chekhov's most common solution to the conflict between the desire for narrative closure and his belief in the relative changelessness of human beings, and because so many of his best stories employ it—and employ it in combination with other closing strategies to achieve different effects—I would like to comment briefly on four stories that are particularly powerful examples of it: "A Gentleman Friend," "Terror," "The Murder," and "The Darling."

"A Gentleman Friend" employs a false climax in order to convey its protagonist's relapse from a true climax. In this story, a prostitute who goes by the name of Vanda (her actual name is Nastasya) has just been released from the hospital, and after paying her medical bills she is too poor to afford the fancy clothes she needs to go to nightclubs and ply her trade. To solve this problem, she decides to ask one of her "gentlemen friends," a dentist named Finkel, for some money. But when she goes to his office, Finkel fails to recognize her and she is so embarrassed that she pretends she has a toothache, and he pulls out a perfectly good tooth—and then charges her for it. When she leaves his office, she is in pain and poorer than when she arrived. As a result of this humiliating experience, she sees herself clearly for the first time and realizes that she has misspent her life, that she has been too concerned with material things, and that she has lost her true self as a result.

If this were a conventional story, Vanda's epiphany would lead her to become Nastasya again and she would remain her true self for the rest of her life. In Chekhov's stories, however, epiphanies typically have the staying power of New Year's resolutions, and he swiftly subverts our expectation of Vanda's "rebirth" by showing her relapse into her former behavior at a club ironically named the "Renaissance":

> But the next day she was at the *Renaissance* and she danced there. She wore a new, immense red hat, a new jacket à la mode and a pair of brown shoes. She was treated to supper by a young merchant from Kazan.

As this ending suggests, the actual climax of this story occurs offstage, when Vanda convinces the young merchant to buy her the clothes she desires, and it is a false climax, for the problem it resolves is a trivial, materialistic one, not the essential, spiritual one that she resolved only temporarily when she realized the error of her ways. Her essential problem, then, remains unresolved, just as Iona's essential problem remains unresolved at the end of "Misery." But whereas Chekhov did not go on to show Iona back at work the next day, facing his fellow human beings' indifference to his suffering, in this story he shows Vanda back where she started, doing her best not to face her true conflict.

In the neglected masterpiece "Terror," Chekhov combines the relapse plot with a more traditional plot. The story opens with a man named Dmitri confessing to his best friend, the story's narrator, that he has a disease, "the fear of life." "I don't understand life and I am afraid of it," he says, and compares himself to a beetle "which was born yesterday and understands nothing" yet continues about his life. He is terrorized by "the common routine of life from which none of us can escape," but his "chief terror" is that his beloved wife does not care for him, much less love him. Later that night, when he goes to his guest's bedroom to fetch a cap he left there, Dmitri sees his wife leave the bedroom and realizes that she and his friend have betrayed him. But this discovery does not enlighten him; he says to his friend, "I suppose it must be my fate that I should understand nothing. . . . If you understand anything, I congratulate you. It's all darkness before my eyes." Nor does this discovery lead Dmitri to escape "the common routine of life" he abhors; as the story's final sentence reveals, he continues to live with his wife, presumably with even more terror than before.

The story's narrator does change, however, and does so in the manner of a traditional plot. As a result of the events of the story, he is infected with the same kind of terror at the incomprehensibility of human behavior that his friend Dmitri feels. As the story ends, he asks himself, "in bewilderment and despair," "Why have I done this? . . . Why has it turned out like this and not differently? To whom and for what was it necessary that she should love me in earnest, and that he should come into my room to fetch his cap? What had a cap to do with it?" The darkness that was before Dmitri's eyes is now before his.

The similarly under-appreciated story "The Murder" is a particularly interesting example of a relapse plot because it uses several of Chekhov's innovative modes of closure—a false climax, an echo ending, and an implied analogy—to reveal the protagonist's relapse. The story ends with Yakov, a religious fanatic, imprisoned for killing his cousin Matvey over a violation of Lenten rules. Now, after years of thinking himself more religious than priests—he even conducted his own religious services at his home—he has found what he believes to be "the true faith." Chekhov writes: "He knew it all now and understood where God was, and how He was to be served" and he "longed to go back home and tell them there of his new faith to save from ruin if only one man." To the best of my knowledge, critics have universally taken Yakov's climactic "epiphany" at face value and so have focused on the irony that he cannot act upon his new faith since he is condemned to a lifetime in prison. But I believe Chekhov wants us to doubt the authenticity of Yakov's alleged epiphany. He tips us off that this is a false climax by prefacing the "annunciation" of it with the tell-tale words "it seemed to him" and by adding, after the selfless-seeming words "to save from ruin if only one man," the clearly selfish words "and to live without suffering if only for one day."

Furthermore, by echoing the story's opening, Chekhov's final sentences imply that Yakov's change, whether it is genuine or not, will be temporary at best. The story opens and closes with references to storms, and as we have seen, an echo of this sort is usually a sign that a character has either failed to change or relapsed back to his old ways. Also, as in so many of Chekhov's stories, an implicit analogy—in this case, between the storm and irreligious beliefs and behavior—communicates the ending's true significance. The story opens with "the howling of the snow-storm that was aimlessly disporting itself outside, regardless of the fact that it was the Eve of the Annunciation." As this sentence suggests, the storm is associated with indifference or opposition to religion. In addition, as the story progresses, Chekhov tells us that stormy weather "disposed one to depression, and to quarreling and to hatred" and he compares abusive behavior to a "storm."

Because of these associations, Chekhov's ending has ominous overtones. The story concludes: "A strong piercing wind was blowing by now; somewhere on the steep cliff overhead the trees were creaking. Most likely a storm was coming." The echo ending suggests that Yakov's climactic belief that he has found the true faith is as false as his earlier belief that he alone had the true faith, and it also suggests that acting upon this false belief would lead him not to serve God but to commit further acts of violence. For although he believes he has changed, he remains a religious fanatic of the most dangerous sort: one who does not know the darkness of his own soul.

"The Darling" provides yet another example of an innovative relapse plot; indeed, it could be called a relapse plot on steroids, for it consists of repeated relapses, each preceded by a false climax. In novella-like fashion, Chekhov repeats one central dramatic action—one movement from conflict to (false) climax—four times and thereby suggests the essential changelessness of his protagonist. The story recounts Olenka's parasitic love for two husbands, a lover, and, eventually, a surrogate son. Its title is a translation of a Russian term of endearment that means, literally, "Little Soul," and clearly, Olenka's soul is so little as to be virtually nonexistent. Only when she is in love, and adopting the opinions of her loved one, does she come to life—and that life is a borrowed life, one that, Chekhov hints, comes at the expense of the person she loves. (Her husbands grow thin and die while she grows fat and healthy.) When she is married to a theatre owner, all she can talk about is the theatre; when she is married to the manager of a lumberyard, she talks endlessly of lumber and disparages the theatre just as he does. And it is clear that she is not consciously adopting their opinions merely to please them, for even her dreams echo the concerns of her current loved one. Because she has no self, Olenka is doomed to repeat not only her loved one's words but also the parasitic pattern Chekhov traces throughout the story. Repetition, then, is at the heart of her character, as well as at the heart of Chekhov's form and theme.

The story ends with the fourth false climax it has recounted—after a long, despairing period of solitude, Olenka finds another object for her love: Sasha, the son of a former lover. In the final moments of the story, she lies in bed listening to him cry out in his dreams, "I'll give it to you! Get away! Shut up!"—words that, in the context of the story, compare Olenka to something like a schoolyard bully, demanding love of her victim. Her essential conflict—her utter lack of a self—remains unresolved, and the story's repetitive structure suggests that the cycle of conflict, false climax, and relapse will continue until her death. What's more, Olenka's final false climax has created a conflict in Sasha, a fact that further undermines the reader's desire for a conclusive resolution.

9. Complication-Creating Climaxes

In some of Chekhov's stories, the characters do change without relapsing, but often their change only complicates the conflict further. "Neighbours" illustrates this brand of inconclusive conclusion superbly. Its protagonist, Pyotr, is enraged that his married neighbor, Vlassitch, has "seduced and abducted" Pyotr's unmarried sister Zina, thereby shaming him and his family. Impulsively, he leaves for Vlassitch's house, intending to horsewhip him and demand that Zina return home. But Pyotr is afflicted with one of the most severe cases of irresolution in Chekhov's fiction, so the intensity of his resolve dwindles instead of builds as the story progresses, thereby making the story consist largely of "falling action" rather than "rising action." By the time Pyotr reaches his neighbor's house, his rage has passed and, although he makes a few feeble attempts to reignite it, he succumbs to his irresolution and does nothing. And as he parts from his sister, he makes matters worse by telling her, falsely, that he approves of what she has done. The climax, then, serves to prolong and intensify the conflict rather than to resolve it. As Pyotr realizes, "I went to solve the question and I have only made it more complicated . . ."

The most renowned Chekhov story that ends not with the resolution of a conflict but with a further, more intense complication of it is, of course, "The Lady with the Little Dog." As Vladimir Kataev has said, "No questions are resolved for Gurov and Anna once 'this love of theirs had changed them both.' On the contrary, only then does the full seriousness of the problems become truly apparent." The story ends with the beginning of a new phase of Gurov and Anna's conflict; indeed, its final word is "beginning." The story concludes: "And it seemed that, just a little more—and the solution would be found, and then a new, beautiful life would begin; and it was clear to both of them that the end was still far, far off, and that the most complicated and difficult part was just beginning." In Frydman's words, the story "builds toward an ending that overturns the assumption that there will be an end." And as Vladimir Nabokov notes, in words that are apropos to so many of Chekhov's stories, "The story does not really end, for as long as people are alive, there is no possible and definite conclusion to their troubles or hopes or dreams." Once again, Chekhov has created a conclusion that provides a sense of closure without resolution, a conclusion that returns his characters to life and its continuing conflicts and complications.

10. Conflict-Creating Climaxes

Sometimes Chekhov replaces the conventional climax of a plot not with a further complication of the conflict but with the creation of a new conflict. As I noted earlier, "The Darling" ends with a reference to the conflict Olenka's parasitic love has created for Sasha. In most of the stories that follow this pattern, however, the new conflict belongs to the protagonist, not a secondary character.

"Sleepy" exemplifies this strategy for closure. In this story, a thirteen-year-old nanny named Varka is exhausted from overwork and unable to sleep because the baby she is tending has been crying for hours. In her semi-delirious state, she strangles the baby. This act resolves her immediate conflict, enabling her to fall asleep at long last, but it creates a new and far greater conflict, for when she wakes, we know, she will be arrested for murder. Chekhov's concluding sentence both reveals her false sense of relief and resolution and hints at the fate that awaits her once she is convicted of murder: "After strangling him, she quickly lies down on the floor, laughing with joy that she can sleep, and a moment later is already fast asleep, like the dead . . ."

Although Chekhov was nothing if not skeptical about those climactic, life-altering revelations we call epiphanies, some of his stories do contain bona fide epiphanies, but they, too, tend to create new, often greater conflicts. "The Kiss" is a superb example of this kind of Chekhovian ending. Like Vanda in "A Gentleman Friend," Ryabovitch, the protagonist of this story, suddenly sees the error of his ways, but instead of ignoring his insight and relapsing into his old habits and beliefs, as Vanda does, he overreacts to it and thereby squelches any chance he might have of profiting from it. At the end of the story, Ryabovitch returns to the site of a party he attended several months before, fully expecting to meet the woman who, mistaking him for someone else, kissed him in a dark room that night. Since the party, he has given in to fantasies about the woman, about whom he knows nothing, and he has not only concocted a composite image of her in his mind but also imagined a future marriage and family. But now, her absence causes him to recognize the difference between reality and fantasy, and he sees "the incident of the kiss, his impatience, his vague hopes and disappointment . . . in a clear light. It no longer seemed to him strange that . . . he would never see the girl who had accidentally kissed him instead of someone else; on the contrary, it would have been strange if he had seen her." When we read this passage, we are relieved that Ryabovitch has finally recognized the truth. But Chekhov makes sure our relief is short-lived, for Ryabovitch immediately overreacts to his insight: "And the whole world, the whole of life, seemed to Ryabovitch an unintelligible, aimless jest," Chekhov writes. A few sentences later, when Ryabovitch learns he and his fellow officers have been invited to a party at the home of a general who lives nearby, his disillusionment leads him to refuse the invitation, and therefore forgo his chance at a real romance: "For an instant there was a flash of joy in Ryabovitch's heart, but he quenched it at once, got into bed, and in his wrath with his fate, as though to spite it, did not go to the General's."

In "A Gentleman Friend," we are disappointed that Vanda's epiphany isn't conclusive—we would like her to stay true to her epiphany—but Chekhov wisely denies us the easy assurance that insight inevitably leads to positive change. In "The Kiss," however, we are disappointed that Ryabovitch's epiphany *is* conclusive—or rather, that he responds to it as if it were conclusive and thereby dooms himself to a miserable, lonely life. Chekhov's ending makes us lament that Ryabovitch has learned what we have been wanting him to learn all along, for he has resolved his initial conflict in such a way that he now faces an even greater one.

11. Extended Anticlimaxes

Yet another way Chekhov subverts our expectations about endings is by giving us the climax relatively early in the story, so that much of the story is quite literally anticlimactic. As Popkin has said, stories that follow this pattern shift the reader's attention away from the "headlines" of life to "the small print that follows, where the real story is told." Because the anticlimactic "small print" dominates the story, the climactic "headline" loses much, if not all, of its impact. As this fact suggests, in stories that end like this, Chekhov returns his characters to the "real story" of life more extensively than anywhere else in his fiction.

"The Teacher of Literature" is an excellent example of this strategy. The story builds toward the conventional happy ending of a wedding, but then goes beyond it to the mundane disappointment that follows. In a diary entry that Nikitin, the titular teacher of literature, writes the day of his wedding, he acknowledges the "storybook" nature of his happiness: "the happiness which at one time . . . seemed to me possible only in novels and stories, I was now experiencing in reality." But even as he asserts that his happiness is real and not the illusory result of looking at his life as if it were a novel, he uses a metaphor for happiness that ironically makes us think of a book (especially since he is, as he writes this entry, holding one in his hand): "I was now, as it were, holding it [happiness] in my hands." As this metaphor subtly implies, the happiness he feels on his wedding day is based on an illusion and cannot last. Indeed, in the fourteen pages that follow the story's climax, we realize that the wedding was a false climax, for within a year, Nikitin begins to find himself bored by "their quiet domestic happiness": it now yields him "only sensations so monotonous" that he feels the desire to "escape" and start "a new life." It is clear, however, that no new life is possible for Nikitin—that, too, is an illusion—and we realize that the life to which Chekhov has returned him will be one extended anticlimax of sorrow and regret for the loss of a happiness that was never real in the first place.

The climax "The Story of an Unknown Man" builds toward—the narrator's transformation into a new person—also occurs long before the end of the story, and the subsequent events likewise deflate that climax and extend the character's anticlimactic return to the "small print" of life. This is one of Chekhov's masterpieces, nearly as complex and successful as his other long masterpiece, "Ward No. 6." In the story's climactic scene, the anonymous narrator, who is serving as a footman to a man named Orlov merely to gain access to Orlov's father, a political enemy he intends to murder, finally gets his chance to kill his enemy. He is alone in the house with Orlov's father and could easily kill him and escape. But he doesn't. Instead, he says,

> I prodded myself and clenched my teeth, trying to squeeze from my soul at least a drop of my former hatred; I remembered what a passionate, stubborn, and indefatigable enemy I had been still recently . . . But it's hard to strike a match on a crumbling wall. The sad old face and the cold gleam of the stars [on his uniform] called up only petty, cheap, and useless thoughts about the frailty of all earthly things, about the proximity of death . . .

And after the old man leaves, he ponders his sudden change: "It was no longer possible to doubt it: a change had taken place in me, I had become different . . ." And he responds to his transformation with euphoric anticipation of a brand-new life, one full of innumerable possibilities. He says,

> How I wanted to live! I was ready to embrace and pack into my short life all that was accessible to man. I wanted to talk, and read, and pound with a hammer somewhere in a big factory, and stand watch, and till the soil. I was drawn to Nevsky Prospect, and to the fields, and to the sea—wherever my imagination could reach.

This is where most writers would have ended the story, but Chekhov immediately shifts his concerns from his protagonist's change to the questions it raises about the rest of his life: "Who am I now? What am I to think about, and what am I to do? Where am I to go? What am I living for?" The story continues for thirty-five more pages, tracing the long, anticlimactic remainder of his life, which consists of the gradual shutting-down of the possibilities for a new life that he imagined during the story's climactic moment. The story ends with the narrator, near the end of his life, disappointed and disillusioned. The questions his climactic change raised so many years ago remain unanswered, and he is still an unknown man, even to himself.

12. Shifts in Address, Tense, and/or Point of View

So far we have been talking chiefly about ways that Chekhov's endings subvert the formal expectations of a traditional plot. Now I would like to point out three ways his endings subvert the technical expectations that his stories have previously established: by abruptly changing the audience addressed, the tense, and/or the point of view. In the final paragraph of "The House with the Mezzanine," for example, the narrator suddenly stops speaking to us and addresses his lost love Zhenya by her nickname: "Missyus, where are you?" The startling shift conveys the intensity of the narrator's sense of loss far more strongly that merely stating "I wish I knew where

Zhenya was" possibly could. "A Boring Story" likewise ends with its narrator suddenly addressing his lost love, but more significantly the ending also shifts to past tense, a shift which reveals the overwhelming sense of loss that he has tried to stave off throughout the story by using the present tense to describe past events. Conversely, "Expensive Lessons" shifts to the present tense for its final paragraph, a shift that suggests the protagonist, a scholar whose failed attempts to learn French have been chronicled in past tense, will continue to fail no matter how long he takes lessons, just as his attempts to win the love of his teacher will also continue to fail.

As effective as Chekhov's shifts in address and/or tense are, his shifts in point of view are far more dramatic and powerful. The early story "A Trifle from Real Life" is a particularly effective example. As I note in my essay "From Long Shots to X-Rays: Distance and Point of View," for the bulk of this story, the narrator reports the thoughts and feelings of a man named Nikolai, who discovers during a conversation with his lover's eight-year-old son Aliosha that the boy has been secretly seeing his father against her wishes. Nikolai promises not to reveal this secret to the boy's mother, but as soon as she returns home he breaks his promise. Then, in the story's final sentence, Chekhov shifts into Aliosha's point of view, telling us that "This was the first time in his life that he had come roughly face to face with deceit; he had never imagined till now that there were things in this world besides pastries and watches and sweet pears, things for which no name could be found in the vocabulary of childhood." The point-of-view shift makes us realize that the story isn't really about Nikolai's trifling grievance but rather about Aliosha's life-changing discovery of deceit and betrayal. And it also makes us realize, with a shiver of guilt, that we, like Nikolai, have been wrongly assuming that the adult's experience was more important than the child's.

An even more dramatic and powerful point-of-view shift occurs at the end of "Gusev." After Gusev dies, Chekhov shifts his point of view away from him not to another character but to sea creatures and, ultimately, to the sea itself.[26] In the story's penultimate paragraph, Chekhov describes Gusev's sailcloth-covered corpse sinking into the sea from the perspective of pilot fish and a shark:

> Seeing the dark body, the little fish stop as though petrified and suddenly all turn round together and disappear. In less than a minute they rush back at Gusev, swift as arrows, and begin zigzagging round him in the water. Then another dark body appears. It is a shark. With dignity and reluctance, seeming not to notice Gusev, as it were, it swims under him; then while he, moving downward, sinks upon its back, the shark turns, belly upward, basks in the warm transparent water and languidly opens its jaws with two rows of teeth. The pilot fish are in ecstasy; they stop to see what will happen next.

When the shark rips the sailcloth in preparation for feasting on Gusev's body, it releases one of the gridirons placed in the cloth to weight the corpse down. Chekhov follows the gridiron to the bottom of the sea, then abruptly leaps to the world above the sea. Here is the final paragraph:

> Meanwhile, up above, in that part of the sky where the sun is about to set, clouds are massing, one resembling a triumphal arch, another a lion, a third a pair of scissors. A broad shaft of green light issues from the clouds and reaches to the middle of the sky; a while later, a violet beam appears alongside of it and then a golden one and a pink one.... The heavens turn a soft lilac tint. Looking at this magnificent enchanting sky, the ocean frowns at first, but soon it, too, takes on tender, joyous, passionate colors for which is it hard to find a name in the language of man.

As Richard Bausch has said, "There is no more audacious or shocking short story in the world," thanks in large part to "the radical way it shifts in the last paragraphs, from the limited omniscience of Gusev's consciousness, to a kind of omniscience that includes even the sea and the sky. The way it leaves the province of human thought and action, as Gusev is dropped into the ocean, and enters the animal kingdom." The purpose of this shift, Bausch points out, is "to lead us into a perception we do not want: the enormity of the world and the universe, and our puny place in it." Chekhov achieves this effect not only by shifting the point of view to nature but by personifying nature. In the story's opening scene, Pavel, one of the other men in the ship's infirmary, attacks Gusev for his ignorant personification of the wind, but in the story's ending, Chekhov himself goes well beyond Gusev's use of personification, conveying the pilot fish and shark's points of view toward Gusev's sinking corpse and depicting the ocean as capable of looking at the sky and even *frowning*. By personifying impersonal nature, Chekhov depersonalizes Gusev, and further emphasizes the meaninglessness of both his death and his life—and by extension, our deaths and our lives.

It is interesting that both "Gusev" and "A Trifle in Real Life" end not only with dramatic point-of-view shifts but also with similar comments about language. "A Trifle in Real Life" ends with a reference to "the vocabulary of childhood" (as opposed to the vocabulary of adulthood) and "Gusev" ends with a reference to "the language of man" (as opposed to the language of nature). The implication, perhaps, is that adults stand in relation to nature as children stand in relation to adults—unable to comprehend its language. By shifting from one point of view, one "language," to another at the ends of these stories, Chekhov conveys his meaning with astonishing power.

In an excellent essay on "the ideology of closure," Douglas Glover asks, "What is the nature and form of . . . an ending that draws into question the idea of endings?" More than any other writer I can think of, Chekhov explored this question, and his stories reveal numerous answers, virtually all of which serve to "return his characters to life." As Frydman has said, "He creates endings that overturn the idea of an ending, either by suggesting infinite repetition, or the beginning of something, or the lack of an end to difficulties."

Virginia Woolf has described the effects of these inconclusive endings better, perhaps, than anyone. When we finish a Chekhov story, she says, we feel "as if a tune had stopped short without the expected chords to close it." But, she goes on to say, the more we become accustomed to his work, the more we are able to hear the subtle music of Chekhov's meaning and the more the traditional conclusions of fiction—"the general tidying up of the last chapter, the marriage, the death, the statement of values so sonorously trumpeted forth"—all "fade into thin air" and "show like transparencies with a light behind them—gaudy, glaring, superficial." His endings, she concludes, "never manipulate the evidence so as to produce something fitting, decorous, agreeable to our vanity," and therefore, "as we read these little stories about nothing at all, the horizon widens; the soul gains an astonishing sense of freedom." It is my hope that careful study of Chekhov's endings will similarly free writers and readers of fiction from the constraints of conventional expectations about conclusions.

The Flowers of Afterthought:
Premises and Strategies for Revision

I rewrite in order to be reread.
—André Gide

I'll begin this essay with an admission that I fear won't surprise many of my readers: I have little or no talent for writing. Nothing (not even the simple sentence you just read) comes easily to me. Whenever I've taken part in timed writing exercises—which, for the record, I have always loathed—I produce a few clumsy sentences while virtually everyone around me writes pages of glittering prose. It would take me a week to write something half as good as what others can write in ten minutes. But although I lack natural writing talent, I do have a talent—or at least an aptitude—for *rewriting*, and I owe whatever small success I've had as a writer to it. I love what Bernard Malamud called "the flowers of afterthought," the discoveries, both large and small, that transform a barren patch of land into a garden. I revel in those afterthoughts, spending months and occasionally even years revising a story, poem, or essay before submitting it for publication. And speaking of stories, poems, and essays, my goal in this essay is to pass along practical strategies for revision that I and others have found useful in all of these genres, although most of my references will be to fiction. But before we turn to these strategies, I'd like to discuss ten premises that I believe should guide us as we practice the art of revision.

Premises

1. First Thought, Worst Thought

Beginning writers sometimes buy into Allen Ginsberg's mantra "first thought, best thought"[27] and assume that revision will only make their work worse. (Lucky for us, Ginsberg didn't follow his own advice; as the facsimile edition of his various drafts of *Howl* reveals, that poem underwent numerous and extensive revisions.) Me, I'd argue that our first thought is the worst thought. If, for example, we write the words *flat as a*, our first thought will most likely be to write *pancake* next, but if we choose that word, we're guilty of a cliché. The same principle applies to all other aspects of literature: if we don't reject our first thoughts, we'll end up with red-haired characters with fiery tempers; plots in which boy meets girl, boy loses girl, and boy gets girl again; rhymes like *love / dove* and *June / moon*; and potted themes like "love conquers all" and "crime doesn't pay." And just as our first thoughts tend to be our worst thoughts, so too our first drafts tend to be our worst drafts.

Hemingway once said, "The first draft of anything is shit," and I believe that's true. But revision can turn that shit to 24-karat gold. Many great works of literature were rewritten numerous times. I'll give you a long list of examples later, but for now, let me just point out that Tolstoy wrote five separate drafts of *Anna Karenina*, each significantly different. As Edward Dahlberg said, "Books are not written; they are rewritten." And if our first drafts seem shitty, we shouldn't let that fact discourage us too much. As the songwriter Mike Smith has said, "When your work seems terrible, you should be grateful, because it proves you still have taste."

2. Revision Is Play, Not Work

In *Homo Ludens*, his classic study of the play-element in culture, Johan Huizinga argues that play is at the heart of all human activity and therefore Homo ludens—*ludens* being Latin for *playing*—would be a more accurate name for our species than Homo sapiens. "All poetry is born of play," he says, and I'd argue that the same is true of any mode of writing that is imaginative rather than expository or journalistic. The word *play* might suggest a lack of seriousness, but whereas "seriousness seeks to exclude play," Huizinga says, play "includes seriousness." Indeed, "serious play" is perhaps the best short definition of literature I can think of, akin to Robert Frost's definition of poetry as "play for mortal stakes." And while we associate play with childhood, play is not mere "child's play." Huizinga believes that play is the highest expression of the adult imagination, and I agree. So does a fellow named Nietzsche, who said that "A man's maturity" is the result of "having rediscovered the seriousness that he had as a child at play."

Perhaps the characteristic of play that is most pertinent to writing is the disproportionate relationship between effort and return. If we approach writing as play, we are willing to put in the maximum amount of effort for the minimum amount of return; we're willing to write dozens, maybe even hundreds, of pages to get a handful of keepers. But if we approach writing as work, our goal is to receive the maximum amount of return for the minimum amount of effort; we want every page we write to be a keeper. We often hear writers praised for their work ethic, but what writers really need is a *play* ethic. If we approach revision as work, we're not in the right frame of mind to create anything of value. "Rewriting," Robert Olen Butler wisely maintains, "is redreaming." No matter if we're writing our second, third, or fortieth draft, we should be employing the same playful, imaginative process we used to produce our first draft.

It's important to note that approaching revision as play doesn't mean it's going to be nothing but fun. Like any form of play, frustration is an essential element of it. If there's no impediment to serving an ace, hitting a home run, or writing a stellar sentence, there's also no pleasure. And writing involves a nearly infinite number of impediments. Solving one problem often creates another—and when that problem is resolved, it, too, creates another. Anne Lamott was right to compare revision to putting an octopus to bed. "You get a bunch of the octopus's arms neatly tucked under the covers," she says, "but two arms are still flailing around." And when "you finally get those arms under the sheets, too, and are about to turn off the lights," that's when "another long sucking arm breaks free." In revision, we need to expect, even welcome, many long sucking arms.

3. Revision Is Not a Separate Stage in the Writing Process

Edgar Allan Poe advised writers to imitate "the old Goths of Germany . . . who used to debate matters of importance to their State twice, once when drunk, and once when sober." The implication, of course, is that the writing process has two distinct and diametrically opposed stages, the first wildly enthusiastic, spontaneous, and creative and the second highly restrained, thoughtful, and critical. Hence many writers think they're supposed to turn off their left brain while writing their first draft, then turn off their right brain while they revise it. They slop down a first draft, then try to salvage it with their intellect. As Catherine Brady notes, "Despite all the advice books that recommend settling for a sloppy first draft and trusting to revision, a practice of indifference toward" the quality of our writing in our first draft will inevitably lead to a sloppy revision. "One sentence leads to another," she says, "and a bad sentence leads to another like itself."

So we should write and revise *both* drunk and sober, alternating between left brain and right brain. As Jesse Lee Kercheval says, the rhythm of writing is "rather like marching: left brain, right brain, left brain, right brain. Your critical sense alternates with your creative sense." Thus, she adds, "it's an artificial distinction to think of revision as a separate stage in the writing process. When I am writing a short story or chapter, I am revising all the time."

In short, revision takes place during *all* of the drafts we write, including the first. Many, if not all, of the strategies for revision I'll discuss in this essay could be employed in the first draft as well as in any subsequent draft.

4. Revision Is a Collaboration Between Our Conscious and Unconscious Selves

Just as the revision process alternates between our left and right brains, it alternates between our conscious and unconscious selves. In an essay on the role the unconscious plays in the creative process, Oliver Sacks recounts an experience the French mathematician Henri Poincaré had in 1880. For fifteen days Poincaré worked intensively on a complex mathematical problem, then his labors were interrupted by a lengthy trip, during which he forgot all about the problem—at least consciously. One day late in his trip, he stepped onto an omnibus and the solution to the problem popped into his head. This "sudden realization," Poincaré wrote, was "a manifest sign of long, unconscious prior work." This and other similar incidents in Poincaré's life convinced the great mathematician that, as Sacks says,

> There must be active and intense unconscious activity even during the period when a problem is lost to conscious thought, and the mind is empty or distracted with other things. This is not the dynamic or "Freudian" unconscious, boiling with repressed fears and desires, nor the "cognitive" unconscious, which enables one to drive a car or to utter a grammatical sentence with no conscious idea of how one does it. It is instead the incubation of hugely complex problems performed by an entire hidden, creative self.

And this hidden, creative self is our wiser self. As Poincaré said, "The subliminal self . . . knows better how to divine than the conscious self, since it succeeds where that has failed. In a word, is not the subliminal self superior to the conscious self?"

As Poincaré's experience suggests, an essential part of the creative process is to stop thinking consciously about the work so it can incubate in our unconscious. Hemingway certainly agreed; he advised writers not to think about their stories when they weren't actually writing them. "That way your subconscious will work on it all the time," he said. "But if you think about it consciously or worry about it you will kill it and your brain will be tired" when you return to your writing desk. Not thinking about your story is not easy. As Andre Dubus said, it's "as hard as writing, maybe harder; I spend most of my waking time doing it." We all want to solve our story's problems, so it's difficult to turn our conscious thoughts off and let our unconscious do its work. But if you do this, the solution will often pop into your mind, seemingly unbidden, at a later time. As Einstein said, "I think 99 times and find nothing. I stop thinking, swim in silence, and the truth comes to me."

While we need to acknowledge the primacy of the unconscious self, we also need to remember the all-important role the conscious self plays in generating the unconscious work. As Poincaré stressed, the unconscious work "is possible, and of a certainty it is only fruitful, if it is on the one hand preceded and on the other hand followed by a period of conscious work." Intense conscious labor forces problems into the unconscious, which then solves them days, weeks, months, or even years later. We aren't always aware of the source of these solutions, or even of the fact that they are solutions—they don't always arrive as "sudden realizations"—but if we put in the requisite conscious labor, we can trust the unconscious to supply what we need. What's more, the conscious effort we put into revising even a small part of a work can ultimately lead us to solve the formal problems of the whole. As Michelle Huneven has said, "Sometimes I'll be stuck on the same three pages for a month," but that time is not wasted, she believes, for "deeper work" is "being done at the same time, a kind of subterranean accumulating and organization," and "an entire novel is taking shape." I suspect *War and Peace* began to take shape in this subterranean way during the year Tolstoy spent writing fifteen drafts of its opening thirty pages.

Peter Markus has said, "I always tell my students that the story is smarter than you, that it knows where it wants to go." But it's not really the story that's smarter than we are; it's our unconscious self that is smarter than our conscious self, and we need to recognize the hints and clues it weaves into our drafts, to intuit what our deeper self wants us to write. The principal goal of revision, then, is to discover in what we have already written what we *should* have written.

5. Revision Is a Quest for Meaning

We tend to think of revision as primarily, if not solely, an aesthetic matter, something we do to improve the work's literary value, and as a result we tend to read our drafts with an eye toward aesthetic enhancement. But revision is not merely a quest for aesthetic perfection; it's also a quest for meaning. Tolstoy didn't revise *Anna Karenina* repeatedly merely in order to polish its prose; as the substantial differences in characterization and plot in his five separate versions reveal, he was searching for his novel's meaning. Butler sums it all up succinctly: "The point of revision is to find meaning." Obviously, we can't do this if we think we already know what our story means. Hence, as Jane Smiley says, "The first idea you need to give up when you begin to revise is that you know what this story is about."

The main reason we don't always, if ever, know what our story is truly about is that the writing process is a collaboration between our conscious and unconscious selves, and by definition we are unaware of our unconscious intentions. Given the role the unconscious plays in the creative process, it's inevitable that our stories come out differently than we consciously intended. All too often we consider this difference a failure that needs to be corrected in revision, and so we struggle in draft after draft to make the story come out the way we intended when what really needs revision is our initial conception. If a story turns out differently than we intended, that's a sign that our unconscious self wants to write a different story.

For me, then, the first step in revision is to try to see what the story is doing to *subvert* my conscious intentions for it. I look for details, characters, and scenes that in some way contradict or ignore my intentions. I consider them clues to the story that I, deep down, really want to write. The more we try to impose our initial conscious intentions on the story, the more we delay our discovery of what truly brought us to the material at hand—and thus our discovery of our work's meaning. So my advice is to set aside, as much as possible, your conscious intentions when you look at what you've actually written. As T.S. Eliot says, between the idea and the reality falls the shadow—and the shadow is where the story is.

In order to discover the story within the shadow, the real story underlying the original draft, we have to be open to discovering new meanings, especially meanings that contradict our initial intentions, and to do that we sometimes have to write several additional drafts that may be no better than the first one and might even be worse. We like to think of revision as a way of heightening the virtues and eliminating the vices of a work—and that of course is our ultimate goal—but revision is often far messier than that: it's a plunge back into the material, and it can roil up everything. When a revision seems more like a step backward than forward, it's important to remember that, as Richard Bausch has said, "You cannot permanently ruin a piece of writing. You cannot damage it or break it. At worst, you only render it as needing for you to go over it again. That's what revision is all about, and that's where the real artistry is, anyway."

As discombobulating as the revision process can be, it can also be exhilarating, because it's the only way we can find what's at the hidden heart of our original effort. And finding that hidden heart, that previously unconscious meaning, should be the principal goal of revision, one more important even than aesthetic improvement. Saul Bellow said the revisions that made him happiest were not "stylistic" revisions but "revisions in my own understanding." And that kind of revision can only result from discovering your meaning.

6. You're Not Just Revising Your Work, You're Revising Yourself

As Bellow's comment suggests, what we're revising is not just a story and its characters; we're also revising our opinions and beliefs—and therefore we're revising ourselves. As the obsessive reviser William Butler Yeats said,

> The friends that have it I do wrong
> When ever I remake a song,
> Should know what issue is at stake:
> It is myself that I remake.

George Saunders echoes this point when he says that revision makes him "better than I am in 'real life'—funnier, kinder, less full of crap, more empathetic, with a clearer sense of virtue, both wiser and more entertaining." However "laborious" and "obsessive" revision may be, he adds, it becomes "addictive" when you discover that it can create "a better version of yourself." And creating a better version of ourselves just may be the single most important reason to revise.

7. Don't Trust Your Brother, Trust Your Own Bad Eye

While it's always wise to consider the advice offered by your teachers, workshop classmates, and friends, there's nothing more deadly to the creative process than following someone else's suggestions for revision as if they were instructions. As I see it, my job as a teacher is to tell my students as honestly and clearly as possible what I think they should do to improve a story, and their job is to sift through that advice and decide what, if anything, will help them achieve their vision. In his Nobel Lecture, Alexander Solzhenitsyn urged writers to follow the advice of the Russian proverb "Don't trust your brother, trust your own bad eye." Your teachers, classmates, and friends may have your best interests at heart, and you may be all too painfully aware that you don't see your work clearly enough, but ultimately all we have as writers is our instinct about what is right for our story and what isn't.

This is not to say that we'll always be right, of course. As Janet Burroway has said, sometimes the advice "you resist the hardest may be exactly what you need." But I'd argue that you should follow your instincts nonetheless. If someone's advice feels right, adopt it. If it doesn't, don't. You may eventually realize your instincts were wrong, but if you assume from the start that they are and robotically follow the advice you receive, your chances of becoming a better writer are greatly diminished. Bum Phillips, the former coach of the Houston Oilers and the New Orleans Saints, once said there were two kinds of football players who weren't "worth a damn"—the kind who never does anything he's told and the kind who does *everything* he's told. Be careful not to become either kind of writer.

8. A Work Is Never Finished

Paul Valéry once said, "A work is never . . . finished, for he who made it is never complete." W.H. Auden translated this comment as "A poem is never finished; it is only abandoned," but Valéry actually said nothing about abandoning a work. Rather, he stressed the almost infinite possibility for revising and improving it. He said that "the power and agility [the writer] has drawn from [writing the work] confer on him . . . the power to improve it" and that each draft he writes teaches him how to "remake it" yet again. A writer might abandon a work, true, but if so, it's not because the work can no longer be improved. Ultimately, Valéry argues that both a work and its author are works in progress, and neither are ever truly "complete." And if that's the case—and I believe it is—we should feel free to revise our work throughout our life.

Some writers disagree. They argue that the revision process should end when a work is published, not when we stop breathing. Richard Hugo disparaged writers who revise old work, calling them "time effacers" because revision inevitably distorts who they were and what they felt and thought at a certain time in their lives. And likewise, Mark Doty says he doesn't revise any of his published poems because "There's a certain degree of respect you have to give to the person you were then, to the fact that you made a shape out of experience and language that stood for something about that hour in your life." Me, I don't think the purpose of a work of literature is to be a snapshot of who I was at a given time. All I'm concerned about is making the work as good as I possibly can. "Perfection is something you're always after," Tobias Wolff has noted, "but as you change over time, so does your notion of perfection"—and therefore we can almost always go back to a previously published work and improve it. In short, I'm with good old "spontaneous" Whitman, who revised the poems in *Leaves of Grass* throughout his life, producing nine vastly different versions of the book in the thirty-seven years between its first publication and his death, and I'm with Jack Kerouac, the so-called champion of "spontaneous prose" who claimed he wrote *On the Road* in a three-week flurry of creativity fueled by coffee and Benzedrine but actually wrote at least six different drafts of the novel between 1951 and 1957. And I'm with Tolstoy, Proust, James, Yeats, Fitzgerald, and Oates, all of whom revised their work after it was published, and with Louise Erdrich, who says she revises previously published work "at every opportunity." And I'm also with Akhil Sharma, who said he rewrote his PEN/Hemingway Award-winning novel *An Obedient Father* twenty-two years after he first published it because he felt he had "betrayed [his] characters" and thus "committed a moral injury" to himself. "Even though the characters are imaginary," he said, he felt he needed to revise his novel to give them "the opportunity to be their full selves" and he compared this feeling to what a father wants to give his children. I feel a similar responsibility toward my characters—and toward the people who may one day read their stories—so I revise my work to make it as good as I can. And if that means returning to a story years after it was originally published and revising it significantly, well, I'm more than willing to do that. Since time plans to efface me, I don't feel the least bit guilty about effacing as much of it as I can.

9. Revision Can Be (Too) Seductive

While revision is, as Malamud said, "one of the exquisite pleasures of writing," and while a given work can be revised and improved virtually infinitely, it's important to keep in mind that revision can seduce us away from generating new work. As Will Allison has said, "For me, revision is the most satisfying aspect of writing and the most seductive form of procrastination." We need to make sure we're continuing to revise for the right reasons, not merely to avoid the difficult task of launching into the blank page and writing something new.

10. You Can't Step into the Same Revision Twice

Eudora Welty once said, "Each story teaches me how to write it, but not the one afterward." Similarly, each story teaches us how to revise it, but not how to revise the next story. As George Saunders has said, "It feels like every story has . . . its own necessary revision process." As we turn to a survey of fourteen strategies for revision, please keep in mind that the revision process will of necessity be somewhat different for each story.

STRATEGIES

I. *Preparation*

1. Defamiliarize Your Draft

The more familiar we are with the words on the page, the harder it is to recognize how they should be changed. So the first step of any revision should be to defamiliarize your draft. The ideal way to do this is to let a significant amount of time pass before you look at it again. This not only gives your unconscious self the time it needs to work on the problems your conscious self has overlooked, it allows you to become, as Zadie Smith says, "its reader instead of its writer." She suggests we wait at least three months and ideally a year or more before rereading what we considered a "finished" draft. Andre Dubus III recommends that we wait "at *least* six months" before reading our draft. "Have two seasons go between you," he says. "And then when you pick it up and read it, you actually forget some of what happens in the story. You forget how hard it was to write those twelve pages. And you become tougher on it. You see closer to what the reader is going to see."

But what if you're a student and have a story due in two weeks, not six months? How can you defamiliarize your draft in that little time? One way is to print it out in a different font, preferably one you think is ugly. And if that doesn't do the trick, I suggest you also try printing it on different-colored paper or with different-colored ink.

Another approach is to tape record your story. Most people hate to hear their tape-recorded voice, so if you listen to a tape of yourself reading the story, you're almost certain to hear things you'll want to change.

And one other possibility: do the equivalent of putting your iPod on Shuffle: read and revise paragraphs or scenes of your story in random order. If you intentionally eliminate the story's narrative arc, you can focus more intently on its parts, and what would otherwise be all too familiar just might seem unfamiliar, even new.

2. Look for Clues to Your Story's Meaning

Once we've defamiliarized our draft, we'll be better able to discover its meaning. As I said earlier, the first thing I do when I revise is look for details, characters, and scenes that in some way subvert or ignore my conscious intentions. I consider them clues to the story my unconscious self wants me to write, as opposed to the one my conscious self intended.

In my early years as a writer, I automatically cut anything that didn't seem to fit my intentions. Then something Eudora Welty said made me realize that was a mistake. She said, "It's strange how in revision you find some little unconsidered thing which is so essential that you not only keep it in but give it preeminence when you revise." Her comment led me to interrogate each seemingly "unconsidered" or inessential aspect of a draft, trying to discover if it were a clue to something essential about the story. We may not have a conscious reason for including a certain detail, but we often have an unconscious one, and a major part of the revision process is discovering what led us to include details that don't seem to serve any obvious purpose. I suggest you not cut these extraneous-seeming details, at least not until you've fully explored their possible significance. Those details are often our unconscious self's way of telling us to consider something, and sometimes the detail that seems the most extraneous is the one that holds the story's deepest and most important secret. Our drafts are like treasure maps, and the "little unconsidered things" are often clues to the location of the buried treasure.

II. *Expansion*

The process of discovering our story and its meaning continues throughout every draft we write, but once we've scoured our initial draft for clues to what the story is truly about and have a fairly clear understanding of our story's meaning, we can begin revising in earnest. The temptation is to go through our story line by line, deleting this, adding that, and changing the wording here and there, and while this approach almost invariably leads to an improved draft, the result is not a true revision; it's just a premature editing job. "Revise" means to "re-see," and to re-see our story we have to do more than just edit what we've already written; we have to imagine what we haven't yet written.

Revising a story is a bit like playing an accordion: just as you have to expand and contract the bellows of an accordion to make music, you have to alternate between expansion and contraction in order to create a story. Most talk about revision focuses on contraction, but unless you begin the revision process by expanding your story, you may not discover what you need to contract. As Lee Martin has said, "I find that the first revisions I make often center on an opening up of aspects of the piece that are under-developed or not developed at all. . . . I keep asking myself what the piece hasn't yet said. I keep poking at the character relationships and the plot to see what might surprise me." Only after he feels he's discovered what's missing does he start to think about what he can leave out. We'll look at ways to compress shortly, but for now, here's some advice for expanding.

3. Revise Blind

In my experience, the single most helpful strategy for revision is to revise blind—that is, without looking at your previous draft. As Peter Selgin has said, "Old words can block fresh insights," so if your story isn't working, I suggest you rewrite it—or at least the problematic parts of it—without looking at your old words. Try to forget what you already wrote and reimagine it. (Even better, wait until you've actually forgotten most of what you wrote in previous drafts, then try to write the passage, scene, or even the whole story from memory. Lewis Hyde calls this "revision by forgetting," and he says, "Great chunks will have fallen into oblivion, while others will have returned clarified.") After you've finished, compare the original and the revision to see what you've lost and gained (it's rarely all one or the other) and mix and match the two versions to create a new version. Don't do this just once; do it as many times as necessary until the story feels right to you.

If you need any further encouragement to try this approach, consider the fact that D.H. Lawrence wrote *Lady Chatterley's Lover* three times, each time beginning from scratch and without "referring to the existent versions." If this approach is good enough for Lawrence, I think it ought to be good enough for the rest of us.

4. Write Outside the Story

Another way to discover how to expand and deepen a given scene without looking at what you've already written is to write "outside the story" for a while—in other words, write something that you don't intend to use in the story but that might help you better understand your characters and plot. Elizabeth Libbey recommends writing outside the story as a way "to return to working inside it," and she suggests various ways of doing this, including "exploring the inner life of your main character through diary entries, letters, dreams, or lists" and writing "a scene that occurred before the beginning of the story" or after it ends. Referring to Hemingway's theory of omission, she says, "Even if you don't use this material in the story, it will, as Hemingway said, make itself felt."

Often, a scene I've written won't work because the protagonist is the only character in it that I even somewhat know, so I'll rewrite the scene from the point of view of one or more of the other characters in the scene. I do this not because I intend to change the story's point of view (though I keep that possibility open) but because I want to get to know the characters well enough to make the scene work. Once I have a better idea of what they'd think, say, and do, I can generally go back to the original scene and make it stronger.

5. Slow Down Where It Hurts

All too often, we skip over, speed through, or summarize our stories' most dramatic moments. We do this partly out of a legitimate fear of melodrama but mostly, I suspect, out of a desire to avoid depicting our characters' emotional pain. In life, avoiding conflict and pain is usually a virtue, but in fiction, it's always a vice. Fiction thrives on the torquing up of tension, not the avoidance of it. So, as Steve Almond wisely says, we should "Slow down where it hurts" and allow not only our characters but our readers and ourselves to experience the pain. The moments that hurt the most are the moments that most deserve expansion.

6. Write Vertically

In his essay "The Habit of Writing," Andre Dubus talks about writing "horizontally" for his first twenty-five years as a writer, trying to get from point A to point Z in a draft as quickly as possible, then going back to revise everything five or six times. His goal during those years was to write five pages per day, but one day, while working on his story "Anna," he began writing "vertically," trying, as he said, "to move down, as deeply as I could" into whatever moment he was writing about and capture all of his character's thoughts and physical sensations. Instead of five pages a day, he wrote just one or two, but slowing down allowed him to discover his story faster and finish it in fewer drafts. If there's a moment in our draft that feels underdeveloped or unexplored, we should follow Dubus's lead and try to write it "vertically" instead of horizontally. In short, sometimes we need to slow down even where it *doesn't* hurt. And sometimes by slowing down we discover a hurt we've overlooked.

7. Take Out the Highlighters

As Flannery O'Connor once said, a scene doesn't come to life unless it evokes at least three of the five senses. "If you're deprived of any of them, you're in a bad way," she said, "but if you're deprived of more than two at once, you almost aren't present." To make sure your readers will be present in your scenes, go through your story and highlight each of the five senses with a different color, and if you find a scene evokes fewer than three senses, add more sensory details.

Also, writers tend to belong to one of two camps—the eye-oriented or the ear-oriented—and both camps tend to over-rely on two of the four principal modes of narration and under-rely on the other two. Eye-oriented writers over-rely on action and description, and ear-oriented writers over-rely on dialogue and thought. In life we generally talk, think, act, and perceive the world around us pretty much simultaneously, so fiction that weaves all four modes of narration together with relative balance tends to best replicate life as we experience it. To achieve this balance, eye-oriented writers often need to expand their scenes by adding dialogue and thought, and ear-oriented writers often need to expand theirs by adding action and description. I suggest you go through your scenes and highlight each of the four modes with different colors, so you can see which modes you overuse and which you underuse.

8. Employ Oppositional Thinking

Expansion is not only literal; we don't just need to expand our scenes, we also need to expand our characters, make them as life-like as possible, and I think oppositional thinking is the key to doing this. As Burroway says, to create three-dimensional characters we need to put at least one of the four modes of narration into opposition with the others. A character who talks, thinks, acts, and looks arrogant is a one-dimensional stereotype, but if he talks, acts, and looks arrogant but thinks insecure thoughts, he instantly becomes more complex. And if we put a single mode of narration into opposition with itself—if, say, the character believes in God one moment and another moment is racked with doubt—he becomes even more complex. The more contradictions a character contains, the more complex and compelling he becomes.

Oppositional thinking can also help us expand the significance of our plots. When you revise a story, ask yourself at every significant moment of the plot "If the character did, said, or thought the opposite thing here, how would the rest of the story change?" If you write a "counter-version" of a key moment of your story, you can often find a larger and more compelling story than the one you initially intended. Jonathan Raban reports that Robert Lowell followed this strategy often: "His favorite method of revision," he says, "was simply to introduce a negative into a line, which absolutely reversed its meaning but very often would improve it."

So if you decide you took a wrong turn at some point in the story, I suggest you try reversing whatever happened at that point, then try to discover what would happen next. I've done this in many of my stories, and rightly or wrongly, I think it's improved them. And I'm a rank amateur when it comes to oppositional thinking. I've changed old characters to young ones, and vice versa, and turned weddings into funerals, but other writers have taken oppositional thinking a lot farther in their revision process. Tobias Wolff, for example, has even "changed the gender of [his] characters halfway through a story."

9. Fine-Tune Your Soundtrack

I wholeheartedly second Stuart Dybek's advice that we "try for the impossible: to make the piece of writing itself have its own interior soundtrack, one that a reader who listens might almost detect." We should be creating this soundtrack during our initial draft too, of course, but in the early stages of the process we are often distracted by matters of characterization and plot and so don't give the music of our prose the full attention it deserves. And that music is all-important. As Konstantin Stanislavski, the Russian actor, director, and method-acting guru, has said, "Vowels are the rivers of the soul and consonants are the banks," and therefore in revision we should take the time to expand and fine-tune our story's soundtrack, making sure the sounds of our vowels and consonants are appropriate for the emotion we want to create.

According to the poet John Frederick Nims, vowel sounds are even more important than consonants for creating our soundtrack. He thought vowels were so inherently musical that he created the following "vowel scale," arranging the vowels on a musical staff according to the frequency of their sounds.

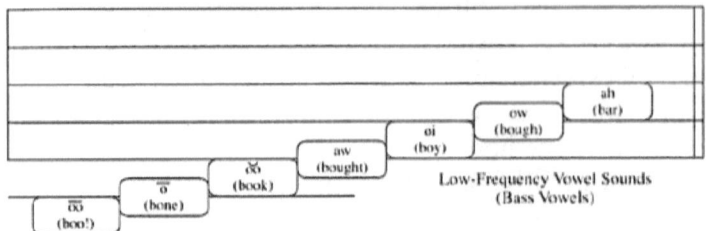

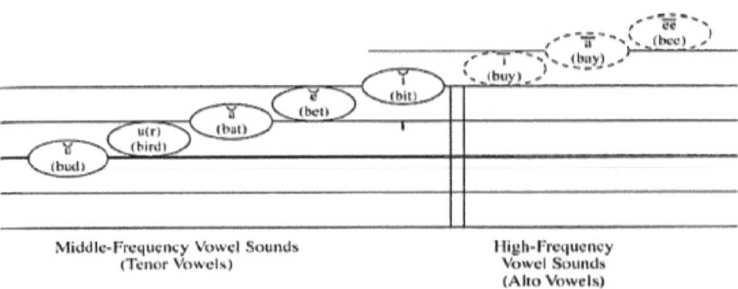

Fig. 1 Frequency Scale of English Vowel Sounds, *Western Wind: An Introduction to Poetry*

If we want to convey a happy, excited, intense, agitated, or fearful mood, we should use, wherever possible, words with "alto" vowels—words like *cry*, *yea*, and *eek*. Conversely, if we want to convey a somber, dejected, or depressed mood, we should use words with "bass" vowels—words like *gloom*, *moan*, *lost*, and *frown*.

If you aren't convinced by Mr. Stanislavski or Mr. Nims, maybe you'll find Keith Richards more persuasive. Here's what he says on the subject of vowels:

> [Mick Jagger and I] also composed using what we called vowel movement—very important for songwriters. . . . Many times you don't know what the word [you're looking for] is, but you know the word has got to contain this vowel, this sound. . . . There's a place to go *ooh* and there's a place to go *daah*. And if you get it wrong, it sounds like crap. It's not necessarily that it rhymes with anything at the moment, and you've got to look for that rhyming word too, but you know there's a particular vowel involved.

As Stanislavski suggested, we need to pay close attention to our consonants too, for they are the "banks" that fortify the river of the soul and prevent it from flooding. The dictionary may define *grief* and *sorrow* as synonyms, but the difference in their consonants and vowels affects our emotional response to them. *Grief* is harder and harsher than *sorrow* because of its plosive *g* and fricative *f* consonants and alto vowel *e* (and the fact that it consists of a single syllable) and *sorrow* is more subdued, thanks to its sibilant *s* and rhotic *r* consonants and its bass vowels *aw* and *o*. The words aren't interchangeable; we should choose the one that carries the emotional connotations we want the reader to feel. If we're after a calm, serene mood, a preponderance of hard, plosive consonants like *b, d, g, k, p,* and *t* will work against that mood. If we want to put the reader on the edge of her seat with terror, we should avoid using relatively soft, soothing consonants like *h, j, l, m, n, s,* and *w*.

We also need to pay close attention to the rhythms created by the placement of stressed and unstressed syllables in our sentences and, even more, the rhythms created by the variations in our syntax. Syntax and music are very closely related—and I mean that literally. As Ellen Bryant Voigt has pointed out, neurolinguists have discovered that the brain's "syntax centers" are "adjacent to where we process music." Pascal said, "Words differently arranged have different meanings, and meanings differently arranged produce different effects"—and to a large extent those effects are musical. But all too often we over-rely on one pet sentence structure and that compromises the rhythm of our soundtrack. If we overuse short simple sentences, for example, we create an overly choppy, staccato rhythm, and if we overuse long, periodic sentences, we can create a sense of stasis, of treading linguistic water, that hinders the story's narrative momentum. One way to find out if you're relying too much on certain sentence structures is to take out your highlighters again and highlight your simple, compound, complex, and compound-complex sentences with different colors. I also suggest highlighting the left-, mid-, and right-branching modifiers in your sentences to see which ones you overuse.[28] And once you've identified problematic sentences and passages, you can combine or divide sentences to create rhythms that are both more various and appropriate to your story's soundtrack.

Just as we need to pay attention to the rhythms of our sentences, we should also pay attention to the tempo of our scenes and chapters. Milan Kundera says that parts of his novels "could carry a musical indication: *moderato, presto, adagio*, and so on." He describes Part Five of *Life Is Elsewhere* as having "a slow, tranquil . . . *moderato*" pace, and Part Four as having "a feeling of great speed: *prestissimo*." Tempo is a complex thing with many variables, but it is largely defined by the relation between the length of a given passage and the amount of "real time" it covers. When Proust recounts a three-hour-long party in a leisurely 190 pages of *In Search of Lost Time*, the tempo is *lento* to the nth power, and when he dispatches an entire decade in one whiplash-inducing sentence, it is as *prestissimo* as *prestissimo* can get. So look at the relationship between the length of your scenes and the "real" time they cover, and if the tempo seems too slow or too fast to create the feeling you're after, adjust the tempo accordingly.

III. *Contraction*

To go back to my accordion analogy, once we've expanded the bellows, we need to compress them to make music. As Lee Martin has said,

> Experience has taught me that sooner or later during the additive part of the [revision] process, something will click, and I'll know the piece more fully than I did when I first began writing it. It's that click that then gives me permission to start subtracting, cutting anything that doesn't belong, anything that slackens the pace, anything that bloats the narrative, anything that makes the language vague and loose.

As we'll discuss later, writers often write hundreds, even thousands, of pages in the process of producing their work. They do so, Anthony Doerr points out, because "It takes time to learn how much you can get away with *not* saying." In order to discover our characters and plots and their meanings, we always have to write a lot more than the reader needs to read, and a major part of revision is deciding what the reader needs to know as opposed to what we needed to write. But once we've discovered what Martin calls "the heart of the piece," we can begin to cut anything that is superfluous to conveying that heart. And the cutting often leads us not only to greater economy but to discovery of the work's ideal form. As Christine Schutt has said, "it is subtraction that shapes stories."

10. Revise as if You'll be Charged by the Word, Not Paid by It

It's almost impossible to read an interview with an author who doesn't include the admonition to cut, cut, cut. Truman Capote said, "I believe more in the scissors than I do in the pencil"; Vladimir Nabokov said, "My pencils outlast their erasers"; Peter De Vries said, "When I see a paragraph shrinking under my eyes like a strip of bacon in a skillet, I know I'm on the right track"; Milan Kundera said, "Deleting a paragraph calls for even more talent, cultivation, and creative power than writing it does"; and Isaac Bashevis Singer said, "The wastepaper basket is a writer's best friend."

And authors regularly tell us not only to cut but *what* to cut. Chief on the hit list are adjectives and adverbs. "The adjective is the enemy of the noun and the adverb is the enemy of the verb," Voltaire purportedly said, and Chekhov, Twain, and numerous other writers have likewise urged us to cut adjectives and adverbs. But of course none of these writers recommended we cut *all* of them. Twain famously said, "If you catch an adjective, kill it," but he not-so-famously added, "No, I don't mean utterly, but kill most of them—then the rest will be valuable. They weaken when they are close together. They give strength when they are far apart."

There's one other thing that writers typically advise us to cut: our best writing. Virtually everybody who's ever commented on revision has quoted Arthur Quiller-Couch's injunction "Murder your darlings" (and virtually everybody has also falsely attributed this quote to a more famous author). Annie Dillard notes that "Sometimes the part you must jettison is not only the best written part; it is also, oddly, that part which was to have been the very point. It is the original key passage, the passage on which the rest was to hang, and from which you yourself drew the courage to begin." (Philip Metres concurs: "Just remember: the trigger—what inspired the work—is not the bullet. We're after the bullet.") But of course we shouldn't murder *all* of our darlings any more than we should kill every adjective.

In any case, there's a way to murder our darlings that allows them to be resurrected to serve another story. Benjamin Percy keeps what he calls a "Cemetery folder." In this folder, he says,

> I have files—tombstones, I call them—with titles like "Images" or "Metaphors" or "Characters" or "Dialogue." Into these I dump and bury anything excised from a story. For some reason, having a cemetery makes it easier to cut, to kill. Perhaps it's because I know the writing isn't lost—it has a place—and I can always return to the freshly shoveled grave and perform a voodoo ceremony.

So sometimes a writer's best friend is a cemetery folder, not a wastepaper basket.

11. Purge Your Superfluities

Michelangelo, who knew a thing or two about beauty, defined it as "the purgation of superfluities." He clearly believed that less is more. Some writers, however, think more is, well, more, and they'd rather give us the entire iceberg, not just the one-eighth of it that Hemingway recommends. In the debate about whether writers should be putter-inners or taker-outers, I cast my vote for Fitzgerald, who preferred taker-outers, not Thomas Wolfe, who defended his putter-inner instincts in an often-cited letter to Fitzgerald. There are of course many great fiction writers who were putter-inners—Wolfe mentions Cervantes, Sterne, Dickens, and Dostoevsky, and we could easily add many others to that list—but I believe their works would be even greater if they'd purged more of their superfluities. Mark Twain, who at times is quite a putter-inner himself, would have taken Fitzgerald's side in this argument. As evidence, I offer his wryly ironic one-sentence critique of the everything-but-the-kitchen-samovar approach that Tolstoy takes in *War and Peace*. "Tolstoy," he complained, "carelessly neglects to include a boat race." I hope all of you will carelessly neglect to include not only boat races but anything else equally superfluous.

12. Play a Cutting Game

To achieve a leaner draft, Burroway recommends we "play a cutting game" and shorten our draft by some arbitrary amount. Sarah Stone and Ron Nyren are a little more specific; they say, "Imagine that the editor of your favorite magazine has called up and said, 'I'll take it, if you can make it 20 percent shorter.' See if you can meet this challenge without harming the story." I'd go one step further: play this game more than once.

13. Downsize Your Cast of Characters

Stone and Nyren also advocate downsizing your cast. "Examine the characters in your story, major and minor," they advise, and "consider the story without each one." Obviously, if two characters are performing the same function, one is expendable. And if a character's actions or dialogue could "be appropriately assigned to another character," you could give one of the characters a pink slip. Also, if you have "two underdeveloped characters," they suggest combining them to "form a [single] complex character."

Jesse Lee Kercheval also has a valuable suggestion: "Count lines to see if the space the characters take up is proportional to their importance in the story." I've found in my own initial drafts that some of my minor characters take up almost as much space as my protagonist, and that fact led me not only to recognize the story's lack of proportion but also my failure to explore the central character as fully as I should.

14. Start Later and End Earlier

Chekhov said, "Once a story has been written, one has to cross out the beginning and the end." All too often beginnings are little more than throat-clearings. We hem and haw for a few pages, then the story truly starts. As Kurt Vonnegut advises, we should "throw away the first six pages" of our draft because "all the reader really wants is for the story to get started as soon as possible." Chekhov goes even further; he says, "Rip out the first half of your story; you'll only have to change the beginning of the second half a little bit and the story will be totally comprehensible."

And whereas openings tend to be unnecessary throat-clearings, endings tend to be unnecessary explanations or clarifications. The real ending of a story, the ending that implies all that follows it, often occurs a paragraph or a page or even several pages earlier. A good ending reverberates with what is unsaid, unexplained, but nonetheless deeply conveyed. But the problem isn't always with the ending per se: as Margot Livesey has said, "Sometimes the reason the ending isn't working is because of something earlier in the story, not because of what's on the last page."

Livesey further notes, "Beginnings and endings are also crucial on a smaller scale." She suggests that we "scrutinize the first and last sentences" of our paragraphs, sections, and chapters. If we do, we may often find sentences that are the equivalent of throat-clearings and unnecessary explanations.

IV. *Rinse and Repeat*

Revision is best understood as a singular term for a plural process. After we finish a revision, we need to begin the process again by once more defamiliarizing our text in order to continue discovering our meaning and to judge more accurately what needs further expansion and contraction. As I've already mentioned, Tolstoy wrote five versions of *Anna Karenina* and D.H. Lawrence wrote three versions of *Lady Chatterley's Lover*. (All three versions of Lawrence's novel have been published, in case you'd like to compare them for insight into his revision process. All five versions of Tolstoy's novel have been published in Russian but are not yet available in English.) Here are some other examples of writers who felt the need to "rinse and repeat" numerous times:

Frank O'Connor said, "Most of my stories have been rewritten a dozen times, a few of them fifty times."

Zadie Smith spent almost two years reworking the first twenty pages of *On Beauty*.

Hemingway rewrote the first part of *A Farewell to Arms* "at least fifty times" and wrote thirty-nine drafts of its final page.

Dan Chaon typically writes more than a hundred pages in order to produce a fifteen-page story.

Andre Dubus spent fourteen months writing his story "Waiting." It was more than one hundred pages in early manuscript form, but when it was published in *The Paris Review*, it was only seven pages long.

Isaac Babel wrote twenty-two separate versions of his story "Lyubka the Cossack." All told, he wrote over two hundred pages to create a six-page story.

James Thurber wrote fifteen complete drafts of his story "The Train on Track Six," composing a total of 240,000 words in the process of creating what was eventually a 20,000-word story.

Margot Livesey wrote eight drafts of her novel *Faces from the Fire*, and "the four words of the title were the only part of the original" draft that appeared in the final version.

Gabriel García Márquez once used up five hundred sheets of paper in the process of writing a fifteen-page story.

Charles Johnson wrote more than 3,000 pages in the process of writing his 210-page National Book Award-winning novel *Middle Passage*.

Flaubert wrote 4,561 pages in the process of writing his 400-page novel *Madame Bovary*.

Tolstoy wrote over 7,000 pages in the process of composing his 450-page novel *Resurrection*.

One caveat to the "rinse and repeat" mantra: as Toni Morrison has said, "I've revised six times, seven times, thirteen times. But there's a line between revision and fretting, just working it to death. It is important to know when you are fretting it; when you are fretting it because it is not working, it needs to be scrapped."

If you're truly revising, not fretting, you should wait until you feel you can't improve the work further—at least at this stage of your writing life—before you submit it for publication. (And we should follow Livesey's advice and not trust "the I-can't-do-anything-more feeling" until we've "experienced it several times.") In his *Ars Poetica*, Horace advises us to wait nine years before publishing, just to make sure our draft is truly the final one, but I doubt very many of us would be willing to take that advice. If you've already followed the advice of Zadie Smith and Andre Dubus III and waited several months before rereading your draft and all you've been doing for weeks is taking out a comma in the morning and putting it back in the afternoon, I think your work's ready to go out into the world, hat in hand, and knock on editors' doors.

I hope some of the premises and strategies I've discussed here help you improve your work. But my main advice is to cultivate perseverance. As the Japanese proverb says, "Fall seven times, stand up eight." And I also urge you to keep in mind what Will Shetterly has said is the greatest thing about revision: "It's your opportunity to fake being brilliant."

NOTES AND WORKS CITED

HOMO FICTUS VS. HOMO SAPIENS

[1] Some scholars believe, however, that in an earlier incarnation of the play, Hamlet was sixteen. They note that, in the First Quarto of *Hamlet*, Yorick has been dead for only twelve years. The fact that Hamlet attends the University of Wittenberg makes sense, they argue, if he is a teenager but not if he is thirty, and they therefore argue that the reference to Wittenberg in the later versions, in which Hamlet is clearly identified as being thirty, is an anachronistic remnant of an earlier version of the play. (The play, however, doesn't exclude the possibility that Hamlet is a scholar or teacher, not a student, at Wittenberg, in which case being thirty would not be unusual.) Scholars further theorize that Shakespeare changed Hamlet's age so that the thirty-two-year-old Richard Burbage could play the role. (Burbage was the first to perform the role, so if an earlier version included a sixteen-year-old Hamlet, that version was never performed.) If this is true, it should make it all the more clear that Shakespeare didn't believe that Hamlet's youth, much less his underdeveloped frontal lobes, was the cause of his indecision.

[2] In addition to Burroway's *Writing Fiction*, the books and essays that recommend this approach (and often offer their own sample questions) include: Tom Bailey, *On Writing Short Stories*; Nicholas Delbanco, *The Sincerest Form: Writing Fiction by Imitation*; John Dufresne, *The Lie That Tells a Truth*; Julia Fierro, "Get Closer: Exposing Your Characters (with Compassion)," in Bret Anthony Johnston, *Naming the World and Other Exercises for the Creative Writer*; Robin Hemley, *Turning Life into Fiction*; Anne Lamott, *Bird by Bird: Some Instructions on Writing and Life*; Josip Novakovich, *Fiction Writer's Workshop*; Ann Packer, "Interviewing Your Character," in Bret Anthony Johnston, *Naming the World and Other Exercises for the Creative Writer*; Brandi Reissenweber, "Character: Casting Shadows," in Gotham Writers' Workshop, *Writing Fiction: The Practical Guide from New York's Acclaimed Creative Writing School*; and Adam Sexton, *Master Class in Fiction Writing*. Other "character questionnaires" can be found at the Gotham Writers' Workshop website; see http://www.writingclasses.com/InformationPages/index.php/PageID/106

Alameddine, Rabih. Quoted in Daniel Alarcón, *The Secret Miracle: The Novelist's Handbook* (New York: Henry Holt, 2010), 183.

Aristotle. Quoted in Tom Bailey, *On Writing Short Stories* (New York: Oxford U Press, 2000), 30.

Bailey, Tom. *On Writing Short Stories* (New York: Oxford U Press, 2000), 30, 46.

Baxter, Charles. "Counterpointed Characterization," *Burning Down the House: Essays on Fiction* (St. Paul, MN: Graywolf Press, 1997), 119.

Bender, Aimee. "Character Motivation," *The Writer's Notebook: Craft Essays from Tin House* (Portland, OR: Tin House Books, 2009), 53.

Boswell, Robert. "The Half-Known World," *The Half-Known World: On Writing Fiction* (St. Paul, MN: Graywolf Press, 2008), 5, 7, 9, 13, 22.

Bronowski, Jacob. *The Ascent of Man* (Boston, MA: Little, Brown, 1974), 424.

Burroway, Janet. *Imaginative Writing: The Elements of Craft* (New York: Penguin, 2003), 87, 97.

_____. *Writing Fiction: A Guide to Narrative Craft*, 4th ed. (New York: HarperCollins, 1996), 95.

Butler, Robert Olen. *From Where You Dream: The Process of Writing Fiction*, ed. Janet Burroway (New York: Grove Press, 2005), 42.

Carver, Raymond. "Cathedral," *Cathedral* (New York: Vintage, 1984).

Chekhov, Anton. Quoted in Francine Prose, *Reading Like a Writer* (New York: Harper Perennial, 2007), 245.

_____. "The Darling," *Stories*, tr. Richard Pevear and Larissa Volokhonsky (New York: Bantam Books, 2000), 343.

_____. "A Gentleman Friend," *Anton Chekhov's Short Stories*, ed. Ralph E. Matlaw, tr. Constance Garnett (New York: Norton, 1979).

_____. "The Lady with the Dog," *The Lady with the Dog & Other Stories*, tr. Constance Garnett (New York: Ecco Press, 1984).

_____. "Terror," *The Party & Other Stories*, tr. Constance Garnett (New York: Ecco Press, 1986), 83.

Cohen, Richard. *Writer's Mind: Crafting Fiction* (Lincolnwood, IL: NTC Publishing Group, 1995), 37.

Cook, K.L., excerpt from an interview conducted by Lucrecia Guerrero, *Writers Ask*, No. 64 (Summer 2014), 7.

Cooper, T. Quoted in Daniel Alarcón, *The Secret Miracle: The Novelist's Handbook* (New York: Henry Holt, 2010), 196.

Delbanco, Nicholas. *The Sincerest Form: Writing Fiction by Imitation* (Boston, MA: McGraw-Hill, 2004), 74.

DeMarinis, Rick. *The Art and Craft of the Short Story* (Cincinnati, OH: Story Press, 2000), 85, 86, 88.

Dubus, Andre. *Meditations from a Movable Chair* (New York: Knopf, 1998), 64-65.

Dufresne, John. *The Lie That Tells a Truth* (New York: Norton, 2003), 170, 171, 182-196.

Eagleman, David. *Incognito: The Secret Lives of the Brain* (New York: Pantheon, 2011), 4, 5, 30, 109, 128.

Edwards, Kim. "Icebergs, Glaciers, and Arctic Dreams: Developing Characters," *Creating Fiction: Instruction and Insights from Teachers of the Associated Writing Programs*, ed. Julie Checkoway (Cincinnati, OH: Story Press, 1999), 45.

Eliot, T.S. "Hamlet and His Problems," in William Shakespeare, *Hamlet*, ed. Cyrus Hoy (New York: Norton, 1963), 177-178.

Emmons, John. Quoted in Daniel Alarcón, *The Secret Miracle: The Novelist's Handbook* (New York: Henry Holt, 2010), 171.

Fierro, Julia. "Get Closer: Exposing Your Characters (with Compassion)," in Bret Anthony Johnston, *Naming the World and Other Exercises for the Creative Writer* (New York: Random House, 2007), 107-112.

Forster, E.M. *Aspects of the Novel* (New York: Harcourt, 1985), 43-65, 78.

Gardner, John. *The Art of Fiction* (New York: Vintage, 1991), 45.

Gass, William H. "The Concept of Character in Fiction," *Fiction and the Figures of Life* (Boston, MA: Nonpareil Books, 1971), 34-54.

Greenblatt, Stephen. *Will in the World: How Shakespeare Became Shakespeare* (New York: Norton, 2004), 323-324.

Harvey, W.J. *Character and the Novel* (Ithaca, NY: Cornell U Press, 1968), 52.

Hemingway, Ernest. "In Another Country" and "Indian Camp," *The Complete Stories of Ernest Hemingway: The Vinca Figia Edition* (New York: Scribner, 1998).

Hemley, Robin. *Turning Life into Fiction* (Cincinnati, OH: Story Press, 1994), 79-81.

Hills, Rust. *Writing in General and the Short Story in Particular: An Informal Textbook*, rev. ed. (Boston, MA: Houghton Mifflin, 1987), 76.

Johnson, Denis. "Car Crash While Hitchhiking," *Jesus' Son* (New York: Picador, 2009).

Kafka, Franz. "A Hunger Artist," *The Complete Stories*, ed. Nahum N. Glatzer (New York: Schocken Books, 1995), 277.

Keats, John. Letter to George and Tom Keats, December 21, 1817, *The Letters of John Keats, 1814-1821*, Vol. 1, ed. Edward D. McDonald (New York: Viking, 1936), 193.

Lamott, Anne. *Bird by Bird: Some Instructions on Writing and Life* (New York: Anchor Books, 1994), 45, 48.

Maisel, Eric and Ann Maisel. *What Would Your Character Do?: Personality Quizzes for Analyzing Your Characters* (Cincinnati, OH: Writer's Digest Books, 2006).

Melville, Herman. *Moby-Dick, or The Whale*, ed. Charles Feidelson, Jr. (New York: Bobbs-Merrill, 1964), 563.

Novakovich, Josip. *Fiction Writer's Workshop* (Cincinnati, OH: Story Press, 1995), 48.

Oates, Joyce Carol. "Where Are You Going, Where Have You Been?," *High Lonesome: New and Selected Stories*, 1966-2006 (New York: Harper Perennial, 2007).

O'Brien, Tim. "The Magic Show," *Writers on Writing*, ed. Robert Pack and Jay Parini (Hanover, NH: Middlebury College Press, 1991), 182.

O'Connor, Flannery. "A Good Man Is Hard to Find," *The Complete Stories* (New York: Farrar, Straus & Giroux, 1981).

_____. "The Nature and Aim of Fiction" and "A Reasonable Use of the Unreasonable," *Mystery and Manners: Occasional Prose*, ed. Sally and Robert Fitzgerald (New York: Farrar, Straus & Giroux, 1981), 70, 112, 113.

O'Keeffe, Georgia. Quoted in *What If?: Writing Exercises for Fiction Writers*, 2nd ed., ed. Anne Bernays and Pamela Painter (New York: Pearson/Longman, 2004), 197.

Packer, Anne. "Interviewing Your Character," in Bret Anthony Johnston, *Naming the World and Other Exercises for the Creative Writer* (New York: Random House, 2007), 86-88.

Percy, Benjamin. "Meltdown," *Refresh, Refresh* (St. Paul, MN: Graywolf Press, 2007), 127.

Pound, Ezra. Quoted by Wayne Dodd in "An Interview with Wayne Dodd" by Kevin Bezner, *Denver Quarterly*, Vol. 26, No. 3 (1992), 112.

Reissenweber, Brandi. "Character: Casting Shadows," Gotham Writers' Workshop, *Writing Fiction: The Practical Guide from New York's Acclaimed Creative Writing School*, ed. Alexander Steele (New York: Bloomsbury, 2003), 27, 28, 38-39.

Salinger, J.D. *The Catcher in the Rye* (Boston, MA: Little, Brown, 1991), 1, 6, 9, 17-18, 39, 64, 125, 173, 196.

Saunders, George. *Writers Write* (Dec. 2, 2013) https://www.writerswrite.co.za/literary-birthday-2-december-george-saunders/

Sexton, Adam. *Master Class in Fiction Writing* (New York: McGraw-Hill, 2005), 46, 54-55.

Shakespeare, William. *Hamlet*, ed. Cyrus Hoy (New York: Norton, 1963), 69, 84-85.

Voltaire. "Sept discourse en vers sur l'homme." Quoted in John Gross, *The Oxford Book of Aphorisms* (Oxford, UK: Oxford U Press, 1983), 208.

Wolff, Tobias. "Bullet in the Brain," *Our Story Begins: New and Selected Stories* (New York: Vintage Books, 2009).

_____. "A Conversation with Tobias Wolff," *Story Matters: Contemporary Short Story Writers Share the Creative Process*, ed. Margaret-Love Denman and Barbara Shoup (Boston, MA: Houghton Mifflin, 2006), 476.

Wood, James. *How Fiction Works* (New York: Farrar, Straus & Giroux, 2009), 121, 128.

WHO'S AFRAID OF THE BIG BAD ABSTRACTION?: CONVEYING EMOTION IN FICTION

[3]For a summary of various studies, see the Introduction to Albert M. Kataaz and Virginia T. Kataaz's *Foundations of Nonverbal Communication: Readings, Exercises, and Commentary* (Carbondale: Southern Illinois U Press, 1983).

[4]Although for years I thought I was describing a scene from Flaubert's *Madame Bovary*, no such scene actually exists, though Emma does spend an inordinate amount of time gazing pensively out of windows.

*

Bausch, Richard. "Wise Men at Their End," *The Stories of Richard Bausch* (New York: HarperCollins, 2003), 242.

Butler, Robert Olen. "The American Couple," *A Good Scent from a Strange Mountain* (New York: Penguin, 1993), 164, 220-221.

———. *From Where We Dream: The Process of Writing Fiction*, ed. Janet Burroway (New York: Grove Press, 2005), 14, 28, 64-65.

Chaon, Dan. *Await Your Reply* (New York: Ballantine, 2009), 136, 173.

Darwin, Charles. *The Expression of the Emotions in Man and Animals* (Chicago, IL: U of Chicago Press, 1965), 176.

DeMarinis, Rick. "Culture Shocks," "disneyland," "Pagans," "Red Chair," and "The Handgun," *The Coming Triumph of the Free World* (New York: Norton, 1991), 1, 28, 46, 115.

Doctorow, E.L. Quoted in Robert Medak, "Writing Quotes," http://rjmedak.wordpress.com/quotes-about-writing/

Doerr, Anthony. "A Tangle by the Rapid River," "Mknondo," "The Caretaker," and "The Hunter's Wife," *The Shell Collector* (New York: Scribner, 2002), 42, 172, 177, 207.

Dunn, Stephen. "Some Reflections on the Abstract and the Wise," *Walking Light: Essays and Memoirs* (New York: Norton, 1993).

Dybek, Stuart. "Blight," *The Coast of Chicago* (New York: Picador, 1990), 47-48.

Echols, Damien. Unpublished death row journal.

Evans, Danielle. "Virgins," *Before You Suffocate Your Own Fool Self* (New York: Riverhead, 2011), 20.

Exley, Frederick. *A Fan's Notes* (New York: Random House, 1968), 73, 88.

Faulkner, William. "A Rose for Emily" and "That Evening Sun," *Collected Stories of William Faulkner* (New York: Vintage, 1995), 119, 303-304.

Fitzgerald, F. Scott. *The Great Gatsby* (New York: Collier Books, 1980), 30, 37, 177-178.

Harfenist, Jean. "The Gift," *A Brief History of the Flood* (New York: Knopf, 2002), 65.

Haslett, Adam. "Devotion," "Notes to My Biographer," and "The Beginnings of Grief," *You Are Not a Stranger Here* (New York: Anchor, 2005), 5, 7, 53, 73.

Havazelet, Ehud. "Like Never Before," *Like Never Before* (New York: Anchor, 1999), 223.

Hemingway, Ernest. *The Old Man and the Sea* (New York: Scribner, 2020), 44.

Irwin, Michael. *Picturing: Description and Illusion in the Nineteenth-Century Novel* (London: Allen and Unwin, 1979), 20.

James, Henry. *The Portrait of a Lady* (New York: Penguin, 2003), 458.

Jauss, David. "Glossolalia," *Glossolalia: New & Selected Stories* (Winston-Salem, NC: Press 53, 2013), 230.

Jin, Ha. "Saboteur," *The Bridegroom: Stories* (New York: Pantheon, 2000), 6, 12.

Johnson, Denis. "Two Men," *Jesus' Son: Stories* (New York: Picador, 1992), 17.

Kataaz, Albert M. and Virginia T. Kataaz. "Introduction," *Foundations of Nonverbal Communication: Readings, Exercises, and Commentary* (Carbondale: Southern Illinois U Press, 1983), xv.

Klineberg, Otto. "Emotional Expression in Chinese Literature," *Journal of Abnormal and Social Psychology*, No. 33 (1938), 518.

Korte, Barbara. *Body Language in Literature*, tr. Erica Ens (Toronto, Ontario: U of Toronto Press, 1997), 3-4, 14, 38-39, 89.

Kress, Nancy. *Character, Emotion & Viewpoint* (Cincinnati, OH: Writer's Digest Books, 2005), 121, 122.

Lahiri, Jhumpa. *The Namesake* (New York: Mariner Books, 2004), 27.

Le Guin, Ursula K. *Steering the Craft: A 21st-Century Guide to Sailing the Sea of Story* (Boston, MA: Mariner Books, 2015), 112.

Lessing, Doris. *In Pursuit of the English* (London: MacGibbon & Kee, 1960), 173.

Lowry, Malcolm. *Under the Volcano* (Philadelphia, PA: J.B. Lippincott Co., 1965), 320.

Malamud, Bernard. "God's Wrath," *The Complete Stories* (New York: Farrar, Straus & Giroux, 1998), 65, 509.

Munro, Alice. "Dance of the Happy Shades," *Selected Stories* (New York: Vintage, 1997), 29.

Quade, Kirstin Valdez. "The Five Wounds," *Night at the Fiestas: Stories* (New York: Norton, 2015), 70.

_____. *The Five Wounds* (New York: Norton, 2021), 70.

McEwan, Ian. *The Comfort of Strangers* (New York: Vintage, 1994), 14.

McGuane, Thomas. "A Man in Louisiana," *Cloudbursts: Collected and New Stories* (New York: Vintage, 2019), 28.

McIlwain, Jolene. "The Steep Side," *Sidle Creek: Stories* (New York: Melville House, 2023), 231-232.

Millhauser, Steven. "The Wizard of West Orange," *Best American Short Stories 2008*, ed. Salman Rushdie (Boston, MA: Houghton Mifflin, 2008), 161.

Moore, Lorrie. *A Gate at the Stairs* (New York: Knopf, 2009), 40, 63, 125, 130, 209, 226, 259, 297.

Morrison, Toni. *Beloved* (New York: Vintage, 2004), 3.

Nabokov, Vladimir. *Lolita* (New York: G.P. Putnam's Sons, 1955), 207-208.

Newton-John, Olivia. "Physical." From *Physical* (EMI 1981); music by Stephen Alan Kipner, lyrics by Terry Shaddick. Lyrics © EMI Music Publishing, Terry Shaddick Music.

O'Connor, Flannery. "The Nature and Aim of Fiction" and "Writing Short Stories," *Mystery and Manners: Occasional Prose*, ed. Sally and Robert Fitzgerald (New York: Farrar, Straus & Giroux, 1962), 68, 92.

Orringer, Julie. "Care," *How to Breathe Underwater* (New York: Vintage, 2005), 136.

Peacock, Thomas Love. *Nightmare Abbey & Crotchet Castle* (New York: Penguin, 1982), 106.

Peelle, Lydia. "Phantom Pain" and "Kidding Season," *Reasons for and Advantages of Breathing* (New York: Harper Perennial, 2009), 39, 152.

Percy, Benjamin. "The Woods," *Refresh, Refresh* (St. Paul, MN: Graywolf Press, 2007), 57.

Pound, Ezra. "A Retrospect," *Literary Essays of Ezra Pound* (New York: New Directions, 1968), 5.

Powers, Richard. *The Echo Maker* (New York: Picador, 2007), 428, 430.

____. *Gold Bug Variations* (New York: Harper Perennial, 1992), 382.

Puchner, Eric. "Mission," *Music through the Floor* (New York: Scribner, 2005), 196.

Rash, Ron. "The Woman at the Pond," *Something Rich and Strange: Selected Stories* (New York: Ecco Press, 2014), 265.

Ruskin, John. "Of the Pathetic Fallacy" (*Modern Painters*, Vol. 3, Part 4), §4, §5, §11, §16. http://www.ourcivilisation.com/smartboard/shop/ruskinj/

Schoemperlen, Diane. "Body Language," *Forms of Devotion* (New York: Viking, 1998), 44, 49.

Shakespeare, William. *Coriolanus*, Act 3, scene 2, line 76.

Sneed, Christine. "Quality of Life," *Best American Short Stories 2008*, ed. Salman Rushdie (Boston, MA: Houghton Mifflin, 2008), 276.

Stein, Gertrude. "Poetry and Grammar," *Writings, 1932-1946* (New York: Library of America, 1998), 323.

Strout, Elizabeth. "Criminal," "Incoming Tide," "Pharmacy," "River," and "Tulips," *Olive Kittredge* (New York: Random House, 2008), 8-9, 33, 45, 144, 243, 270.

Thon, Melanie Rae. "Necessary Angels," *In This Light: New & Selected Stories* (St. Paul, MN: Graywolf Press, 2011), 146.

Tower, Wells. "Door in Your Eye," *Everything Ravaged, Everything Burned* (New York: Farrar, Straus & Giroux, 2009), 138.

Updike, John. *Roger's Version* (Harmondsworth, UK: Penguin, 1987), 37-38.

Vaz, Katherine. "Math Bending unto Angels," *Fado & Other Stories* (Pittsburgh, PA: U of Pittsburgh Press, 1997), 50, 79.

Williams, John. *Stoner* (New York: New York Review Books, 2003), 121.

Wood, James. "A Snack Before I Die," *London Review of Books*, Vol. 19, No. 16 (Aug. 21, 1997), 20.

Yates, Richard. "Doctor Jack-o'-Lantern," *The Collected Stories of Richard Yates* (New York: Picador, 2002), 13.

The Art of Description

[5] See Robert Paul Lamb, *Art Matters: Hemingway, Craft, and the Creation of the Modern Short Story* (Baton Rouge: Louisiana State U Press, 2011), especially chapter three, and Raymond S. Nelson, *Hemingway: Expressionist Artist* (Ames: Iowa State U Press, 1979).

[6] Vermeer, Johannes. *The Music Lesson*, http://www.essentialvermeer.com/catalogue/music_lesson.html#.V7JciU0krX4

[7] Goings, Ralph. *Double Ketchup*, http://www.magnoliaeditions.com/artworks/double-ketchup/

[8] Morisot, Berthe. *English Seascape*, http://www.the-athenaeum.org/art/detail.php?ID=1623

[9] Pissarro, Camille. The Boulevard Montmartre at Night, http://www.galleryintell.com/artex/the-boulevard-montmartre-at-night-by-camille-pissarro/

[10] Monet, Claude. *Waterloo Bridge, Sunlight in the Fog*, http://www.claudemonetgallery.org/Waterloo-Bridge,-Sunlight-in-the-Fog.html

[11] Munch, Edvard. *The Scream*, http://www.edvardmunch.org/the-scream.jsp

[12] Dix, Otto. *Trench*, http://www.wikiart.org/en/Search/Trench

[13] Meidner, Ludwig. *I and the City*, http://weimarart.blogspot.com/2010/07/ludwig-meidner.html

[14] Cézanne, Paul. *Rocks at Fontainebleau*, http://www.paul-cezanne.org/Rocks-At-Fountainebleau.html

[15] ———. *Mont Sainte Victoire Seen from Les Lauves*, http://www.paul-cezanne.org/Mont-Sainte-Victoire-Seen-From-Les-Lauves.html

[16] For a side-by-side comparison of Cézanne's *Gardanne 2* and a photograph of Gardanne, see http://www.edwardtufte.com/bboard/images/00009H-239.jpg, and compare both images to *Gardanne* at http://www.paul-cezanne.org/Gardanne.html

[17] Cézanne, Paul. *The Village of Gardanne*, http://www.paul-cezanne.org/The-Village-Of-Gardanne.html

[18] ———. *The Lane of Chestnut Trees at the Jas de Bouffon* https://www.paul-cezanne.org/The-Lane-Of-Chestnut-Trees-At-The-Jas-De-Bouffan.html

[19] Picasso, Pablo. *Still Life with Liqueur Bottle*, http://www.moma.org/rails4/collection/works/78986?locale=en

Anonymous. *Encyclopedia of World Biography* (Farmington Hills, MI: The Gale Group, 2004), http://www.encyclopedia.com/topic/Alain_Robbe-Grillet.aspx#2

Cather, Willa. *My Ántonia*, in *Willa Cather: Early Novels and Stories*, ed. Sharon O'Brien (New York: Library of America, 1987), 790.

_____. "The Novel *Démeublé*," *Willa Cather: Stories, Poems, and Other Writings*, ed. Sharon O'Brien (New York: Library of America, 1992), 837.

Cézanne, Paul. Quoted in Forrest Gander, *A Faithful Existence: Reading, Memory, and Transcendence* (Berkeley, CA: Counterpoint Press, 2005), 141.

_____. Quoted in Paul Machotka, *Cézanne: Landscape into Art* (New Haven, CT: Yale U Press, 1996), 148.

_____. Quoted in Joyce Medina, *Cézanne and Modernism: The Poetics of Painting* (Albany, NY: SUNY Press, 1995), 67.

_____. Quoted in Emily Stipes Watts, *Ernest Hemingway and the Arts* (Urbana: U of Illinois Press, 1971), 34.

Conrad, Joseph. *Lord Jim*, ed. Thomas C. Moser (New York: Norton, 1968), 5.

_____. Preface to *The Nigger of the Narcissus*, in *Joseph Conrad on Fiction*, ed. Walter F. Wright (Lincoln: U of Nebraska Press, 1964), 162.

Crane, Stephen. Quoted in Ford Madox Ford, "Techniques," *Critical Writings of Ford Madox Ford* (Lincoln: U of Nebraska Press, 1964), 67.

_____. *The Red Badge of Courage*, in *Stephen Crane: Prose and Poetry* (New York: Library of America, 1984), 126.

Doty, Mark. *The Art of Description: World into Word* (St. Paul, MN: Graywolf Press, 2010), 19, 33, 90, 111.

Eliot, T.S. "Hamlet and His Problems," *The Sacred Wood: Essays on Poetry and Criticism* (London: Methuen, 1920), 92.

Gaillard, Jr., Theodore L. "Hemingway's Debt to Cézanne: New Perspectives," *Twentieth Century Literature*, Vol. 45, No. 1 (1999), 68.

Gallix, Andrew. "In Theory: Towards a New Novel," *The Guardian*, May 13, 2010, http://www.theguardian.com/books/booksblog/2010/may/13/in-theory-alain-robbe-grillet-fiction

Greene, Robert W. *The Poetic Theory of Pierre Reverdy* (Berkeley: U of California Press, 1967), 12.

Hagemann, Meyly Chin. "Hemingway's Secret: Visual to Verbal Art," *Journal of Modern Literature*, Vol. 7, No. 1 (Feb. 1979), 89, 111-112.

Hejinian, Lyn. "The Rejection of Closure," *The Language of Inquiry* (Berkeley: U of California Press, 2010), 56.

Hemingway, Ernest. "An Alpine Idyll," "Big Two-Hearted River," "Soldier's Home," "Up in Michigan," and "Wine of Wyoming," *The Complete Short Stories of Ernest Hemingway: The Finca Vigía Edition* (New York: Scribner, 1987), 59, 115, 163-164, 263, 342.

———. "The Art of Fiction: Ernest Hemingway," interview by George Plimpton, *Conversations with Ernest Hemingway*, ed. Matthew J. Bruccoli (Oxford: U Press of Mississippi, 1986), 118, 120, 126, 129.

———. *Death in the Afternoon* (New York: Scribner, 1932), 2.

———. *Islands in the Stream* (New York: Scribner, 1997), 148.

———. Letter to Gertrude Stein, August, 1924, and Letter to Bernard Berenson, March 20-22, 1953, *Selected Letters, 1917-1961*, ed. Carlos Baker (New York: Scribner, 1961), 122, 809.

———. *A Moveable Feast* (New York: Scribner, 1964), 12-13, 75.

———. "On Writing," *The Nick Adams Stories*, ed. Philip Young (New York: Scribner, 1972), 239-40.

James, Henry. "The Art of Fiction," *Partial Portraits* (Ann Arbor: U of Michigan Press, 1970), 260.

Jillette, Penn and Raymond Teller. *Tim's Vermeer* (High Delft Pictures, 2013).

Jobst, Jack. "Hemingway in Seney," *Michigan History*, Vol. 74, No. 6 (Nov./Dec. 1990), 22, 25. http://www.michiganhemingwaysociety.org/articlelinks/EHin%20Seney.htm

Johnston, Kenneth G. "Hemingway and Cézanne: Doing the Country," *American Literature*, Vol. 56, No. 1 (March 1984), 35.

Lamb, Robert Paul. *Art Matters: Hemingway, Craft, and the Creation of the Modern Short Story* (Baton Rouge: Louisiana State U Press, 2011), 54-55, 57, 59, 63-64, 70-71, 77.

Lane, Jerome. "Landscapes of the Mind: Physical Landscapes as Maps of the Psyche in Hemingway, Munro, and Cheever," MFA Critical Thesis, Vermont College of Fine Arts, 2015.

Loran, Erle. *Cézanne's Composition*, 3rd ed. (Berkeley: U of California Press, 1963).

Machotka, Pavel. *Cézanne: Landscape into Art*, 2nd ed. (Prague, Czech Republic: Arbor Vitae, 2014), 202.

Mallarmé, Stéphane. Letter to Henri Cazalis, October 1864, in *Mallarmé: Selected Prose Poems, Essays, and Letters* (Baltimore, MD: Johns Hopkins U Press, 1956), 83.

Montgomery, Constance Cappel. *Hemingway in Michigan* (New York: Fleet, 1966), 121.

Murphy, Richard W. *The World of Cézanne 1839-1906* (New York: Time-Life Books, 1968), 7-8, 33, 75, 77.

Nagel, James. "Stephen Crane and the Narrative Methods of Impressionism," *Studies in the Novel*, Vol. 10, No. 1 (Spring 1979), 76.

Nelson, Raymond S. *Hemingway: Expressionist Artist* (Ames: Iowa State U Press, 1979).

Poe, Edgar Allan. "The Fall of the House of Usher," *Complete Tales and Poems* (Minneapolis, MN: Castle Books, 2009), 171.

Robbe-Grillet, Alain. *For a New Novel: Essays on Fiction*, tr. Richard Howard (New York: Grove Press, 1965), 145-146.

_____. *The Voyeur*, tr. Richard Howard (New York: Grove Press, 1958), 7, 149.

Ross, Lillian. *Portrait of Hemingway* (New York: Scribner, 2015), 60.

Solnit, Rebecca. *River of Shadows: Eadweard Muybridge and the Technological Wild West* (New York: Penguin, 2003), 196.

Stein, Gertrude. "A Carafe, That Is a Blind Glass," *Tender Buttons: The Corrected Centennial Edition* (San Francisco, CA: City Lights Publishers, 2014), 11.

_____. *Everybody's Autobiography* (New York: Random House, 1937), 180.

_____. Quoted in Carolyn Faunce Copeland, *Language & Time & Gertrude Stein* (Iowa City: U of Iowa Press, 1975), 79.

_____. Quoted in Donald Sutherland, *Gertrude Stein: A Biography of Her Work* (New Haven, CT: Yale U Press, 1951), 88-89.

Svoboda, Frederic J. "Landscapes real and imagined: 'Big Two-Hearted River,'" *Hemingway Review*, Vol. 16, No. 1 (Fall 1996), 36, http://www.michiganhemingwaysociety.org/articlelinks/BTHRSvoboda.htm

Weaver, Alfred. "Roger Fry's Discovery of Cézanne," in Roger Fry, *Cézanne: A Study of His Development* (New York: Noonday Press, 1960), iii.

"What We See With": Redefining Plot

[20] For example, Gustave Freytag favors the terms *exposition, rising action, climax, falling action*, and *denouement*; E.M. Forster, *complication, crisis*, and *solution*; Frank O'Connor, *exposition, development*, and *drama*; Robie Macauley and George Lanning, *introduction of oppositions, deepening of the oppositions, the flash point or crisis*, and *the resolution*; Rust Hills, *initiation, complication*, and *resolution*; John Gardner, *exposition, development*, and *denouement*; and Sarah Stone and Ron Nyren, *ground situation, complication or inception, rising action, crisis, climax, and falling action*.

[21] This distinction, which is virtually nonexistent in fiction writing articles and textbooks, is common in scholarly discussion of short stories. According to Jean Pickering, scholars attending a roundtable discussion on the short story at the Université d'Angers in 1983 first "came up with the term *revelation* to describe the essential nature of the short story and *evolution* for the novel."

[22] Part of the following discussion of "The Things They Carried" is borrowed from my essay "Beyond Plot: Structuring Fiction" in *Alone with All That Could Happen: On Writing Fiction*, revised & expanded ed. (Winston-Salem, NC: Press 53, 2022), 88-90.

[23] Here is the chronological timeline of the principal events in "The Things They Carried," each followed by the section or sections in which they're mentioned:

Before the war (Cross's memories of Martha)—sections 1, 3, 4, 7, 10, and 13

Before April (general-time events)—parts of most sections but especially 5, 8, 9, and 12

Before April (specific-time event: Sanders cuts a thumb off a Vietnamese corpse)—8, 12

First week of April (Cross gets a good-luck pebble from Martha)—6

April 16 (Strunk searches a tunnel near the village of Than Khe)—7

April 16 (Lavender's death)—2, 4, 5, 7, 10, 11, 12, 13

April 16 (they call for a chopper to evacuate Lavender's body)—4

April 16 (they wait for the chopper)—12

April 16 (they load Lavender's body onto the chopper)—2, 4

April 16 (the chopper takes Lavender's body away)—10

April 16 (they burn the village of Than Khe)—4, 10

April 16 (Kiowa describes the death of Lavender)—4, 10, 11, 13

April 16 (Cross weeps after hearing Kiowa describe Lavender's death)—10, 11

April 17 (Cross burns Martha's letters and photographs)—13

April 17 (Cross prepares to lead the men toward the villages west of Than Khe)—13

*

Alison, Jane. *Meander, Spiral, Explode: Design and Pattern in Narrative* (New York: Catapult, 2019), 6, 95-96.

Allison, Dorothy. "River of Names," *Trash* (New York: Penguin, 2002), 11, 12.

Atwood, Margaret. "Happy Endings," *Murder in the Dark: Short Fictions and Prose Poems* (Dallas: Texas Bookman, 1996), 63, 70.

Bailey, Tom. "The 'Why?' Behind the Power of Plot: Shaping the Short Story," *On Writing Short Stories*, ed. Tom Bailey (New York: Oxford U Press, 2000), 48

Bakhtin, Mikhail. "Tolstoy's *Three Deaths*," *Tolstoy's Short Fiction*, 2nd ed., ed. and tr. Michael R. Katz (New York: Norton, 2008), 397.

Baldeshwiler, Eileen. "The Lyric Short Story: The Sketch of a History," *The New Short Story Theories*, ed. Charles E. May (Athens: Ohio U Press, 1994), 231, 234-235.

Barthelme, Donald. "A Symposium on Fiction," *Not-Knowing: The Essays and Interviews of Donald Barthelme*, ed. Kim Herzinger (New York: Vintage, 1999), 76.

———. "The Balloon" and "Views of My Father Weeping," *Sixty Stories* (New York: Penguin, 2003), 46, 48, 50, 51.

Baxter, Charles. *The Feast of Love* (New York: Pantheon, 2000).

Bell, Madison Smartt. *Narrative Design: Working with Imagination, Craft, and Form* (New York: Norton, 1997), 30.

Bennett, Claire-Louise. "Morning, Noon & Night," *Pond* (New York: Riverhead, 2016), 3, 6, 7, 10, 11, 12, 14, 15, 16, 18, 25, 26, 27.

Berlin, Lucia. "A Manual for Cleaning Women" and "Point of View," *A Manual for Cleaning Women: Selected Stories*, ed. Stephen Emerson (New York: Picador, 2016), 38, 51, 52, 53, 54, 55.

Bishop, Elizabeth. "In the Village," *Prose*, ed. Lloyd Schwartz (New York: Farrar, Straus & Giroux, 2011), 62.

Boccaccio, Giovanni. *The Decameron*, ed. and tr. G.H. McWilliam (New York: Penguin, 2003).

Borges, Jorge Luis. "Pierre Menard, Author of *Don Quixote*," tr. Anthony Bonner, *Ficciones* (New York: Grove Press, 1962), 52, 54.

Borges, Jorge Luis and Adolfo Bioy-Casares, *Chronicles of Bustos Domecq*, tr. Norman Thomas Di Giovanni (New York: Dutton, 1979).

Brockmeier, Kevin. "The Ceiling," *Things that Fall from the Sky* (New York: Vintage, 2003), 113, 117.

Brown, Larry. "The Rich," *Tiny Love: The Complete Stories of Larry Brown* (Chapel Hill, NC: Algonquin Books, 2019).

Burroway, Janet. *Imaginative Writing: The Elements of Craft* (New York: Penguin, 2003), 183.

Chekhov, Anton. "The Darling," *The Darling and Other Stories*, tr. Constance Garnett (New York: Ecco Press, 1984), 4, 6, 11, 15, 16, 19, 20, 21.

———. "Gooseberries," *Anton Chekhov's Short Stories*, tr. Ivy Litvinov, ed. Ralph E. Matlaw (New York: Norton, 1979), 192, 193.

———. "Lights" and "A Story Without an End," *Love & Other Stories*, tr. Constance Garnett (New York: Ecco Press, 1987), 68, 73, 81, 82, 83.

Conrad, Joseph. *Heart of Darkness and Other Tales*, rev. ed. (New York: Oxford U Press, 2008), 105, 111, 129, 168, 178, 182, 183, 185, 186.

Coover, Robert. "The Babysitter" and "The Elevator," *Pricksongs & Descants* (New York: Signet, 1970).

DeMarinis, Rick. "Rudderless Fiction: Lesson One," *Harper's Magazine* (April 1991), 54.

Dybek, Stuart. "Pet Milk," *The Coast of Chicago* (New York: Picador, 1990), 167-169, 172, 173.

Ebenbach, David Harris. "Writing Toward the Light," *The Writer*, Vol. 123, No. 12 (2010), 15.

Faulkner, William. "Dry September," *Collected Stories* (New York: Vintage, 1995), 172.

Fisher, Dorothy Canfield. "Sex Education," *The Bedquilt and Other Stories*, ed. Mark J. Madigan (Columbia: U of Missouri Press, 1997).

Flaubert, Gustave. "A Simple Heart" and "The Legend of St. Julian Hospitator," tr. Robert Baldick, *Three Tales* (Harmondsworth, UK: Penguin, 1973), 50, 54, 56, 87.

_____. Feb. 1, 1852 letter to Louise Colet, in *Madame Bovary*, ed. Paul de Man (New York: Norton, 1965), 309-10.

_____. Quoted in Rosellen Brown, "Notes on This Issue's Issue: Women on Men/Men on Women," *A Rosellen Brown Reader* (Hanover, NH: Middlebury College Press, 1992), 233.

Forster, E.M. *Aspects of the Novel* (New York: Harcourt, 1985), 26, 85, 86, 97.

Freytag, Gustave. Quoted in Madison Smartt Bell, *Narrative Design: Working with Imagination, Craft, and Form* (New York: Norton, 1997), 27.

Friedman, Norman. "Forms of the Plot," *The Theory of the Novel*, ed. Philip Stevick (New York: Free Press, 1967).

Frye, Northrop. *Anatomy of Criticism: Four Essays*, ed. David Damrosch (Princeton, NJ: Princeton U Press, 2020).

Gardner, John. *The Art of Fiction* (New York: Vintage, 1991), 84, 165, 185, 186, 188.

Gass, William H. "The Concept of Character in Fiction," *Fiction and the Figures of Life* (Boston, MA: Nonpareil Books, 1971), 36.

Gogol, Nikolai. "The Nose," *The Overcoat and Other Short Stories*, tr. Mary Struve (Mineola, NY: Dover Publications, 2012), 61, 68, 77, 78.

Gordon, Caroline. "Summer Dust," *The Forest of the South* (New York: Scribner, 1945).

Hanson, Clare. *Short Stories and Short Fictions, 1880-1980* (New York: St. Martin's Press, 1985), 7-8, 36, 107.

Hempel, Amy. "The Harvest," *The Collected Stories* (New York: Scribner, 2007).

Hills, Rust. *Writing in General and the Short Story in Particular*, rev. ed. (Boston, MA: Houghton Mifflin, 1987), 95, 97.

Homer. *The Odyssey*, tr. Robert Fagles (New York: Penguin, 1999).

Hughes, Langston. "Radioactive Red Caps," *The Collected Works of Langston Hughes, Vol. 8: The Later Simple Stories* (Columbia: U of Missouri Press, 2002), 50, 51, 52.

Joyce, James. Chapter 18 (Penelope), *Ulysses* (New York: Vintage, 1961), 738-783.

Lefer, Diane. "Breaking the 'Rules' of Story Structure," *Words Overflown by Stars: Creative Writing Instruction and Insight from the Vermont College of Fine Arts MFA Program*, ed. David Jauss (Cincinnati, OH: Writer's Digest Books, 2009), 63, 66.

Macauley, Robie and George Lanning. *Technique in Fiction*, 2nd ed. (New York: St. Martin's Press, 1987), 201, 203, 214, 238.

Machado, Carmen Maria. "Inventory," *Her Body and Other Parties* (St. Paul, MN: Graywolf Press, 2017).

Martone, Michael. *The Blue Guide to Indiana* (Normal/Tallahassee, FL: FC2, 2001).

Millhauser, Steven. "The Barnum Museum," *We Others: New and Selected Stories* (London: Corsair, 2011), 233, 234-235.

Minot, Susan. "Lust," *Lust & Other Stories* (New York: Washington Square Press, 1990), 17.

Moody, Rick. "Boys," *Demonology: Stories* (Boston, MA: Back Bay Books, 2002).

O'Brien, John. "Birds," *The Iowa Review*, Vol. 3, No. 3 (1972).

O'Brien, Tim. "The Things They Carried" and "How to Tell a True War Story," *The Things They Carried* (New York: Broadway Books, 1998), 21, 25, 26, 76, 77, 79, 87, 89, 91.

O'Connor, Flannery. "The Nature and Aim of Fiction," *Mystery and Manners: Occasional Prose*, ed. Sally and Robert Fitzgerald (New York: Farrar, Straus & Giroux, 1981), 79.

O'Connor, Frank. *The Lonely Voice: A Study of the Short Story* (New York: Melville House, 2004), 9.

Olesha, Yuri. "Lyompa," tr. Andrew R. MacAndrew, *Extreme Fiction: Fabulists and Formalists*, ed. Robin Hemley and Michael Martone (New York: Pearson/Longman, 2004), 107, 108, 109.

Olsen, Tillie. "I Stand Here Ironing," *Tell Me a Riddle* (New York: Delta Books, 1981), 1.

O'Rourke, Meghan. "As Far as the Mind Can See," *The New York Times Book Review* (July 24, 2016), 17.

Paley, Grace. "A Conversation with My Father," *Enormous Changes at the Last Minute* (New York: Farrar, Straus & Giroux, 1974), 162, 166.

Pickering, Jean. "Time and the Short Story," *Re-reading the Short Story*, ed. Clare Hanson (New York: St. Martin's Press, 1989), 49-50.

Poe, Edgar Allan. "The Power of Words," *Complete Tales and Poems* (Minneapolis, MN: Castle Books, 2009), 389-392.

Pound, Ezra. *Make It New: Essays* (London: Faber and Faber, 1934).

Robbe-Grillet, Alain. "On Several Obsolete Notions," tr. Richard Howard, *For a New Novel: Essays on Fiction* (New York: Grove Press, 1965), 25, 31-33.

Scholes, Robert. Quoted in Jane Alison, *Meander, Spiral, Explode: Design and Pattern in Narrative* (New York: Catapult, 2019), 13.

Singer, Isaac Bashevis. "The Boarder," *The New Yorker* (May 7, 2018), 60-63.

Stone, Sarah and Ron Nyren. *Deepening Fiction: A Practical Guide for Intermediate and Advanced Writers* (New York: Pearson/ Longman, 2005), 73, 86, 88.

Tolstoy, Leo. "Three Deaths," *Tolstoy's Short Fiction*, 2nd ed., ed. and tr. Michael R. Katz (New York: Norton, 2008), 52, 55, 56.

Vonnegut, Kurt. Quoted in Mark Baechtel, *Shaping the Story: A Step-by-Step Guide to Writing Fiction* (New York: Pearson/ Longman, 2004), 137.

Welty, Eudora. "The Reading and Writing of Short Stories," *Short Story Theories*, ed. Charles E. May (Athens: Ohio U Press, 1976), 170.

Woolf, Virginia. "Modern Fiction," *The Common Reader—First Series* (New York: Harcourt, Inc., 2002), 150.

_____. "Moments of Being: 'Slater's Pins Have No Points'," *The Complete Shorter Fiction of Virginia Woolf*, ed. Susan Dick (New York: Harcourt Brace Jovanovich, 1985), 215, 217, 220.

Returning Characters to Life:
What Chekhov Teaches Us about Endings

[24] For sample complaints about Chekhov's endings made by literary critics of his time, see Ann Frydman, *A Study of the Endings of Anton Chekhov's Short Stories*, PhD dissertation, Columbia U, 1978, 22-25.

[25] Barthelme ends his story "Views of My Father Weeping" with a succinct version of one of Chekhov's signature closing strategies, the revelation that the protagonist's life will continue unchanged. Its final section consists simply of the word "Etc." The endings of Barth's "Title" and "Life-Story" echo two of Chekhov's other favorite strategies for "endless" endings, the anti-epilogue and the "dead-end."

[26] A similar strategy occurs in Chekhov's "A Day in the Country," which shifts in its final sentence to the point of view of the moon. Another early story, "A Country Cottage," also employs the moon's point of view, although it does so throughout the story, not just in its conclusion.

*

Aiken, Conrad. "Anton Chekhov," *Critical Essays on Anton Chekhov*, ed. Thomas A. Eekman (Boston, MA: G.K. Hall & Co., 1989), 22.

Barth, John. "Life-Story" and "Title," *Lost in the Funhouse* (New York: Anchor Books, 1988), 113, 129.

Barthelme, Donald. "Views of My Father Weeping," *Sixty Stories* (New York: Penguin, 2003), 120.

Bartlett, Rosamund. "Introduction," *About Love and Other Stories*, tr. Rosamund Bartlett (Oxford, UK: Oxford U Press, 2004), xiii.

Bausch, Richard. "On Gusev," *The Norton Anthology of Short Fiction*, 6th ed., ed. R.V. Cassill and Richard Bausch (New York: Norton, 2000), 259, 260.

Byron, Lord George Gordon. *Don Juan*, canto 1, stanza 133 (New York: Penguin, 2005).

Chekhov, Anton. Quoted in Avram B. Derman, "Structural Features in Chekhov's Poetics," *Critical Essays on Anton Chekhov*, ed. Thomas A. Eekman (Boston, MA: G.K. Hall & Co., 1989), 40.

_____. Quoted in Ehud Havazelet, "Chekhov and Form," *Bringing the Devil to His Knees: The Craft of Fiction and the Writing Life*, ed. Charles Baxter and Peter Turchi (Ann Arbor: U of Michigan Press, 2001), 89.

_____. "Aborigines," "A Country Cottage," "A Story Without an End," and "Lights," *Love & Other Stories*, tr. Constance Garnett (New York: Ecco Press, 1987), 19, 68, 82-83, 186, 261-263.

_____. "A Boring Story," "Anyuta," "Sleepy," "The House with the Mezzanine," and "The Lady with the Little Dog," *Stories*, tr. Richard Pevear and Larissa Volokhonsky (New York: Bantam, 2000), 27, 30-31, 54, 107, 281, 297, 376.

_____. "The Chorus Girl," "The Little Joke" and "The Witch," *Early Stories*, tr. Patrick Miles and Harvey Pitcher (Oxford, UK: Oxford U Press, 1999), 79, 105, 114.

_____. "The Darling" and "The Two Volodyas," *The Darling & Other Stories*, tr. Constance Garnett (New York: Ecco Press, 1984), 22, 113.

_____. "A Day in the Country," *The Cook's Wedding & Other Stories*, tr. Constance Garnett (New York: Ecco Press, 1986), 115.

_____. "Expensive Lessons" and "Neighbours," *The Duel & Other Stories*, tr. Constance Garnett (New York: Ecco Press, 1984), 232, 255, 290.

_____. "Fortune," *About Love and Other Stories*, tr. Rosamund Bartlett (Oxford, UK: Oxford U Press, 2004), 35, 38, 41-42, 44.

_____. "A Gentleman Friend" and "Gusev," tr. Avrahm Yarmolinsky, *A Doctor's Visit: Short Stories by Anton Chekhov*, ed. Tobias Wolff (New York: Bantam, 1988), 48, 107, 118-119.

_____. "In a Strange Land," *The Schoolmaster & Other Stories*, tr. Constance Garnett (New York: Ecco Press, 1986), 302.

_____. "Misery," *The Schoolmistress & Other Stories*, tr. Constance Garnett (New York: Ecco Press, 1986), 62, 65.

_____. "The Murder," *The Bishop & Other Stories*, tr. Constance Garnett (New York: Ecco Press, 1985), 89, 109, 113, 131-132.

_____. "The Steppe," "The Story of an Unknown Man," "Three Years," and "Ward No. 6," *The Complete Short Novels*, tr. Richard Pevear and Larissa Volokhonsky (New York: Vintage, 2005), 113, 217, 220, 291-292, 432.

_____. "Terror," "The Kiss," and "The Teacher of Literature," *The Party & Other Stories*, tr. Constance Garnett (New York: Ecco Press, 1984), 70, 74, 82-83, 204-205, 260, 270-274.

_____. "A Trifle from Real Life," *Russian Silhouettes: More Stories of Russian Life by Anton Tchekoff*, tr. Marian Fell (New York: Scribner, 1915), 27-28.

Evdokimova, Svetlana. "'The Darling': Femininity Scorned and Desired," *Reading Chekhov's Text*, ed. Robert Louis Jackson (Evanston, IL: Northwestern U Press, 1993), 190.

Frydman, Ann. *A Study of the Endings of Anton Chekhov's Short Stories*, PhD dissertation, Columbia U, 1978, 22-25, 65, 109-110, 118, 123, 159, 258, 274, 275.

Glover, Douglas. "*Don Quixote, Rosemary's Baby, Alien*, and *The French Lieutenant's Woman*: Meditations on the Ideology of Closure and the Comforting Lie," *upstreet*, No. 4 (2008), 49.

James, Henry. Quoted in Ann Frydman, *A Study of the Endings of Anton Chekhov's Short Stories*, PhD dissertation, Columbia U, 1978, 28.

Jauss, David. "From Long Shots to X-Rays: Distance and Point of View," *Alone with All that Could Happen: On Writing Fiction*, revised and expanded ed. (Winston-Salem, NC: Press 53, 2022), 52-54.

Kataev, Vladimir. *If Only We Could Know!: An Interpretation of Chekhov*, tr. and ed. Harvey Pitcher (Chicago, IL: Ivan R. Dee, 2002), 224.

Kunitz, Stanley. "The Art of Poetry, No. 29," interview by Chris Busa, *The Paris Review*, No. 83 (Spring 1982), https://www.theparisreview.org/interviews/3185/the-art-of-poetry-no-29-stanley-kunitz

Nabokov, Vladimir. "Chekhov's Prose," *Critical Essays on Anton Chekhov*, ed. Thomas A. Eekman (Boston, MA: G.K. Hall & Co., 1989), 33.

Paley, Grace. "A Conversation with My Father," *Enormous Changes at the Last Minute* (New York: Farrar, Straus & Giroux, 1974), 162.

Popkin, Cathy. *The Pragmatics of Insignificance: Chekhov, Zoshchenko, Gogol* (Stanford, CA: Stanford U Press, 1993), 38, 44.

Tolstoy, Leo. "The Death of Ivan Ilych," *The Raid and Other Stories*, tr. Louise and Alymer Maude, ed. P.N. Furbank (Oxford, UK: Oxford U Press, 1982), 278-279.

Woolf, Virginia. "The Russian Point of View," *The Common Reader: First Series, Annotated Edition*, ed. Andrew McNeillie (Boston, MA: Mariner Books, 2002), 172-174.

The Flowers of Afterthought:
Premises and Strategies for Revision

[27] Ginsberg credited the motto "First thought, best thought" at various times to William Blake, Jack Kerouac, Ghögyam Trungpa, and others.

[28] For a discussion of branching modifiers and their role in syntax, see chapter nine of Virginia Tufte's *Artful Sentences: Syntax as Style* (Cheshire, CT: Graphics Press, 2006).

*

Allison, Will. "Throw Up, Then Clean Up," *Rules of Thumb: 73 Authors Reveal Their Fiction Writing Fixations*, ed. Michael Martone and Susan Neville (Cincinnati, OH: Writer's Digest Books, 2006), 234.

Almog, Ruth. "The Right Words, the Last Words," *Haaretz*, Oct. 18, 2002, https://www.haaretz.com/israel-news/the-right-words-the-last-words-1.31065

Almond, Steve. *This Won't Take But a Minute, Honey: Essays* (Boston, MA: Harvard Bookstore, 1995), 17.

Auden, W. H. *Collected Poems*, ed. Edward Mendelson (New York: Vintage, 1991), xxvi.

Bausch, Richard. Facebook post, Feb. 20, 2022.

Bellow, Saul. Quoted in Maggie Simmons, "Free to Feel: Conversation with Saul Bellow," *Conversations with Saul Bellow*, ed. Gloria Cronin and Ben Siegel (Oxford: U Press of Mississippi, 1994), 165.

Bodwell, Joshua. "The Art of Reading Andre Dubus," *Poets & Writers* (July/Aug. 2008), 22.

Brady, Catherine. *Story Logic and the Craft of Fiction* (New York: Palgrave/Macmillan, 2010), 169.

Burroway, Janet. *Imaginative Writing: The Elements of Craft* (New York: Longman, 2003), 225, 228.

_____. *Writing Fiction: A Guide to Narrative Craft*, 5th ed. (New York: Longman, 2000), 139.

Butler, Robert Olen. *From Where You Dream: The Process of Writing Fiction*, ed. Janet Burroway (New York: Grove Press, 2005), 38, 58.

Capote, Truman. *Conversations with Capote*, ed. Lawrence Grobel (New York: New American Library, 1986), 205.

Chekhov, Anton. Quoted in A.B. Derman, "Compositional Elements in Chekhov's Poetics," *Anton Chekhov's Short Stories*, ed. Ralph E. Matlaw (New York: Norton, 1979), 302.

_____. Quoted in Valerie Miner, "Revising Revision," *Rules of Thumb: 73 Authors Reveal Their Fiction Writing Fixations*, ed. Michael Martone and Susan Neville (Cincinnati, OH: Writer's Digest Books, 2006), 132.

Dahlberg, Edward. *The Carnal Myth: A Search into Classical Sensuality* (New York: Weybright & Talley, 1968), 11.

De Vries, Peter. Quoted in Leonore Fleischer, "De Vries on Rewriting," *Life* (Dec. 13, 1968), 18.

Dillard, Annie. *The Writing Life* (New York: HarperCollins, 1989), 4.

Doerr, Anthony. "Manufacturing Dreams: An Interview with Anthony Doerr," interview by Richard Farrell, *Numéro Cinq*, Vol. 3, No. 1 (Jan. 2012), http://numerocinqmagazine.com/2012/01/13/manufacturing-dreams-an-interview-with-anthony-doerr/

Doty, Mark. "Mark Doty: An Interview," interview by Jona Colson, *The Writer's Chronicle*, Vol. 44, No. 1 (Sept. 2011), 20.

Dubus, Andre. "The Habit of Writing," *On Writing Short Stories*, ed. Tom Bailey (New York: Oxford U Press, 2000), 90, 92-93.

Dubus III, Andre. "The Case for Writing a Story Before Knowing How It Ends," theatlantic.com/entertainment/print/2013/10/the-case-for-writing-a-story-before-knowing-how-it-ends/280387/

Dybek, Stuart. Interview by Jennifer Levasseu and Kevin Rabalais, *Glimmer Train Stories*, No. 44 (Fall 2002), 88-89.

Einstein, Alfred. https://www.goodreads.com/quotes/842695-i-think-99-times-and-find-nothing-i-stop-thinking

Eliot, T.S. "The Hollow Men," *The Complete Poems and Plays, 1909-1950* (New York: Harcourt, Brace & World, 1971), 58.

Erdrich, Louise. "The Art of Fiction, No. 208," interview by Lisa Halliday, *The Paris Review*, No. 195 (Winter 2010).

Frost, Robert. "Two Tramps in Mud Time," *The Poetry of Robert Frost*, ed. Edward Connery Lathem (New York: Holt, Rinehart and Winston, 1969), 277.

García Márquez, Gabriel. Quoted in Marlise Simons, "Love and Age: A Talk with García Márquez," *The New York Times Review of Books*, April 7, 1985, http://www.nytimes.com/1985/04/07/books/love-and-age-a-talk-with-garcia-marquez.html?pagewanted=all

Genette, Gérard. "Time and Narrative in *A la recherché du temps perdu*," *Essentials of the Theory of Fiction*, ed. Michael J. Hoffmann and Patrick D. Murphy (Durham, NC: Duke U Press, 1988), 284.

Gide, André. Quoted in Dan Albergotti, "The Traveling Word File (A Virtual Interview with David Kirby)," *storySouth*, No. 8 (Summer 2003), http://storysouth.com/stories/the-traveling-word-file-a-virtual-interview-with-david-kirby/

Ginsberg, Allen. *Howl: Original Draft Facsimile, Transcript, and Variant Versions*, ed. Barry Miles (New York: HarperCollins, 2006).

Grauman, Brigid. "Madame Bovary goes interactive," *Prospect Magazine*, May 2009, http://www.prospectmagazine.co.uk/magazine/madamebovarygoesinteractive

Hemingway, Ernest. "The Art of Fiction," interview by George Plimpton, *The Paris Review*, No. 18 (Spring 1958).

———. *By-Line: Selected Articles and Dispatches of Four Decades*, ed. William White (New York: Scribner, 1998), 216.

———. Quoted in Arnold Samuelson, *With Hemingway: A Year in Key West and Cuba* (New York: Random House, 1984), 11.

Horace. *Ars Poetica*, lines 389-391, tr. by A.S. Kline, https://www.poetryintranslation.com/PITBR/Latin/HoraceArsPoetica.php

Hugo, Richard. From a fall 1980 conversation with the author.

Huizinga, Johan. *Homo Ludens: A Study of the Play-Element in Culture* (Mansfield Centre, CT: Martino Publishing, 2014), 129.

Huneven, Michelle. Quoted in Eric Olsen and Glenn Schaeffer's *We Wanted to Be Writers: Life, Love, and Literature at the Iowa Writer's Workshop* (New York: Skyhorse Publishing, 2011), 116.

Hyde, Lewis. *A Primer for Forgetting* (New York: Farrar, Straus & Giroux, 2019), 264.

Japanese proverb. Quoted in *The Poet's Notebook: Excerpts from the Notebooks of 26 American Poets*, ed. Stephen Kuusisto, Deborah Tall, and David Weiss (New York: Norton, 1997), 26.

Kercheval, Jesse Lee. *Building Fiction: How to Develop Plot and Structure* (Madison: U of Wisconsin Press, 2003), 131, 136.

Kundera, Milan. *The Art of the Novel*, tr. Linda Asher (New York: Harper Perennial, 2000), 88.

———. *Testament Betrayed: An Essay in Nine Parts*, tr. Linda Asher (New York: Harper Perennial, 2001), 267.

Lamott, Anne. *Bird by Bird: Some Instructions on Writing and Life* (New York: Anchor Books, 1995), 93-94.

Lawrence, D.H. *The First and Second Lady Chatterley Novels*, ed. Dieter Mehl and Christa Jansohn (Cambridge, UK: Cambridge U Press, 1999).

_____. *Lady Chatterley's Lover* (New York: Penguin, 2010).

Libbey, Elizabeth. "Writing Outside the Story," *What If?: Writing Exercises for Fiction Writers*, ed. Anne Bernays and Pamela Painter (New York: Harper Perennial, 1991), 164.

Livesey, Margot. *The Hidden Machinery: Essays on Writing* (Portland, OR: Tin House Books, 2017), 295.

Malamud, Bernard. Interview by Daniel Stern, *Writers at Work: The Paris Review Interviews*, Sixth Series, ed. George Plimpton (New York: Viking, 1984), 167.

_____. "The Train Stops Here: The Optimism of Revision," *As We Were Saying: Sewanee Writers on Writing*, ed. Wyatt Prunty, Megan Roberts, and Adam Latham (Baton Rouge: Louisiana State U Press, 2021), 117, 124.

Markus, Peter. "How to End," https://www.writingclasses.com/toolbox/articles/how-to-end

Martin, Lee. "The Addition and Subtraction of Revision," https://leemartinauthor.com/2018/01/29/addition-subtraction-revision/

Metres, Philip. "The Art of Losing (and Other Visions of Revision)," *The Writer's Chronicle*, Vol. 51, No. 5 (March/April 2019), 62.

Michelangelo. Quoted in *Wordsworth Dictionary of Quotations*, ed. Connie Robertson (Ware, UK: Wordsworth Editions, 1998), 275.

Morrison, Toni. "The Art of Fiction," *The Paris Review Interviews, II*, ed. Philip Gourevitch (New York: Picador, 2007), 361.

Nabokov, Vladimir. *Strong Opinions* (New York: McGraw-Hill, 1973), 4.

Nietzsche, Friedrich. *Beyond Good and Evil: Prelude to a Philosophy of the Future*, tr. Marion Faber (Oxford, UK: Oxford U Press, 1999), 94.

Nims, John Frederick and David Mason. *Western Wind: An Introduction to Poetry*, 5th ed. (New York: McGraw-Hill, 2005), 154-155.

O'Connor, Flannery. "The Nature and Aim of Fiction," *Mystery and Manners: Occasional Prose*, ed. Sally and Robert Fitzgerald (New York: Farrar, Straus & Giroux, 1981), 69.

O'Connor, Frank. *The Lonely Voice: A Study of the Short Story* (Brooklyn, NY: Melville House, 2004), 211.

Pascal, Blaise. *Pensées*, tr. and ed. Roger Ariew (Cambridge, MA: Hackett Publishing Co., 2005), 192.

Percy, Benjamin. "Home Improvement: Revision as Renovation," *Thrill Me: Essays on Fiction* (St. Paul, MN: Graywolf Press, 2016), 165-166.

Phillips, Bum. https://www.sbnation.com/nfl/2013/10/19/4855684/bum-phillips-quotes

Poe, Edgar Allan. "Letter to B-----," *Selections from the Critical Writings of Edgar Allan Poe*, ed. Frederick C. Prescott (New York: Henry Holt, 1909), 1-10 and 323-325.

Poincaré, Henri. "Mathematical Creation," tr. George Bruce Halsted, *The Creative Process: A Symposium*, ed. Brewster Ghiselin (New York: New American Library, 1952), 38, 39.

Quiller-Couch, Arthur. *On the Art of Writing* (Mineola, NY: Dover Publications, 2006), 203.

Raban, Jonathan. Quoted in Ian Hamilton, *Robert Lowell* (New York: Vintage, 1983), 431.

Richards, Keith and James Fox. *Life* (Boston, MA: Back Bay Books, 2011), 267.

Russian proverb. Quoted in Alexander Solzhenitsyn, *Nobel Lecture*, tr. F.D. Reeve (New York: Farrar, Straus & Giroux, 1972).

Sacks, Oliver. "The Creative Self," *The River of Consciousness* (New York: Knopf, 2017), 144.

Saunders, George. https://www.goodreads.com/author/quotes/8885.George_Saunders?page=9

———. Quoted in Adam Vitcavage, "George Saunders Likes a Challenge," *Electric Literature*, Feb. 14, 2017, https://electricliterature.com/george-saunders-likes-a-challenge-bb92c31fc8b40

Schutt, Christine. "The Directing Sentence," *As We Were Saying: Sewanee Writers on Writing*, ed. Wyatt Prunty, Megan Roberts, and Adam Latham (Baton Rouge: Louisiana State U Press, 2021), 227.

Selgin, Peter. "Revision: Real Writers Revise," *Gotham Writers' Workshop, Writing Fiction: The Practical Guide from New York's Acclaimed Creative Writing School*, ed. Alexander Steele (New York: Bloomsbury, 2003), 218.

Sharma, Akhil. Quoted in Wyatt Mason, "His First Novel Was a Critical Hit. Two Decades Later, He Rewrote It," *The New York Times Magazine*, July 12, 2022, https://www.nytimes.com/2022/07/12/magazine/akhil-sharma-an-obedient-father.html?referringSource=articleShare&utm_source=Sailthru&utm_medium=email&utm_campaign=Lit%20Hub%20Daily:%20July%2012%2C%202022&utm_term=lithub_master_list

Shea, Andrea. "Jack Kerouac's Famous Scroll, 'On the Road' Again," *All Things Considered* (National Public Radio, July 5, 2007), https://www.npr.org/templates/story/story.php?storyId=11709924&fbclid=IwAR0-_egx-9oAeeGEAxC0NGIEu5g_D0yJlWCmsKJi6ElPCayE-4FpF_B8jfs#:~:text=Between%201951%20and%201957%2C%20Kerouac,his%20work%2C%20according%20to%20Sampas

Shetterly, Will. http://www.azquotes.com/author/38377-Will_Shetterly

Singer, Isaac Bashevis. Quoted in Morton A. Reichek, "'Yiddish,' says Isaac Bashevis Singer, 'contains vitamins other languages don't have,'" *The New York Times* (March 23, 1975), 228, http://www.nytimes.com/1975/03/23/archives/yiddish-says-isaac-bashevis-singer-contains-vitamins-that-other.html

Smiley, Jane. "What Stories Teach Their Writers: The Purpose and Practice of Revision," *Creating Fiction: Instruction and Insights from Teachers of the Associated Writing Programs*, ed. Julie Checkoway (Cincinnati, OH: Story Press, 1999), 248.

Smith, Mike. Quoted by George Saunders in "As It Turns Out, George Saunders Loves Revision Too," *UCWBling*, Feb. 4, 2013, http://ucwbling.chicagolandwritingcenters.org/george-saunders-writing-advice/

Smith, Zadie. *Changing My Mind: Occasional Essays* (New York: Penguin, 2009), 101, 107.

Stanislavski, Konstantin. Quoted in *Introduction to Alternative and Complementary Therapies*, ed. Anne L. Strozier and Joyce Carpenter (Abingdon-on-Thames, UK: Routledge, 2008), 82.

Stone, Sarah and Ron Nyren. *Deepening Fiction: A Practical Guide for Intermediate and Advanced Writers* (New York: Pearson/Longman, 2005), 214.

Thurber, James. "The Art of Fiction," *The Paris Review Interviews, II*, ed. Philip Gourevitch (New York: Picador, 2007), 22.

Turner, C.J.G. *A Karenina Companion* (Waterloo, Ontario: Wilfrid Laurier U Press, 1993), 13.

Twain, Mark. March 20, 1880, letter to D.W. Bowser, *Mark Twain's Notebooks: Journals, Letters, Observations, Wit, Wisdom, and Doodles*, ed. Carlo De Vito (New York: Black Dog & Leventhal, 2015), 58.

_____. Quoted by Richard Bausch in *Glimmer Train Stories* (Spring 2000), 129.

Valéry, Paul. "A Poet's Notebook," *The Poet's Work: 29 Poets on the Origins and Practice of Their Art*, ed. Reginald Gibbons (Chicago, IL: U of Chicago Press, 1989), 173-174.

Voigt, Ellen Bryant. *The Art of Syntax* (St. Paul, MN: Graywolf Press, 2009), 8.

Voltaire. Quoted in Thomas Kennedy, *Realism and Other Illusions: Essays on the Craft of Fiction* (Portland: Wordcraft of Oregon, 2002), 122.

Vonnegut, Kurt. "How to Get a Job Like Mine." Quoted in Tina Zambetis, "Author Vonnegut tells fans how to get a job like his at speech," *Daily Kent Stater*, Vol. 56, No. 109 (April 19, 1983), 9.

Wells, Jeff. "18 Novel Facts about *War and Peace*," *Mental Floss*, Sept. 9, 2018, https://mentalfloss.com/article/85834/18-novel-facts-about-war-and-peace

Welty, Eudora. *Conversations with Eudora Welty*, ed. Peggy Whitman Prenshaw (New York: Washington Square Books, 1984), 346.

_____. Quoted in "A Conversation with Susan Neville," *Story Matters: Contemporary Short Story Writers Share the Creative Process*, ed. Margaret-Love Denman and Barbara Shoup (Boston, MA: Houghton Mifflin, 2006), 358.

Williams, John. "'Middle Passage' at 25," *The New York Times*, July 10, 2015, https://www.nytimes.com/2015/07/12/books/review/middle-passage-at-25.html

Wolfe, Thomas. July 26, 1937, letter to F. Scott Fitzgerald, *The Sons of Maxwell Perkins: Letters of F. Scott Fitzgerald, Ernest Hemingway, Thomas Wolfe, and Their Editor*, ed. Matthew J. Bruccoli and Judith S. Baughman (Columbia: U of South Carolina Press, 2004), 258.

Wolff, Tobias. "A Conversation with Tobias Wolff," *Story Matters: Contemporary Short Story Writers Share the Creative Process*, ed. Margaret-Love Denman and Barbara Shoup (Boston, MA: Houghton Mifflin, 2006), 476.

———. Onstage interview at The Story Prize Award Ceremony in New York, March 4, 2009.

Yeats, William Butler. Untitled poem, *Yeats's Poems*, ed. A. Norman Jeffares (New York: Palgrave/ Macmillan, 1998), 713.

Zelinskiĭ, Korneliĭ. *Soviet Literature* (Moscow: Foreign Languages Publishing House, 1978), 185.

David Jauss is the author of four collections of short stories, most recently *Glossolalia: New & Selected Stories* and *Nice People: New & Selected Stories II*; two collections of poems, *You Are Not Here* and *Improvising Rivers*; and a previous craft book, *Alone with All That Could Happen: On Writing Fiction (Revised & Expanded Edition)*. He has also edited or co-edited three anthologies, *Strong Measures: Contemporary American Poetry in Traditional Forms*; *The Best of* Crazyhorse: *Thirty Years of Poetry and Prose;* and *Words Overflown by Stars*, a collection of essays on the craft of fiction, poetry, and creative nonfiction by the MFA in Writing faculty of Vermont College of Fine Arts. His short stories have been published in numerous magazines and reprinted in such anthologies as *Best American Short Stories, The O. Henry Awards: Prize Stories,* and *The Pushcart Prize: Best of the Small Presses,* as well as in *The Pushcart Book of Short Stories: The Best Stories from the Pushcart Prize*. He is the recipient of a National Endowment for the Arts Fellowship, a James A. Michener / Copernicus Society of America Fellowship, and three fellowships from the Arkansas Arts Council and one from the Minnesota State Arts Board. His collection *Black Maps* received the Associated Writers and Writing Programs Award for Short Fiction. For many years he taught creative writing at the University of Arkansas-Little Rock and in the low-residency MFA in Writing Program at Vermont College of Fine Arts.

www.ingramcontent.com/pod-product-compliance
Lightning Source LLC
Chambersburg PA
CBHW021855230426
43671CB00006B/399